The Ultimate

Air Fryer

2024

COOKBOOK

Margorie L. Carranza

2000 Days Irresistible Air Fryer Recipes for
Healthy and Flavorful Meals | Perfect for
Busy Weeknights and Family Gatherings

Table of Contents

INTRODUCTION

In the heart of every kitchen, where the sizzle of creativity meets the aroma of culinary possibilities, lies a revolutionary appliance that has captured the imagination of home cooks and professional chefs alike – the air fryer. Welcome to The Ultimate 2024 Air Fryer Cookbook, a cookbook designed to guide you through a culinary journey that harnesses the power of this remarkable device to transform your everyday meals into extraordinary delights.

As you hold this cookbook in your hands, you're embarking on a culinary adventure that promises not only the convenience of quick and efficient cooking but also the pleasure of savoring crispy, flavorful dishes with a fraction of the oil traditionally used. The Ultimate 2024 Air Fryer Cookbook is not just a collection of recipes; it's an invitation to reimagine the way you approach cooking, introducing you to a world where health-conscious choices coexist seamlessly with indulgent flavors.

The allure of the air fryer lies in its ability to conjure the crispy texture we all crave, using hot air circulation that envelops your ingredients, ensuring a perfect crunch without the need for excessive oil. Within the pages of The Ultimate 2024 Air Fryer Cookbook, we aim to demystify the art of air frying, empowering you to navigate this innovative cooking technique with ease and confidence.

To embark on this journey, we'll start by unraveling the fundamentals – exploring the different types of air fryers available, understanding key features, and discovering essential accessories that enhance your culinary prowess. Whether you're a seasoned pro or just unboxing your new kitchen companion, our cookbook is crafted to guide you through the basics, ensuring that you feel comfortable and confident as you dive into the world of air frying.

Beyond the technicalities, The Ultimate 2024 Air Fryer Cookbook celebrates the joy of experimentation. Our carefully curated recipes cater to a diverse range of tastes and dietary preferences, ensuring there's something for everyone. From crispy appetizers to succulent main courses, and from innovative side dishes to mouthwatering desserts, each recipe is a testament to the versatility of the air fryer.

In the spirit of fusion cuisine, we've combined traditional flavors with contemporary twists, allowing you to infuse your meals with creativity and flair. Imagine perfectly seasoned sweet potato fries, golden brown and crispy on the outside, yet tender on the inside. Envision juicy, herb-infused chicken wings that boast the crunch of fried perfection without the excess oil. The Ultimate 2024 Air Fryer Cookbook invites you to experience these culinary triumphs and many more.

As you journey through these pages, consider this cookbook not just as a guide but as a companion, inspiring you to explore, innovate, and make every meal a memorable occasion. Alongside our diverse array of recipes, you'll find helpful tips, cooking techniques, and flavor pairing suggestions that empower you to make each dish uniquely yours.

So, whether you're a culinary adventurer seeking new horizons or a busy individual craving quick, wholesome meals, The Ultimate 2024 Air Fryer Cookbook has something extraordinary to offer. Prepare to be captivated by the possibilities that unfold when the art of air frying merges with the joy of culinary exploration. Let your taste buds soar as we embark together on a journey of The Ultimate 2024 Air Fryer Cookbook – where every dish is a celebration of flavors, textures, and the joy of cooking with an air fryer.

Chapter 1

Breakfasts

Chapter 1 Breakfasts

Green Eggs and Ham

Prep time: 5 minutes | Cook time: 10 minutes | Serves 2

- 1 large Hass avocado, halved and pitted
- 2 thin slices ham
- 2 large eggs
- 2 tablespoons chopped green onions, plus more for garnish
- ½ teaspoon fine sea salt
- ¼ teaspoon ground black pepper
- ¼ cup shredded Cheddar cheese (omit for dairy-free)

1. Preheat the air fryer to 400ºF (204ºC). 2. Place a slice of ham into the cavity of each avocado half. Crack an egg on top of the ham, then sprinkle on the green onions, salt, and pepper. 3. Place the avocado halves in the air fryer cut side up and air fry for 10 minutes, or until the egg is cooked to your desired doneness. Top with the cheese (if using) and air fry for 30 seconds more, or until the cheese is melted. Garnish with chopped green onions. 4. Best served fresh. Store extras in an airtight container in the fridge for up to 4 days. Reheat in a preheated 350ºF (177ºC) air fryer for a few minutes, until warmed through.

Bacon, Egg, and Cheese Roll Ups

Prep time: 15 minutes | Cook time: 15 minutes | Serves 4

- 2 tablespoons unsalted butter
- ¼ cup chopped onion
- ½ medium green bell pepper, seeded and chopped
- 6 large eggs
- 12 slices sugar-free bacon
- 1 cup shredded sharp Cheddar cheese
- ½ cup mild salsa, for dipping

1. In a medium skillet over medium heat, melt butter. Add onion and pepper to the skillet and sauté until fragrant and onions are translucent, about 3 minutes. 2. Whisk eggs in a small bowl and pour into skillet. Scramble eggs with onions and peppers until fluffy and fully cooked, about 5 minutes. Remove from heat and set aside. 3. On work surface, place three slices of bacon side by side, overlapping about ¼ inch. Place ¼ cup scrambled eggs in a heap on the side closest to you and sprinkle ¼ cup cheese on top of the eggs. 4. Tightly roll the bacon around the eggs and secure the seam with a toothpick if necessary. Place each roll into the air fryer basket. 5. Adjust the temperature to 350ºF (177ºC) and air fry for 15 minutes.

Rotate the rolls halfway through the cooking time. 6. Bacon will be brown and crispy when completely cooked. Serve immediately with salsa for dipping.

BLT Breakfast Wrap

Prep time: 5 minutes | Cook time: 10 minutes | Serves 4

- 8 ounces (227 g) reduced-sodium bacon
- 8 tablespoons mayonnaise
- 8 large romaine lettuce leaves
- 4 Roma tomatoes, sliced
- Salt and freshly ground black pepper, to taste

1. Arrange the bacon in a single layer in the air fryer basket. (It's OK if the bacon sits a bit on the sides.) Set the air fryer to 350ºF (177ºC) and air fry for 10 minutes. Check for crispiness and air fry for 2 to 3 minutes longer if needed. Cook in batches, if necessary, and drain the grease in between batches. 2. Spread 1 tablespoon of mayonnaise on each of the lettuce leaves and top with the tomatoes and cooked bacon. Season to taste with salt and freshly ground black pepper. Roll the lettuce leaves as you would a burrito, securing with a toothpick if desired.

Southwestern Ham Egg Cups

Prep time: 5 minutes | Cook time: 12 minutes | Serves 2

- 4 (1 ounce / 28 g) slices deli ham
- 4 large eggs
- 2 tablespoons full-fat sour cream
- ¼ cup diced green bell pepper
- 2 tablespoons diced red bell pepper
- 2 tablespoons diced white onion
- ½ cup shredded medium Cheddar cheese

1. Place one slice of ham on the bottom of four baking cups. 2. In a large bowl, whisk eggs with sour cream. Stir in green pepper, red pepper, and onion. 3. Pour the egg mixture into ham-lined baking cups. Top with Cheddar. Place cups into the air fryer basket. 4. Adjust the temperature to 320ºF (160ºC) and bake for 12 minutes or until the tops are browned. 5. Serve warm.

Pumpkin Donut Holes

Prep time: 15 minutes | Cook time: 14 minutes | Makes 12 donut holes

- 1 cup whole-wheat pastry flour, plus more as needed
- 3 tablespoons packed brown sugar
- ½ teaspoon ground cinnamon
- 1 teaspoon low-sodium baking powder
- ⅓ cup canned no-salt-added pumpkin purée (not pumpkin pie filling)
- 3 tablespoons 2% milk, plus more as needed
- 2 tablespoons unsalted butter, melted
- 1 egg white
- Powdered sugar (optional)

1. In a medium bowl, mix the pastry flour, brown sugar, cinnamon, and baking powder. 2. In a small bowl, beat the pumpkin, milk, butter, and egg white until combined. Add the pumpkin mixture to the dry ingredients and mix until combined. You may need to add more flour or milk to form a soft dough. 3. Divide the dough into 12 pieces. With floured hands, form each piece into a ball. 4. Cut a piece of parchment paper or aluminum foil to fit inside the air fryer basket but about 1 inch smaller in diameter. Poke holes in the paper or foil and place it in the basket. 5. Put 6 donut holes into the basket, leaving some space around each. Air fry at 360ºF (182ºC) for 5 to 7 minutes, or until the donut holes reach an internal temperature of 200ºF (93ºC) and are firm and light golden brown. 6. Let cool for 5 minutes. Remove from the basket and roll in powdered sugar, if desired. Repeat with the remaining donut holes and serve.

Fried Cheese Grits

Prep time: 10 minutes | Cook time: 10 to 12 minutes | Serves 4

- ⅔ cup instant grits
- 1 teaspoon salt
- 1 teaspoon freshly ground black pepper
- ¾ cup whole or 2% milk
- 3 ounces (85 g) cream
- cheese, at room temperature
- 1 large egg, beaten
- 1 tablespoon butter, melted
- 1 cup shredded mild Cheddar cheese
- Cooking spray

1. Mix the grits, salt, and black pepper in a large bowl. Add the milk, cream cheese, beaten egg, and melted butter and whisk to combine. Fold in the Cheddar cheese and stir well. 2. Preheat the air fryer to 400ºF (204ºC). Spray a baking pan with cooking spray. 3. Spread the grits mixture into the baking pan and place in the air fryer basket. 4. Air fry for 1o to 12 minutes, or until the grits are cooked and a knife inserted in the center comes out clean. Stir the mixture once halfway through the cooking time. 5. Rest for 5 minutes and serve warm.

Simple Scotch Eggs

Prep time: 5 minutes | Cook time: 25 minutes | Serves 4

- 4 large hard boiled eggs
- 1 (12-ounce / 340-g) package pork sausage
- 8 slices thick-cut bacon
- 4 wooden toothpicks, soaked in water for at least 30 minutes

1. Slice the sausage into four parts and place each part into a large circle. 2. Put an egg into each circle and wrap it in the sausage. Put in the refrigerator for 1 hour. 3. Preheat the air fryer to 450ºF (235ºC). 4. Make a cross with two pieces of thick-cut bacon. Put a wrapped egg in the center, fold the bacon over top of the egg, and secure with a toothpick. 5. Air fry in the preheated air fryer for 25 minutes. 6. Serve immediately.

Strawberry Tarts

Prep time: 15 minutes | Cook time: 10 minutes | Serves 6

- 2 refrigerated piecrusts
- ½ cup strawberry preserves
- 1 teaspoon cornstarch
- Cooking oil spray
- ½ cup low-fat vanilla yogurt
- 1 ounce (28 g) cream cheese,
- at room temperature
- 3 tablespoons confectioners' sugar
- Rainbow sprinkles, for decorating

1. Place the piecrusts on a flat surface. Using a knife or pizza cutter, cut each piecrust into 3 rectangles, for 6 total. Discard any unused dough from the piecrust edges. 2. In a small bowl, stir together the preserves and cornstarch. Mix well, ensuring there are no lumps of cornstarch remaining. 3. Scoop 1 tablespoon of the strawberry mixture onto the top half of each piece of piecrust. 4. Fold the bottom of each piece up to enclose the filling. Using the back of a fork, press along the edges of each tart to seal. 5. Insert the crisper plate into the basket and the basket into the unit. Preheat the unit by selecting BAKE, setting the temperature to 375ºF (191ºC), and setting the time to 3 minutes. Select START/STOP to begin. 6. Once the unit is preheated, spray the crisper plate with cooking oil. Working in batches, spray the breakfast tarts with cooking oil and place them into the basket in a single layer. Do not stack the tarts. 7. Select BAKE, set the temperature to 375ºF (191ºC), and set the time to 10 minutes. Select START/STOP to begin. 8. When the cooking is complete, the tarts should be light golden brown. Let the breakfast tarts cool fully before removing them from the basket. 9. Repeat steps 5, 6, 7, and 8 for the remaining breakfast tarts. 10. In a small bowl, stir together the yogurt, cream cheese, and confectioners' sugar. Spread the breakfast tarts with the frosting and top with sprinkles.

Easy Buttermilk Biscuits

Prep time: 5 minutes | Cook time: 18 minutes | Makes 16 biscuits

◄ 2½ cups all-purpose flour
◄ 1 tablespoon baking powder
◄ 1 teaspoon kosher salt
◄ 1 teaspoon sugar
◄ ½ teaspoon baking soda

◄ 8 tablespoons (1 stick) unsalted butter, at room temperature
◄ 1 cup buttermilk, chilled

1. Stir together the flour, baking powder, salt, sugar, and baking powder in a large bowl. 2. Add the butter and stir to mix well. Pour in the buttermilk and stir with a rubber spatula just until incorporated. 3. Place the dough onto a lightly floured surface and roll the dough out to a disk, ½ inch thick. Cut out the biscuits with a 2-inch round cutter and re-roll any scraps until you have 16 biscuits. 4. Preheat the air fryer to 325ºF (163ºC). 5. Working in batches, arrange the biscuits in the air fryer basket in a single layer. Bake for about 18 minutes until the biscuits are golden brown. 6. Remove from the basket to a plate and repeat with the remaining biscuits. 7. Serve hot.

Breakfast Cobbler

Prep time: 20 minutes | Cook time: 30 minutes | Serves 4

Filling:
◄ 10 ounces (283 g) bulk pork sausage, crumbled
◄ ¼ cup minced onions
◄ 2 cloves garlic, minced
◄ ½ teaspoon fine sea salt
◄ ½ teaspoon ground black pepper
Biscuits:
◄ 3 large egg whites
◄ ¾ cup blanched almond flour
◄ 1 teaspoon baking powder
◄ ¼ teaspoon fine sea salt

◄ 1 (8 ounces / 227 g) package cream cheese (or Kite Hill brand cream cheese style spread for dairy-free), softened
◄ ¾ cup beef or chicken broth

◄ 2½ tablespoons very cold unsalted butter, cut into ¼-inch pieces
◄ Fresh thyme leaves, for garnish

1. Preheat the air fryer to 400ºF (204ºC). 2. Place the sausage, onions, and garlic in a pie pan. Using your hands, break up the sausage into small pieces and spread it evenly throughout the pie pan. Season with the salt and pepper. Place the pan in the air fryer and bake for 5 minutes. 3. While the sausage cooks, place the cream cheese and broth in a food processor or blender and purée until smooth. 4. Remove the pork from the air fryer and use a fork or metal spatula to crumble it more. Pour the cream cheese mixture into the sausage and stir to combine. Set aside. 5. Make the biscuits: Place the egg whites in a medium-sized mixing bowl or the bowl of a stand mixer and whip with a hand mixer or stand mixer until stiff peaks form. 6. In a separate medium-sized bowl, whisk together the

almond flour, baking powder, and salt, then cut in the butter. When you are done, the mixture should still have chunks of butter. Gently fold the flour mixture into the egg whites with a rubber spatula. 7. Use a large spoon or ice cream scoop to scoop the dough into 4 equal-sized biscuits, making sure the butter is evenly distributed. Place the biscuits on top of the sausage and cook in the air fryer for 5 minutes, then turn the heat down to 325ºF (163ºC) and bake for another 17 to 20 minutes, until the biscuits are golden brown. Serve garnished with fresh thyme leaves. 8. Store leftovers in an airtight container in the refrigerator for up to 3 days. Reheat in a preheated 350ºF (177ºC) air fryer for 5 minutes, or until warmed through.

Johnny Cakes

Prep time: 10 minutes | Cook time: 10 to 12 minutes | Serves 4

◄ ½ cup all-purpose flour
◄ 1½ cups yellow cornmeal
◄ 2 tablespoons sugar
◄ 1 teaspoon baking powder
◄ 1 teaspoon salt

◄ 1 cup milk, whole or 2%
◄ 1 tablespoon butter, melted
◄ 1 large egg, lightly beaten
◄ 1 to 2 tablespoons oil

1. In a large bowl, whisk the flour, cornmeal, sugar, baking powder, and salt until blended. Whisk in the milk, melted butter, and egg until the mixture is sticky but still lumpy. 2. Preheat the air fryer to 350ºF (177ºC). Line the air fryer basket with parchment paper. 3. For each cake, drop 1 heaping tablespoon of batter onto the parchment paper. The fryer should hold 4 cakes. 4. Spritz the cakes with oil and cook for 3 minutes. Turn the cakes, spritz with oil again, and cook for 2 to 3 minutes more. Repeat with a second batch of cakes.

Hole in One

Prep time: 5 minutes | Cook time: 6 to 7 minutes | Serves 1

◄ 1 slice bread
◄ 1 teaspoon soft butter
◄ 1 egg
◄ Salt and pepper, to taste

◄ 1 tablespoon shredded Cheddar cheese
◄ 2 teaspoons diced ham

1. Place a baking dish inside air fryer basket and preheat the air fryer to 330ºF (166ºC). 2. Using a 2½-inch-diameter biscuit cutter, cut a hole in center of bread slice. 3. Spread softened butter on both sides of bread. 4. Lay bread slice in baking dish and crack egg into the hole. Sprinkle egg with salt and pepper to taste. 5. Cook for 5 minutes. 6. Turn toast over and top it with shredded cheese and diced ham. 7. Cook for 1 to 2 more minutes or until yolk is done to your liking.

Spinach Omelet

Prep time: 5 minutes | Cook time: 12 minutes | Serves 2

- 4 large eggs
- 1½ cups chopped fresh spinach leaves
- 2 tablespoons peeled and chopped yellow onion
- 2 tablespoons salted butter, melted
- ½ cup shredded mild Cheddar cheese
- ¼ teaspoon salt

1. In an ungreased round nonstick baking dish, whisk eggs. Stir in spinach, onion, butter, Cheddar, and salt. 2. Place dish into air fryer basket. Adjust the temperature to 320°F (160°C) and bake for 12 minutes. Omelet will be done when browned on the top and firm in the middle. 3. Slice in half and serve warm on two medium plates.

Onion Omelet

Prep time: 10 minutes | Cook time: 12 minutes | Serves 2

- 3 eggs
- Salt and ground black pepper, to taste
- ½ teaspoons soy sauce
- 1 large onion, chopped
- 2 tablespoons grated Cheddar cheese
- Cooking spray

1. Preheat the air fryer to 355°F (179°C). 2. In a bowl, whisk together the eggs, salt, pepper, and soy sauce. 3. Spritz a small pan with cooking spray. Spread the chopped onion across the bottom of the pan, then transfer the pan to the air fryer. 4. Bake in the preheated air fryer for 6 minutes or until the onion is translucent. 5. Add the egg mixture on top of the onions to coat well. Add the cheese on top, then continue baking for another 6 minutes. 6. Allow to cool before serving.

Egg White Cups

Prep time: 10 minutes | Cook time: 15 minutes | Serves 4

- 2 cups 100% liquid egg whites
- 3 tablespoons salted butter, melted
- ¼ teaspoon salt
- ¼ teaspoon onion powder
- ½ medium Roma tomato, cored and diced
- ½ cup chopped fresh spinach leaves

1. In a large bowl, whisk egg whites with butter, salt, and onion powder. Stir in tomato and spinach, then pour evenly into four ramekins greased with cooking spray. 2. Place ramekins into air fryer basket. Adjust the temperature to 300°F (149°C) and bake for 15 minutes. Eggs will be fully cooked and firm in the center when done. Serve warm.

Bacon and Spinach Egg Muffins

Prep time: 7 minutes | Cook time: 12 to 14 minutes | Serves 6

- 6 large eggs
- ¼ cup heavy (whipping) cream
- ½ teaspoon sea salt
- ¼ teaspoon freshly ground black pepper
- ¼ teaspoon cayenne pepper
- (optional)
- ¾ cup frozen chopped spinach, thawed and drained
- 4 strips cooked bacon, crumbled
- 2 ounces (57 g) shredded Cheddar cheese

1. In a large bowl (with a spout if you have one), whisk together the eggs, heavy cream, salt, black pepper, and cayenne pepper (if using). 2. Divide the spinach and bacon among 6 silicone muffin cups. Place the muffin cups in your air fryer basket. 3. Divide the egg mixture among the muffin cups. Top with the cheese. 4. Set the air fryer to 300°F (149°C). Bake for 12 to 14 minutes, until the eggs are set and cooked through.

Pork Sausage Eggs with Mustard Sauce

Prep time: 20 minutes | Cook time: 12 minutes | Serves 8

- 1 pound (454 g) pork sausage
- 8 soft-boiled or hard-boiled eggs, peeled
- 1 large egg
- 2 tablespoons milk
- 1 cup crushed pork rinds
- Smoky Mustard Sauce:
- ¼ cup mayonnaise
- 2 tablespoons sour cream
- 1 tablespoon Dijon mustard
- 1 teaspoon chipotle hot sauce

1. Preheat the air fryer to 390°F (199°C). 2. Divide the sausage into 8 portions. Take each portion of sausage, pat it down into a patty, and place 1 egg in the middle, gently wrapping the sausage around the egg until the egg is completely covered. (Wet your hands slightly if you find the sausage to be too sticky.) Repeat with the remaining eggs and sausage. 3. In a small shallow bowl, whisk the egg and milk until frothy. In another shallow bowl, place the crushed pork rinds. Working one at a time, dip a sausage-wrapped egg into the beaten egg and then into the pork rinds, gently rolling to coat evenly. Repeat with the remaining sausage-wrapped eggs. 4. Arrange the eggs in a single layer in the air fryer basket, and lightly spray with olive oil. Air fry for 10 to 12 minutes, pausing halfway through the baking time to turn the eggs, until the eggs are hot and the sausage is cooked through. 5. To make the sauce: In a small bowl, combine the mayonnaise, sour cream, Dijon, and hot sauce. Whisk until thoroughly combined. Serve with the Scotch eggs.

Savory Sweet Potato Hash

Prep time: 15 minutes | Cook time: 18 minutes | Serves 6

- ◀ 2 medium sweet potatoes, peeled and cut into 1-inch cubes
- ◀ ½ green bell pepper, diced
- ◀ ½ red onion, diced
- ◀ 4 ounces (113 g) baby bella mushrooms, diced
- ◀ 2 tablespoons olive oil
- ◀ 1 garlic clove, minced
- ◀ ½ teaspoon salt
- ◀ ½ teaspoon black pepper
- ◀ ½ tablespoon chopped fresh rosemary

1. Preheat the air fryer to 380°F(193°C). 2. In a large bowl, toss all ingredients together until the vegetables are well coated and seasonings distributed. 3. Pour the vegetables into the air fryer basket, making sure they are in a single even layer. (If using a smaller air fryer, you may need to do this in two batches.) 4. Roast for 9 minutes, then toss or flip the vegetables. Roast for 9 minutes more. 5. Transfer to a serving bowl or individual plates and enjoy.

Gold Avocado

Prep time: 5 minutes | Cook time: 6 minutes | Serves 4

- ◀ 2 large avocados, sliced
- ◀ ¼ teaspoon paprika
- ◀ Salt and ground black pepper, to taste
- ◀ ½ cup flour
- ◀ 2 eggs, beaten
- ◀ 1 cup bread crumbs

1. Preheat the air fryer to 400°F (204°C). 2. Sprinkle paprika, salt and pepper on the slices of avocado. 3. Lightly coat the avocados with flour. Dredge them in the eggs, before covering with bread crumbs. 4. Transfer to the air fryer and air fry for 6 minutes. 5. Serve warm.

Veggie Frittata

Prep time: 7 minutes | Cook time: 21 to 23 minutes | Serves 2

- ◀ Avocado oil spray
- ◀ ¼ cup diced red onion
- ◀ ¼ cup diced red bell pepper
- ◀ ¼ cup finely chopped broccoli
- ◀ 4 large eggs
- ◀ 3 ounces (85 g) shredded sharp Cheddar cheese, divided
- ◀ ½ teaspoon dried thyme
- ◀ Sea salt and freshly ground black pepper, to taste

1. Spray a pan well with oil. Put the onion, pepper, and broccoli in the pan, place the pan in the air fryer, and set to 350°F (177°C). Bake for 5 minutes. 2. While the vegetables cook, beat the eggs in a medium bowl. Stir in half of the cheese, and season with the thyme, salt, and pepper. 3. Add the eggs to the pan and top with the remaining cheese. Set the air fryer to 350°F (177°C). Bake for 16 to 18 minutes, until cooked through.

Cinnamon-Raisin Bagels

Prep time: 30 minutes | Cook time: 10 minutes | Makes 4 bagels

- ◀ Oil, for spraying
- ◀ ¼ cup raisins
- ◀ 1 cup self-rising flour, plus more for dusting
- ◀ 1 cup plain Greek yogurt
- ◀ 1 teaspoon ground cinnamon
- ◀ 1 large egg

1. Line the air fryer basket with parchment and spray lightly with oil. 2. Place the raisins in a bowl of hot water and let sit for 10 to 15 minutes, until they have plumped. This will make them extra juicy. 3. In a large bowl, mix together the flour, yogurt, and cinnamon with your hands or a large silicone spatula until a ball is formed. It will be quite sticky for a while. 4. Drain the raisins and gently work them into the ball of dough. 5. Place the dough on a lightly floured work surface and divide into 4 equal pieces. Roll each piece into an 8- or 9-inch-long rope and shape it into a circle, pinching the ends together to seal. 6. In a small bowl, whisk the egg. Brush the egg onto the tops of the dough. 7. Place the dough in the prepared basket. 8. Air fry at 350°F (177°C) for 10 minutes. Serve immediately.

Apple Cider Doughnut Holes

Prep time: 10 minutes | Cook time: 6 minutes | Makes 10 mini doughnuts

Doughnut Holes:
- ◀ 1½ cups all-purpose flour
- ◀ 2 tablespoons granulated sugar
- ◀ 2 teaspoons baking powder
- ◀ 1 teaspoon baking soda
- ◀ ½ teaspoon kosher salt
- ◀ Pinch of freshly grated nutmeg

- ◀ ¼ cup plus 2 tablespoons buttermilk, chilled
- ◀ 2 tablespoons apple cider (hard or nonalcoholic), chilled
- ◀ 1 large egg, lightly beaten
- ◀ Vegetable oil, for brushing

Glaze:
- ◀ ½ cup powdered sugar
- ◀ 2 tablespoons unsweetened applesauce
- ◀ ¼ teaspoon vanilla extract
- ◀ Pinch of kosher salt

1. Make the doughnut holes: In a bowl, whisk together the flour, granulated sugar, baking powder, baking soda, salt, and nutmeg until smooth. Add the buttermilk, cider, and egg and stir with a small rubber spatula or spoon until the dough just comes together. 2. Using a 1 ounce (28 g) ice cream scoop or 2 tablespoons, scoop and drop 10 balls of dough into the air fryer basket, spaced evenly apart, and brush the tops lightly with oil. Air fry at 350°F (177°C) until the doughnut holes are golden brown and fluffy, about 6 minutes. Transfer the doughnut holes to a wire rack to cool completely. 3. Make the glaze: In a small bowl, stir together the powdered sugar, applesauce, vanilla, and salt until smooth. 4. Dip the tops of the doughnuts holes in the glaze, then let stand until the glaze sets before serving. If you're impatient and want warm doughnuts, have the glaze ready to go while the doughnuts cook, then use the glaze as a dipping sauce for the warm doughnuts, fresh out of the air fryer.

Bacon, Broccoli and Cheese Bread Pudding

Prep time: 30 minutes | Cook time: 48 minutes | Serves 2 to 4

- ½ pound (227 g) thick cut bacon, cut into ¼-inch pieces
- 3 cups brioche bread or rolls, cut into ½-inch cubes
- 3 eggs
- 1 cup milk
- ½ teaspoon salt
- freshly ground black pepper
- 1 cup frozen broccoli florets, thawed and chopped
- 1½ cups grated Swiss cheese

1. Preheat the air fryer to 400ºF (204ºC). 2. Air fry the bacon for 6 to 10 minutes until crispy, shaking the basket a few times while it cooks to help it cook evenly. Remove the bacon and set it aside on a paper towel. 3. Air fry the brioche bread cubes for 2 minutes to dry and toast lightly. (If your brioche is a few days old and slightly stale, you can omit this step.) 4. Butter a cake pan. Combine all the ingredients in a large bowl and toss well. Transfer the mixture to the buttered cake pan, cover with aluminum foil and refrigerate the bread pudding overnight, or for at least 8 hours. 5. Remove the casserole from the refrigerator an hour before you plan to cook, and let it sit on the countertop to come to room temperature. 6. Preheat the air fryer to 330ºF (166ºC). Transfer the covered cake pan, to the basket of the air fryer, lowering the dish into the basket using a sling made of aluminum foil (fold a piece of aluminum foil into a strip about 2-inches wide by 24-inches long). Fold the ends of the aluminum foil over the top of the dish before returning the basket to the air fryer. Air fry for 20 minutes. Remove the foil and air fry for an additional 20 minutes. If the top starts to brown a little too much before the custard has set, simply return the foil to the pan. The bread pudding has cooked through when a skewer inserted into the center comes out clean.

Hearty Cheddar Biscuits

Prep time: 10 minutes | Cook time: 22 minutes | Makes 8 biscuits

- 2⅓ cups self-rising flour
- 2 tablespoons sugar
- ½ cup butter (1 stick), frozen for 15 minutes
- ½ cup grated Cheddar cheese, plus more to melt
- on top
- 1⅓ cups buttermilk
- 1 cup all-purpose flour, for shaping
- 1 tablespoon butter, melted

1. Line a buttered 7-inch metal cake pan with parchment paper or a silicone liner. 2. Combine the flour and sugar in a large mixing bowl. Grate the butter into the flour. Add the grated cheese and stir to coat the cheese and butter with flour. Then add the buttermilk and stir just until you can no longer see streaks of flour. The dough should be quite wet. 3. Spread the all-purpose (not self-rising) flour out on a small cookie sheet. With a spoon, scoop 8 evenly sized balls of dough into the flour, making sure they don't touch each other. With floured hands, coat each dough ball with flour and toss them gently from hand to hand to shake off any excess flour. Put

each floured dough ball into the prepared pan, right up next to the other. This will help the biscuits rise, rather than spreading out. 4. Preheat the air fryer to 380ºF (193ºC). 5. Transfer the cake pan to the basket of the air fryer. Let the ends of the aluminum foil sling hang across the cake pan before returning the basket to the air fryer. 6. Air fry for 20 minutes. Check the biscuits twice to make sure they are not getting too brown on top. If they are, re-arrange the aluminum foil strips to cover any brown parts. After 20 minutes, check the biscuits by inserting a toothpick into the center of the biscuits. It should come out clean. If it needs a little more time, continue to air fry for two extra minutes. Brush the tops of the biscuits with some melted butter and sprinkle a little more grated cheese on top if desired. Pop the basket back into the air fryer for another 2 minutes. 7. Remove the cake pan from the air fryer. Let the biscuits cool for just a minute or two and then turn them out onto a plate and pull apart. Serve immediately.

Oat Bran Muffins

Prep time: 10 minutes | Cook time: 10 to 12 minutes per batch | Makes 8 muffins

- ⅔ cup oat bran
- ½ cup flour
- ¼ cup brown sugar
- 1 teaspoon baking powder
- ½ teaspoon baking soda
- ⅛ teaspoon salt
- ½ cup buttermilk
- 1 egg
- 2 tablespoons canola oil
- ½ cup chopped dates, raisins, or dried cranberries
- 24 paper muffin cups
- Cooking spray

1. Preheat the air fryer to 330ºF (166ºC). 2. In a large bowl, combine the oat bran, flour, brown sugar, baking powder, baking soda, and salt. 3. In a small bowl, beat together the buttermilk, egg, and oil. 4. Pour buttermilk mixture into bowl with dry ingredients and stir just until moistened. Do not beat. 5. Gently stir in dried fruit. 6. Use triple baking cups to help muffins hold shape during baking. Spray them with cooking spray, place 4 sets of cups in air fryer basket at a time, and fill each one ¾ full of batter. 7. Cook for 10 to 12 minutes, until top springs back when lightly touched and toothpick inserted in center comes out clean. 8. Repeat for remaining muffins.

Tomato and Mozzarella Bruschetta

Prep time: 5 minutes | Cook time: 4 minutes | Serves 1

- 6 small loaf slices
- ½ cup tomatoes, finely chopped
- 3 ounces (85 g) Mozzarella
- cheese, grated
- 1 tablespoon fresh basil, chopped
- 1 tablespoon olive oil

1. Preheat the air fryer to 350ºF (177ºC). 2. Put the loaf slices inside the air fryer and air fry for about 3 minutes. 3. Add the tomato, Mozzarella, basil, and olive oil on top. 4. Air fry for an additional minute before serving.

Breakfast Pita

Prep time: 5 minutes | Cook time: 6 minutes | Serves 2

- 1 whole wheat pita
- 2 teaspoons olive oil
- ½ shallot, diced
- ¼ teaspoon garlic, minced
- 1 large egg
- ¼ teaspoon dried oregano
- ¼ teaspoon dried thyme
- ⅛ teaspoon salt
- 2 tablespoons shredded Parmesan cheese

1. Preheat the air fryer to 380°F(193°C). 2. Brush the top of the pita with olive oil, then spread the diced shallot and minced garlic over the pita. 3. Crack the egg into a small bowl or ramekin, and season it with oregano, thyme, and salt. 4. Place the pita into the air fryer basket, and gently pour the egg onto the top of the pita. Sprinkle with cheese over the top. 5. Bake for 6 minutes. 6. Allow to cool for 5 minutes before cutting into pieces for serving.

Fried Chicken Wings with Waffles

Prep time: 10 minutes | Cook time: 30 minutes | Serves 4

- 8 whole chicken wings
- 1 teaspoon garlic powder
- Chicken seasoning, for preparing the chicken
- Freshly ground black pepper, to taste
- ½ cup all-purpose flour
- Cooking oil spray
- 8 frozen waffles
- Pure maple syrup, for serving (optional)

1. In a medium bowl, combine the chicken and garlic powder and season with chicken seasoning and pepper. Toss to coat. 2. Transfer the chicken to a resealable plastic bag and add the flour. Seal the bag and shake it to coat the chicken thoroughly. 3. Insert the crisper plate into the basket and the basket into the unit. Preheat the unit by selecting AIR FRY, setting the temperature to 400°F (204°C), and setting the time to 3 minutes. Select START/STOP to begin. 4. Once the unit is preheated, spray the crisper plate with cooking oil. Using tongs, transfer the chicken from the bag to the basket. It is okay to stack the chicken wings on top of each other. Spray them with cooking oil. 5. Select AIR FRY, set the temperature to 400°F (204°C), and set the time to 20 minutes. Select START/STOP to begin. 6. After 5 minutes, remove the basket and shake the wings. Reinsert the basket to resume cooking. Remove and shake the basket every 5 minutes until the chicken is fully cooked. 7. When the cooking is complete, remove the cooked chicken from the basket; cover to keep warm. 8. Rinse the basket and crisper plate with warm water. Insert them back into the unit. 9. Select AIR FRY, set the temperature to 360°F (182°C), and set the time to 3 minutes. Select START/STOP to begin. 10. Once the unit is preheated, spray the crisper plate with cooking spray. Working in batches, place the frozen waffles into the basket. Do not stack them. Spray the waffles with cooking oil. 11. Select AIR FRY, set the temperature to 360°F (182°C), and set the time to 6 minutes. Select START/STOP to begin. 12. When the cooking is complete, repeat steps 10 and 11 with the remaining waffles. 13. Serve the waffles with the chicken and a touch of maple syrup, if desired.

Baked Egg and Mushroom Cups

Prep time: 5 minutes | Cook time: 15 minutes | Serves 6

- Olive oil cooking spray
- 6 large eggs
- 1 garlic clove, minced
- ½ teaspoon salt
- ½ teaspoon black pepper
- Pinch red pepper flakes
- 8 ounces (227 g) baby bella mushrooms, sliced
- 1 cup fresh baby spinach
- 2 scallions, white parts and green parts, diced

1. Preheat the air fryer to 320°F (160°C). Lightly coat the inside of six silicone muffin cups or a six-cup muffin tin with olive oil cooking spray. 2. In a large bowl, beat the eggs, garlic, salt, pepper, and red pepper flakes for 1 to 2 minutes, or until well combined. 3. Fold in the mushrooms, spinach, and scallions. 4. Divide the mixture evenly among the muffin cups. 5. Place into the air fryer and bake for 12 to 15 minutes, or until the eggs are set. 6. Remove and allow to cool for 5 minutes before serving.

Everything Bagels

Prep time: 15 minutes | Cook time: 14 minutes | Makes 6 bagels

- 1¾ cups shredded Mozzarella cheese or goat cheese Mozzarella
- 2 tablespoons unsalted butter or coconut oil
- 1 large egg, beaten
- 1 tablespoon apple cider
- vinegar
- 1 cup blanched almond flour
- 1 tablespoon baking powder
- ⅛ teaspoon fine sea salt
- 1½ teaspoons everything bagel seasoning

1. Make the dough: Put the Mozzarella and butter in a large microwave-safe bowl and microwave for 1 to 2 minutes, until the cheese is entirely melted. Stir well. Add the egg and vinegar. Using a hand mixer on medium, combine well. Add the almond flour, baking powder, and salt and, using the mixer, combine well. 2. Lay a piece of parchment paper on the countertop and place the dough on it. Knead it for about 3 minutes. The dough should be a little sticky but pliable. (If the dough is too sticky, chill it in the refrigerator for an hour or overnight.) 3. Preheat the air fryer to 350°F (177°C). Spray a baking sheet or pie pan that will fit into your air fryer with avocado oil. 4. Divide the dough into 6 equal portions. Roll 1 portion into a log that is 6 inches long and about ½ inch thick. Form the log into a circle and seal the edges together, making a bagel shape. Repeat with the remaining portions of dough, making 6 bagels. 5. Place the bagels on the greased baking sheet. Spray the bagels with avocado oil and top with everything bagel seasoning, pressing the seasoning into the dough with your hands. 6. Place the bagels in the air fryer and bake for 14 minutes, or until cooked through and golden brown, flipping after 6 minutes. 7. Remove the bagels from the air fryer and allow them to cool slightly before slicing them in half and serving. Store leftovers in an airtight container in the fridge for up to 4 days or in the freezer for up to a month.

Breakfast Meatballs

Prep time: 10 minutes | Cook time: 15 minutes | Makes 18 meatballs

- 1 pound (454 g) ground pork breakfast sausage
- ½ teaspoon salt
- ¼ teaspoon ground black pepper
- ½ cup shredded sharp Cheddar cheese
- 1 ounce (28 g) cream cheese, softened
- 1 large egg, whisked

1. Combine all ingredients in a large bowl. Form mixture into eighteen 1-inch meatballs. 2. Place meatballs into ungreased air fryer basket. Adjust the temperature to 400ºF (204ºC) and air fry for 15 minutes, shaking basket three times during cooking. Meatballs will be browned on the outside and have an internal temperature of at least 145ºF (63ºC) when completely cooked. Serve warm.

Bacon Eggs on the Go

Prep time: 5 minutes | Cook time: 15 minutes | Serves 1

- 2 eggs
- 4 ounces (113 g) bacon, cooked
- Salt and ground black pepper, to taste

1. Preheat the air fryer to 400ºF (204ºC). Put liners in a regular cupcake tin. 2. Crack an egg into each of the cups and add the bacon. Season with some pepper and salt. 3. Bake in the preheated air fryer for 15 minutes, or until the eggs are set. Serve warm.

All-in-One Toast

Prep time: 10 minutes | Cook time: 10 minutes | Serves 1

- 1 strip bacon, diced
- 1 slice 1-inch thick bread
- 1 egg
- Salt and freshly ground black pepper, to taste
- ¼ cup grated Colby cheese

1. Preheat the air fryer to 400ºF (204ºC). 2. Air fry the bacon for 3 minutes, shaking the basket once or twice while it cooks. Remove the bacon to a paper towel lined plate and set aside. 3. Use a sharp paring knife to score a large circle in the middle of the slice of bread, cutting halfway through, but not all the way through to the cutting board. Press down on the circle in the center of the bread slice to create an indentation. 4. Transfer the slice of bread, hole side up, to the air fryer basket. Crack the egg into the center of the bread, and season with salt and pepper. 5. Adjust the air fryer temperature to 380ºF (193ºC) and air fry for 5 minutes. Sprinkle the grated cheese around the edges of the bread, leaving the center of the yolk uncovered, and top with the cooked bacon. Press the cheese and bacon into the bread lightly to help anchor it to the bread and prevent it from blowing around in the air fryer. 6. Air fry for one or two more minutes, just to melt the cheese and finish cooking the egg. Serve immediately.

Cheddar Eggs

Prep time: 5 minutes | Cook time: 15 minutes | Serves 2

- 4 large eggs
- 2 tablespoons unsalted butter, melted
- ½ cup shredded sharp Cheddar cheese

1. Crack eggs into a round baking dish and whisk. Place dish into the air fryer basket. 2. Adjust the temperature to 400ºF (204ºC) and set the timer for 10 minutes. 3. After 5 minutes, stir the eggs and add the butter and cheese. Let cook 3 more minutes and stir again. 4. Allow eggs to finish cooking an additional 2 minutes or remove if they are to your desired liking. 5. Use a fork to fluff. Serve warm.

Egg Muffins

Prep time: 10 minutes | Cook time: 11 to 13 minutes | Serves 4

- 4 eggs
- Salt and pepper, to taste
- Olive oil
- 4 English muffins, split
- 1 cup shredded Colby Jack cheese
- 4 slices ham or Canadian bacon

1. Preheat the air fryer to 390ºF (199ºC). 2. Beat together eggs and add salt and pepper to taste. Spray a baking pan lightly with oil and add eggs. Bake for 2 minutes, stir, and continue cooking for 3 or 4 minutes, stirring every minute, until eggs are scrambled to your preference. Remove pan from air fryer. 3. Place bottom halves of English muffins in air fryer basket. Take half of the shredded cheese and divide it among the muffins. Top each with a slice of ham and one-quarter of the eggs. Sprinkle remaining cheese on top of the eggs. Use a fork to press the cheese into the egg a little so it doesn't slip off before it melts. 4. Air fry at 360ºF (182ºC) for 1 minute. Add English muffin tops and cook for 2 to 4 minutes to heat through and toast the muffins.

Pancake Cake

Prep time: 10 minutes | Cook time: 7 minutes | Serves 4

- ½ cup blanched finely ground almond flour
- ¼ cup powdered erythritol
- ½ teaspoon baking powder
- 2 tablespoons unsalted butter, softened
- 1 large egg
- ½ teaspoon unflavored gelatin
- ½ teaspoon vanilla extract
- ½ teaspoon ground cinnamon

1. In a large bowl, mix almond flour, erythritol, and baking powder. Add butter, egg, gelatin, vanilla, and cinnamon. Pour into a round baking pan. 2. Place pan into the air fryer basket. 3. Adjust the temperature to 300ºF (149ºC) and set the timer for 7 minutes. 4. When the cake is completely cooked, a toothpick will come out clean. Cut cake into four and serve.

Cheesy Cauliflower "Hash Browns"

Prep time: 30 minutes | Cook time: 24 minutes | Makes 6 hash browns

- ◄ 2 ounces (57 g) 100% cheese crisps
- ◄ 1 (12-ounce / 340-g) steamer bag cauliflower, cooked according to package

instructions
- ◄ 1 large egg
- ◄ ½ cup shredded sharp Cheddar cheese
- ◄ ½ teaspoon salt

1. Let cooked cauliflower cool 10 minutes. 2. Place cheese crisps into food processor and pulse on low 30 seconds until crisps are finely ground. 3. Using a kitchen towel, wring out excess moisture from cauliflower and place into food processor. 4. Add egg to food processor and sprinkle with Cheddar and salt. Pulse five times until mixture is mostly smooth. 5. Cut two pieces of parchment to fit air fryer basket. Separate mixture into six even scoops and place three on each piece of ungreased parchment, keeping at least 2 inch of space between each scoop. Press each into a hash brown shape, about ¼ inch thick. 6. Place one batch on parchment into air fryer basket. Adjust the temperature to 375°F (191°C) and air fry for 12 minutes, turning hash browns halfway through cooking. Hash browns will be golden brown when done. Repeat with second batch. 7. Allow 5 minutes to cool. Serve warm.

Honey-Apricot Granola with Greek Yogurt

Prep time: 10 minutes | Cook time: 30 minutes | Serves 6

- ◄ 1 cup rolled oats
- ◄ ¼ cup dried apricots, diced
- ◄ ¼ cup almond slivers
- ◄ ¼ cup walnuts, chopped
- ◄ ¼ cup pumpkin seeds
- ◄ ¼ cup hemp hearts
- ◄ ¼ to ⅓ cup raw honey, plus more for drizzling
- ◄ 1 tablespoon olive oil
- ◄ 1 teaspoon ground cinnamon
- ◄ ¼ teaspoon ground nutmeg
- ◄ ¼ teaspoon salt
- ◄ 2 tablespoons sugar-free dark chocolate chips (optional)
- ◄ 3 cups nonfat plain Greek yogurt

1. Preheat the air fryer to 260°F(127°C). Line the air fryer basket with parchment paper. 2. In a large bowl, combine the oats, apricots, almonds, walnuts, pumpkin seeds, hemp hearts, honey, olive oil, cinnamon, nutmeg, and salt, mixing so that the honey, oil, and spices are well distributed. 3. Pour the mixture onto the parchment paper and spread it into an even layer. 4. Bake for 10 minutes, then shake or stir and spread back out into an even layer. Continue baking for 10 minutes more, then repeat the process of shaking or stirring the mixture. Bake for an additional 10 minutes before removing from the air fryer. 5. Allow the granola to cool

completely before stirring in the chocolate chips (if using) and pouring into an airtight container for storage. 6. For each serving, top ½ cup Greek yogurt with ⅓ cup granola and a drizzle of honey, if needed.

Red Pepper and Feta Frittata

Prep time: 10 minutes | Cook time: 20 minutes | Serves 4

- ◄ Olive oil cooking spray
- ◄ 8 large eggs
- ◄ 1 medium red bell pepper, diced
- ◄ ½ teaspoon salt
- ◄ ½ teaspoon black pepper
- ◄ 1 garlic clove, minced
- ◄ ½ cup feta, divided

1. Preheat the air fryer to 360°F(182°C). Lightly coat the inside of a 6-inch round cake pan with olive oil cooking spray. 2. In a large bowl, beat the eggs for 1 to 2 minutes, or until well combined. 3. Add the bell pepper, salt, black pepper, and garlic to the eggs, and mix together until the bell pepper is distributed throughout. 4. Fold in ¼ cup of the feta cheese. 5. Pour the egg mixture into the prepared cake pan, and sprinkle the remaining ¼ cup of feta over the top. 6. Place into the air fryer and bake for 18 to 20 minutes, or until the eggs are set in the center. 7. Remove from the air fryer and allow to cool for 5 minutes before serving.

Turkey Breakfast Sausage Patties

Prep time: 5 minutes | Cook time: 10 minutes | Serves 4

- ◄ 1 tablespoon chopped fresh thyme
- ◄ 1 tablespoon chopped fresh sage
- ◄ 1¼ teaspoons kosher salt
- ◄ 1 teaspoon chopped fennel seeds
- ◄ ¾ teaspoon smoked paprika
- ◄ ½ teaspoon onion powder
- ◄ ½ teaspoon garlic powder
- ◄ ⅛ teaspoon crushed red pepper flakes
- ◄ ⅛ teaspoon freshly ground black pepper
- ◄ 1 pound (454 g) 93% lean ground turkey
- ◄ ½ cup finely minced sweet apple (peeled)

1. Thoroughly combine the thyme, sage, salt, fennel seeds, paprika, onion powder, garlic powder, red pepper flakes, and black pepper in a medium bowl. 2. Add the ground turkey and apple and stir until well incorporated. Divide the mixture into 8 equal portions and shape into patties with your hands, each about ¼ inch thick and 3 inches in diameter. 3. Preheat the air fryer to 400°F (204°C). 4. Place the patties in the air fryer basket in a single layer. You may need to work in batches to avoid overcrowding. 5. Air fry for 5 minutes. Flip the patties and air fry for 5 minutes, or until the patties are nicely browned and cooked through. 6. Remove from the basket to a plate and repeat with the remaining patties. 7. Serve warm.

Chapter 2

Desserts

Chapter 2 Desserts

Blackberry Peach Cobbler with Vanilla

Prep time: 10 minutes | Cook time: 20 minutes | Serves 4

Filling:
- 1 (6-ounce / 170-g) package blackberries
- 1½ cups chopped peaches, cut into ½-inch thick slices

Topping:
- 2 tablespoons sunflower oil
- 1 tablespoon maple syrup
- 1 teaspoon vanilla
- 3 tablespoons coconut sugar
- ½ cup rolled oats
- 2 teaspoons arrowroot or cornstarch
- 2 tablespoons coconut sugar
- 1 teaspoon lemon juice
- ⅓ cup whole-wheat pastry flour
- 1 teaspoon cinnamon
- ¼ teaspoon nutmeg
- ⅛ teaspoon sea salt

Make the Filling: 1. Combine the blackberries, peaches, arrowroot, coconut sugar, and lemon juice in a baking pan. 2. Using a rubber spatula, stir until well incorporated. Set aside. Make the Topping: 3. Preheat the air fryer to 320ºF (160ºC) 4. Combine the oil, maple syrup, and vanilla in a mixing bowl and stir well. Whisk in the remaining ingredients. Spread this mixture evenly over the filling. 5. Place the pan in the air fryer basket and bake for 20 minutes, or until the topping is crispy and golden brown. Serve warm

Caramelized Fruit Skewers

Prep time: 10 minutes | Cook time: 3 to 5 minutes | Serves 4

- 2 peaches, peeled, pitted, and thickly sliced
- 3 plums, halved and pitted
- 3 nectarines, halved and pitted

Special Equipment:
- 8 metal skewers
- 1 tablespoon honey
- ½ teaspoon ground cinnamon
- ¼ teaspoon ground allspice
- Pinch cayenne pepper

1. Preheat the air fryer to 400ºF (204ºC). 2. Thread, alternating peaches, plums, and nectarines, onto the metal skewers that fit into the air fryer. 3. Thoroughly combine the honey, cinnamon, allspice, and cayenne in a small bowl. Brush generously the glaze over the fruit skewers. 4. Transfer the fruit skewers to the air fryer basket. You may need to cook in batches to avoid overcrowding. 5. Air fry for 3 to 5 minutes, or until the fruit is caramelized. 6. Remove from the basket and repeat with the remaining fruit skewers. 7. Let the fruit skewers rest for 5 minutes before serving.

Butter Flax Cookies

Prep time: 25 minutes | Cook time: 20 minutes | Serves 4

- 8 ounces (227 g) almond meal
- 2 tablespoons flaxseed meal
- 1 ounce (28 g) monk fruit
- 1 teaspoon baking powder
- A pinch of grated nutmeg
- A pinch of coarse salt
- 1 large egg, room temperature.
- 1 stick butter, room temperature
- 1 teaspoon vanilla extract

1. Mix the almond meal, flaxseed meal, monk fruit, baking powder, grated nutmeg, and salt in a bowl. 2. In a separate bowl, whisk the egg, butter, and vanilla extract. 3. Stir the egg mixture into dry mixture; mix to combine well or until it forms a nice, soft dough. 4. Roll your dough out and cut out with a cookie cutter of your choice. Bake in the preheated air fryer at 350ºF (177ºC) for 10 minutes. Decrease the temperature to 330ºF (166ºC) and cook for 10 minutes longer. Bon appétit!

Dark Chocolate Lava Cake

Prep time: 5 minutes | Cook time: 10 minutes | Serves 4

- Olive oil cooking spray
- ¼ cup whole wheat flour
- 1 tablespoon unsweetened dark chocolate cocoa powder
- ⅛ teaspoon salt
- ½ teaspoon baking powder
- ¼ cup raw honey
- 1 egg
- 2 tablespoons olive oil

1. Preheat the air fryer to 380°F(193ºC). Lightly coat the insides of four ramekins with olive oil cooking spray. 2. In a medium bowl, combine the flour, cocoa powder, salt, baking powder, honey, egg, and olive oil. 3. Divide the batter evenly among the ramekins. 4. Place the filled ramekins inside the air fryer and bake for 10 minutes. 5. Remove the lava cakes from the air fryer and slide a knife around the outside edge of each cake. Turn each ramekin upside down on a saucer and serve.

Kentucky Chocolate Nut Pie

Prep time: 20 minutes | Cook time: 25 minutes | Serves 8

◀ 2 large eggs, beaten
◀ ⅓ cup butter, melted
◀ 1 cup sugar
◀ ½ cup all-purpose flour
◀ 1½ cups coarsely chopped

pecans
◀ 1 cup milk chocolate chips
◀ 2 tablespoons bourbon
◀ 1 (9-inch) unbaked piecrust

1. In a large bowl, stir together the eggs and melted butter. Add the sugar and flour and stir until combined. Stir in the pecans, chocolate chips, and bourbon until well mixed. 2. Using a fork, prick holes in the bottom and sides of the pie crust. Pour the pie filling into the crust. 3. Preheat the air fryer to 350ºF (177ºC). 4. Cook for 25 minutes, or until a knife inserted into the middle of the pie comes out clean. Let set for 5 minutes before serving.

Olive Oil Cake

Prep time: 10 minutes | Cook time: 30 minutes | Serves 8

◀ 2 cups blanched finely
ground almond flour
◀ 5 large eggs, whisked
◀ ¾ cup extra-virgin olive oil

◀ ⅓ cup granular erythritol
◀ 1 teaspoon vanilla extract
◀ 1 teaspoon baking powder

1. In a large bowl, mix all ingredients. Pour batter into an ungreased round nonstick baking dish. 2. Place dish into air fryer basket. Adjust the temperature to 300ºF (149ºC) and bake for 30 minutes. The cake will be golden on top and firm in the center when done. 3. Let cake cool in dish 30 minutes before slicing and serving.

Maple Bacon Moonshine Bread Pudding

Prep time: 20 minutes | Cook time: 15 minutes | Serves 6

◀ 1 cup whole milk
◀ 1 (4.6-ounce / 130-g)
package cook-and-serve
vanilla pudding and pie
filling
◀ ¼ cup granulated sugar
◀ 2 large eggs, beaten
◀ 1 tablespoon butter, melted
◀ 1 teaspoon ground cinnamon
◀ 1 teaspoon vanilla extract

◀ 4 cups loosely packed cubed
French bread
◀ ¼ cup packed light brown
sugar
◀ ½ cup chopped toasted
pecans
◀ ¾ cup maple bacon
moonshine, plus 3
tablespoons
◀ 1 to 2 tablespoons oil

1. In a large bowl, whisk the milk, pudding mix, granulated sugar,

eggs, melted butter, cinnamon, and vanilla until blended. Add the bread cubes and let soak for 10 minutes. 2. In a small bowl, stir together the brown sugar, pecans, and ¾ cup moonshine. Stir the pecan mixture into the bread mixture. 3. Preheat the air fryer to 355ºF (179ºC). Spritz a baking pan with oil. 4. Transfer the bread mixture to the prepared pan. 5. Bake for 10 minutes. The bottom of the pudding will still be mushy. Stir. Bake for 5 minutes more and stir again. The pudding will be soft, but not runny, and a knife inserted into the middle will have soft crumbs attached. 6. Drizzle the remaining 3 tablespoons of maple bacon moonshine over the pudding.

Pecan Brownies

Prep time: 10 minutes | Cook time: 20 minutes | Serves 6
◀ ½ cup blanched finely
ground almond flour
◀ ½ cup powdered erythritol
◀ 2 tablespoons unsweetened
cocoa powder
◀ ½ teaspoon baking powder

◀ ¼ cup unsalted butter,
softened
◀ 1 large egg
◀ ¼ cup chopped pecans
◀ ¼ cup low-carb, sugar-free
chocolate chips

1. In a large bowl, mix almond flour, erythritol, cocoa powder, and baking powder. Stir in butter and egg. 2. Fold in pecans and chocolate chips. Scoop mixture into a round baking pan. Place pan into the air fryer basket. 3. Adjust the temperature to 300ºF (149ºC) and bake for 20 minutes. 4. When fully cooked a toothpick inserted in center will come out clean. Allow 20 minutes to fully cool and firm up.

Almond Shortbread

Prep time: 10 minutes | Cook time: 12 minutes | Serves 8

◀ ½ cup (1 stick) unsalted
butter
◀ ½ cup sugar

◀ 1 teaspoon pure almond
extract
◀ 1 cup all-purpose flour

1. In bowl of a stand mixer fitted with the paddle attachment, beat the butter and sugar on medium speed until light and fluffy, 3 to 4 minutes. Add the almond extract and beat until combined, about 30 seconds. Turn the mixer to low. Add the flour a little at a time and beat for about 2 minutes more until well-incorporated. 2. Pat the dough into an even layer in a baking pan. Place the pan in the air fryer basket. Set the air fryer to 375ºF (191ºC) for 12 minutes. 3. Carefully remove the pan from air fryer basket. While the shortbread is still warm and soft, cut it into 8 wedges. 4. Let cool in the pan on a wire rack for 5 minutes. Remove the wedges from the pan and let cool completely on the rack before serving.

Brown Sugar Banana Bread

Prep time: 20 minutes | Cook time: 22 to 24 minutes | Serves 4

- 1 cup packed light brown sugar
- 1 large egg, beaten
- 2 tablespoons butter, melted
- ½ cup milk, whole or 2%
- 2 cups all-purpose flour
- 1½ teaspoons baking powder
- 1 teaspoon ground cinnamon
- ½ teaspoon salt
- 1 banana, mashed
- 1 to 2 tablespoons oil
- ¼ cup confectioners' sugar (optional)

1. In a large bowl, stir together the brown sugar, egg, melted butter, and milk. 2. In a medium bowl, whisk the flour, baking powder, cinnamon, and salt until blended. Add the flour mixture to the sugar mixture and stir just to blend. 3. Add the mashed banana and stir to combine. 4. Preheat the air fryer to 350°F (177°C). Spritz 2 mini loaf pans with oil. 5. Evenly divide the batter between the prepared pans and place them in the air fryer basket. 6. Cook for 22 to 24 minutes, or until a knife inserted into the middle of the loaves comes out clean. 7. Dust the warm loaves with confectioners' sugar (if using).

Honeyed Roasted Apples with Walnuts

Prep time: 5 minutes | Cook time: 12 to 15 minutes | Serves 4

- 2 Granny Smith apples
- ¼ cup certified gluten-free rolled oats
- 2 tablespoons honey
- ½ teaspoon ground
- cinnamon
- 2 tablespoons chopped walnuts
- Pinch salt
- 1 tablespoon olive oil

1. Preheat the air fryer to 380°F(193°C). 2. Core the apples and slice them in half. 3. In a medium bowl, mix together the oats, honey, cinnamon, walnuts, salt, and olive oil. 4. Scoop a quarter of the oat mixture onto the top of each half apple. 5. Place the apples in the air fryer basket, and roast for 12 to 15 minutes, or until the apples are fork-tender.

Coconut Macaroons

Prep time: 5 minutes | Cook time: 8 to 10 minutes | Makes 12 macaroons

- 1⅓ cups shredded, sweetened coconut
- 4½ teaspoons flour
- 2 tablespoons sugar
- 1 egg white
- ½ teaspoon almond extract

1. Preheat the air fryer to 330°F (166°C). 2. Mix all ingredients together. 3. Shape coconut mixture into 12 balls. 4. Place all 12 macaroons in air fryer basket. They won't expand, so you can place them close together, but they shouldn't touch. 5. Air fry at 330°F (166°C) for 8 to 10 minutes, until golden.

Pumpkin Cookie with Cream Cheese Frosting

Prep time: 10 minutes | Cook time: 7 minutes | Serves 6

- ½ cup blanched finely ground almond flour
- ½ cup powdered erythritol, divided
- 2 tablespoons butter, softened
- 1 large egg
- ½ teaspoon unflavored gelatin
- ½ teaspoon baking powder
- ½ teaspoon vanilla extract
- ½ teaspoon pumpkin pie spice
- 2 tablespoons pure pumpkin purée
- ½ teaspoon ground cinnamon, divided
- ¼ cup low-carb, sugar-free chocolate chips
- 3 ounces (85 g) full-fat cream cheese, softened

1. In a large bowl, mix almond flour and ¼ cup erythritol. Stir in butter, egg, and gelatin until combined. 2. Stir in baking powder, vanilla, pumpkin pie spice, pumpkin purée, and ¼ teaspoon cinnamon, then fold in chocolate chips. 3. Pour batter into a round baking pan. Place pan into the air fryer basket. 4. Adjust the temperature to 300°F (149°C) and bake for 7 minutes. 5. When fully cooked, the top will be golden brown and a toothpick inserted in center will come out clean. Let cool at least 20 minutes. 6. To make the frosting: mix cream cheese, remaining ¼ teaspoon cinnamon, and remaining ¼ cup erythritol in a large bowl. Using an electric mixer, beat until it becomes fluffy. Spread onto the cooled cookie. Garnish with additional cinnamon if desired.

Zucchini Bread

Prep time: 10 minutes | Cook time: 40 minutes | Serves 12

- 2 cups coconut flour
- 2 teaspoons baking powder
- ¾ cup erythritol
- ½ cup coconut oil, melted
- 1 teaspoon apple cider
- vinegar
- 1 teaspoon vanilla extract
- 3 eggs, beaten
- 1 zucchini, grated
- 1 teaspoon ground cinnamon

1. In the mixing bowl, mix coconut flour with baking powder, erythritol, coconut oil, apple cider vinegar, vanilla extract, eggs, zucchini, and ground cinnamon. 2. Transfer the mixture into the air fryer basket and flatten it in the shape of the bread. 3. Cook the bread at 350°F (177°C) for 40 minutes.

Coconut-Custard Pie

Prep time: 10 minutes | Cook time: 20 to 23 minutes | Serves 4

- 1 cup milk
- ¼ cup plus 2 tablespoons sugar
- ¼ cup biscuit baking mix
- 1 teaspoon vanilla

- 2 eggs
- 2 tablespoons melted butter
- Cooking spray
- ½ cup shredded, sweetened coconut

1. Place all ingredients except coconut in a medium bowl. 2. Using a hand mixer, beat on high speed for 3 minutes. 3. Let sit for 5 minutes. 4. Preheat the air fryer to 330ºF (166ºC). 5. Spray a baking pan with cooking spray and place pan in air fryer basket. 6. Pour filling into pan and sprinkle coconut over top. 7. Cook pie at 330ºF (166ºC) for 20 to 23 minutes or until center sets.

Pumpkin Pudding with Vanilla Wafers

Prep time: 10 minutes | Cook time: 12 to 17 minutes | Serves 4

- 1 cup canned no-salt-added pumpkin purée (not pumpkin pie filling)
- ¼ cup packed brown sugar
- 3 tablespoons all-purpose flour
- 1 egg, whisked

- 2 tablespoons milk
- 1 tablespoon unsalted butter, melted
- 1 teaspoon pure vanilla extract
- 4 low-fat vanilla wafers, crumbled
- Nonstick cooking spray

1. Preheat the air fryer to 350ºF (177ºC). Coat a baking pan with nonstick cooking spray. Set aside. 2. Mix the pumpkin purée, brown sugar, flour, whisked egg, milk, melted butter, and vanilla in a medium bowl and whisk to combine. Transfer the mixture to the baking pan. 3. Place the baking pan in the air fryer basket and bake for 12 to 17 minutes until set. 4. Remove the pudding from the basket to a wire rack to cool. 5. Divide the pudding into four bowls and serve with the vanilla wafers sprinkled on top.

Lush Chocolate Chip Cookies

Prep time: 7 minutes | Cook time: 9 minutes | Serves 4

- 3 tablespoons butter, at room temperature
- ⅓ cup plus 1 tablespoon light brown sugar
- 1 egg yolk
- ½ cup all-purpose flour
- 2 tablespoons ground white chocolate

- ¼ teaspoon baking soda
- ½ teaspoon vanilla extract
- ¾ cup semisweet chocolate chips
- Nonstick flour-infused baking spray

1. In medium bowl, beat together the butter and brown sugar until fluffy. Stir in the egg yolk. 2. Add the flour, white chocolate, baking soda, and vanilla and mix well. Stir in the chocolate chips. 3. Line a 6-by-2-inch round baking pan with parchment paper. Spray the parchment paper with flour-infused baking spray. 4. Insert the crisper plate into the basket and the basket into the unit. Preheat the unit by selecting BAKE, setting the temperature to 300ºF (149ºC), and setting the time to 3 minutes. Select START/STOP to begin. 5. Spread the batter into the prepared pan, leaving a ½-inch border on all sides. 6. Once the unit is preheated, place the pan into the basket. 7. Select BAKE, set the temperature to 300ºF (149ºC), and set the time to 9 minutes. Select START/STOP to begin. 8. When the cooking is complete, the cookie should be light brown and just barely set. Remove the pan from the basket and let cool for 10 minutes. Remove the cookie from the pan, remove the parchment paper, and let cool completely on a wire rack.

Coconut Mixed Berry Crisp

Prep time: 5 minutes | Cook time: 20 minutes | Serves 6

- 1 tablespoon butter, melted
- 12 ounces (340 g) mixed berries
- ⅓ cup granulated Swerve
- 1 teaspoon pure vanilla extract
- ½ teaspoon ground cinnamon
- ¼ teaspoon ground cloves
- ¼ teaspoon grated nutmeg
- ½ cup coconut chips, for garnish

1. Preheat the air fryer to 330ºF (166ºC). Coat a baking pan with melted butter. 2. Put the remaining ingredients except the coconut chips in the prepared baking pan. 3. Bake in the preheated air fryer for 20 minutes. 4. Serve garnished with the coconut chips.

Oatmeal Raisin Bars

Prep time: 15 minutes | Cook time: 15 minutes | Serves 8

- ⅓ cup all-purpose flour
- ¼ teaspoon kosher salt
- ¼ teaspoon baking powder
- ¼ teaspoon ground cinnamon
- ¼ cup light brown sugar, lightly packed
- ¼ cup granulated sugar
- ½ cup canola oil
- 1 large egg
- 1 teaspoon vanilla extract
- 1⅓ cups quick-cooking oats
- ⅓ cup raisins

1. Preheat the air fryer to 360ºF (182ºC). 2. In a large bowl, combine the all-purpose flour, kosher salt, baking powder, ground cinnamon, light brown sugar, granulated sugar, canola oil, egg, vanilla extract, quick-cooking oats, and raisins. 3. Spray a baking pan with nonstick cooking spray, then pour the oat mixture into the pan and press down to evenly distribute. Place the pan in the air fryer and bake for 15 minutes or until golden brown. 4. Remove from the air fryer and allow to cool in the pan on a wire rack for 20 minutes before slicing and serving.

Chocolate Chip-Pecan Biscotti

Prep time: 15 minutes | Cook time: 20 to 22 minutes | Serves 10

- 1¼ cups finely ground blanched almond flour
- ¾ teaspoon baking powder
- ½ teaspoon xanthan gum
- ¼ teaspoon sea salt
- 3 tablespoons unsalted butter, at room temperature
- ⅓ cup Swerve
- 1 large egg, beaten
- 1 teaspoon pure vanilla extract
- ⅓ cup chopped pecans
- ¼ cup stevia-sweetened chocolate chips, such as Lily's Sweets brand
- Melted stevia-sweetened chocolate chips and chopped pecans, for topping (optional)

1. In a large bowl, combine the almond flour, baking powder, xanthan gum, and salt. 2. Line a cake pan that fits inside your air fryer with parchment paper. 3. In the bowl of a stand mixer, beat together the butter and Swerve. Add the beaten egg and vanilla, and beat for about 3 minutes. 4. Add the almond flour mixture to the butter-and-egg mixture; beat until just combined. 5. Stir in the pecans and chocolate chips. 6. Transfer the dough to the prepared pan, and press it into the bottom. 7. Set the air fryer to 325ºF (163ºC) and bake for 12 minutes. Remove from the air fryer and let cool for 15 minutes. Using a sharp knife, cut the cookie into thin strips, then return the strips to the cake pan with the bottom sides facing up. 8. Set the air fryer to 300ºF (149ºC). Bake for 8 to 10 minutes. 9. Remove from the air fryer and let cool completely on a wire rack. If desired, dip one side of each biscotti piece into melted chocolate chips, and top with chopped pecans.

Chapter 3

Snacks and Appetizers

Chapter 3 Snacks and Appetizers

Dark Chocolate and Cranberry Granola Bars

Prep time: 5 minutes | Cook time: 15 minutes | Serves 6

- ◁ 2 cups certified gluten-free quick oats
- ◁ 2 tablespoons sugar-free dark chocolate chunks
- ◁ 2 tablespoons unsweetened dried cranberries
- ◁ 3 tablespoons unsweetened shredded coconut
- ◁ ½ cup raw honey
- ◁ 1 teaspoon ground cinnamon
- ◁ ⅛ teaspoon salt
- ◁ 2 tablespoons olive oil

1. Preheat the air fryer to 360°F(182°C). Line an 8-by-8-inch baking dish with parchment paper that comes up the side so you can lift it out after cooking. 2. In a large bowl, mix together all of the ingredients until well combined. 3. Press the oat mixture into the pan in an even layer. 4. Place the pan into the air fryer basket and bake for 15 minutes. 5. Remove the pan from the air fryer, and lift the granola cake out of the pan using the edges of the parchment paper. 6. Allow to cool for 5 minutes before slicing into 6 equal bars. 7. Serve immediately, or wrap in plastic wrap and store at room temperature for up to 1 week.

Chile-Brined Fried Calamari

Prep time: 20 minutes | Cook time: 8 minutes | Serves 2

- ◁ 1 (8 ounces / 227 g) jar sweet or hot pickled cherry peppers
- ◁ ½ pound (227 g) calamari bodies and tentacles, bodies cut into ½-inch-wide rings
- ◁ 1 lemon
- ◁ 2 cups all-purpose flour
- ◁ Kosher salt and freshly
- ground black pepper, to taste
- ◁ 3 large eggs, lightly beaten
- ◁ Cooking spray
- ◁ ½ cup mayonnaise
- ◁ 1 teaspoon finely chopped rosemary
- ◁ 1 garlic clove, minced

1. Drain the pickled pepper brine into a large bowl and tear the peppers into bite-size strips. Add the pepper strips and calamari to the brine and let stand in the refrigerator for 20 minutes or up to 2 hours. 2. Grate the lemon zest into a large bowl then whisk in the flour and season with salt and pepper. Dip the calamari and pepper strips in the egg, then toss them in the flour mixture until fully coated. Spray the calamari and peppers liberally with cooking spray, then transfer half to the air fryer. Air fry at 400°F (204°C), shaking the basket halfway into cooking, until the calamari is cooked through and golden brown, about 8 minutes. Transfer to a plate and repeat with the remaining pieces. 3. In a small bowl, whisk together the mayonnaise, rosemary, and garlic. Squeeze half the zested lemon to get 1 tablespoon of juice and stir it into the sauce. Season with salt and pepper. Cut the remaining zested lemon half into 4 small wedges and serve alongside the calamari, peppers, and sauce.

Crunchy Basil White Beans

Prep time: 2 minutes | Cook time: 19 minutes | Serves 2

- ◁ 1 (15 ounces / 425 g) can cooked white beans
- ◁ 2 tablespoons olive oil
- ◁ 1 teaspoon fresh sage, chopped
- ◁ ¼ teaspoon garlic powder
- ◁ ¼ teaspoon salt, divided
- ◁ 1 teaspoon chopped fresh basil

1. Preheat the air fryer to 380°F(193°C). 2. In a medium bowl, mix together the beans, olive oil, sage, garlic, ⅛ teaspoon salt, and basil. 3. Pour the white beans into the air fryer and spread them out in a single layer. 4. Bake for 10 minutes. Stir and continue cooking for an additional 5 to 9 minutes, or until they reach your preferred level of crispiness. 5. Toss with the remaining ⅛ teaspoon salt before serving.

Crispy Breaded Beef Cubes

Prep time: 10 minutes | Cook time: 12 to 16 minutes | Serves 4

- ◁ 1 pound (454 g) sirloin tip, cut into 1-inch cubes
- ◁ 1 cup cheese pasta sauce
- ◁ 1½ cups soft bread crumbs
- ◁ 2 tablespoons olive oil
- ◁ ½ teaspoon dried marjoram

1. Preheat the air fryer to 360°F (182°C). 2. In a medium bowl, toss the beef with the pasta sauce to coat. 3. In a shallow bowl, combine the bread crumbs, oil, and marjoram, and mix well. Drop the beef cubes, one at a time, into the bread crumb mixture to coat thoroughly. 4. Air fry the beef in two batches for 6 to 8 minutes, shaking the basket once during cooking time, until the beef is at least 145°F (63°C) and the outside is crisp and brown. 5. Serve hot.

Crunchy Tex-Mex Tortilla Chips

Prep time: 5 minutes | Cook time: 5 minutes | Serves 4

- Olive oil
- ½ teaspoon salt
- ½ teaspoon ground cumin
- ½ teaspoon chili powder
- ½ teaspoon paprika
- Pinch cayenne pepper
- 8 (6-inch) corn tortillas, each cut into 6 wedges

1. Spray fryer basket lightly with olive oil. 2. In a small bowl, combine the salt, cumin, chili powder, paprika, and cayenne pepper. 3. Place the tortilla wedges in the air fryer basket in a single layer. Spray the tortillas lightly with oil and sprinkle with some of the seasoning mixture. You will need to cook the tortillas in batches. 4. Air fry at 375ºF (191ºC) for 2 to 3 minutes. Shake the basket and cook until the chips are light brown and crispy, an additional 2 to 3 minutes. Watch the chips closely so they do not burn.

Stuffed Figs with Goat Cheese and Honey

Prep time: 5 minutes | Cook time: 10 minutes | Serves 4

- 8 fresh figs
- 2 ounces (57 g) goat cheese
- ¼ teaspoon ground cinnamon
- 1 tablespoon honey, plus more for serving
- 1 tablespoon olive oil

1. Preheat the air fryer to 360°F(182ºC). 2. Cut the stem off of each fig. 3. Cut an X into the top of each fig, cutting halfway down the fig. Leave the base intact. 4. In a small bowl, mix together the goat cheese, cinnamon, and honey. 5. Spoon the goat cheese mixture into the cavity of each fig. 6. Place the figs in a single layer in the air fryer basket. Drizzle the olive oil over top of the figs and roast for 10 minutes. 7. Serve with an additional drizzle of honey.

Onion Pakoras

Prep time: 30 minutes | Cook time: 10 minutes per batch | Serves 2

- 2 medium yellow or white onions, sliced (2 cups)
- ½ cup chopped fresh cilantro
- 2 tablespoons vegetable oil
- 1 tablespoon chickpea flour
- 1 tablespoon rice flour, or 2 tablespoons chickpea flour
- 1 teaspoon ground turmeric
- 1 teaspoon cumin seeds
- 1 teaspoon kosher salt
- ½ teaspoon cayenne pepper
- Vegetable oil spray

1. In a large bowl, combine the onions, cilantro, oil, chickpea flour, rice flour, turmeric, cumin seeds, salt, and cayenne. Stir to combine.

Cover and let stand for 30 minutes or up to overnight. (This allows the onions to release moisture, creating a batter.) Mix well before using. 2. Spray the air fryer basket generously with vegetable oil spray. Drop half of the batter in 6 heaping tablespoons into the basket. Set the air fryer to 350ºF (177ºC) for 8 minutes. Carefully turn the pakoras over and spray with oil spray. Set the air fryer for 2 minutes, or until the batter is cooked through and crisp. 3. Repeat with remaining batter to make 6 more pakoras, checking at 6 minutes for doneness. Serve hot.

Root Veggie Chips with Herb Salt

Prep time: 10 minutes | Cook time: 8 minutes | Serves 2

- 1 parsnip, washed
- 1 small beet, washed
- 1 small turnip, washed
- ½ small sweet potato, washed
- 1 teaspoon olive oil
- Cooking spray
- Herb Salt:
- ¼ teaspoon kosher salt
- 2 teaspoons finely chopped fresh parsley

1. Preheat the air fryer to 360ºF (182ºC). 2. Peel and thinly slice the parsnip, beet, turnip, and sweet potato, then place the vegetables in a large bowl, add the olive oil, and toss. 3. Spray the air fryer basket with cooking spray, then place the vegetables in the basket and air fry for 8 minutes, gently shaking the basket halfway through. 4. While the chips cook, make the herb salt in a small bowl by combining the kosher salt and parsley. 5. Remove the chips and place on a serving plate, then sprinkle the herb salt on top and allow to cool for 2 to 3 minutes before serving.

Spiced Nuts

Prep time: 5 minutes | Cook time: 25 minutes | Makes 3 cups

- 1 egg white, lightly beaten
- ¼ cup sugar
- 1 teaspoon salt
- ½ teaspoon ground cinnamon
- ¼ teaspoon ground cloves
- ¼ teaspoon ground allspice
- Pinch ground cayenne pepper
- 1 cup pecan halves
- 1 cup cashews
- 1 cup almonds

1. Combine the egg white with the sugar and spices in a bowl. 2. Preheat the air fryer to 300ºF (149ºC). 3. Spray or brush the air fryer basket with vegetable oil. Toss the nuts together in the spiced egg white and transfer the nuts to the air fryer basket. 4. Air fry for 25 minutes, stirring the nuts in the basket a few times during the cooking process. Taste the nuts (carefully because they will be very hot) to see if they are crunchy and nicely toasted. Air fry for a few more minutes if necessary. 5. Serve warm or cool to room temperature and store in an airtight container for up to two weeks.

Roasted Mushrooms with Garlic

Prep time: 3 minutes | Cook time: 22 to 27 minutes | Serves 4

- 16 garlic cloves, peeled
- 2 teaspoons olive oil, divided
- 16 button mushrooms
- ½ teaspoon dried marjoram
- ⅛ teaspoon freshly ground black pepper
- 1 tablespoon white wine or low-sodium vegetable broth

1. In a baking pan, mix the garlic with 1 teaspoon of olive oil. Roast in the air fryer at 350°F (177°C) for 12 minutes. 2. Add the mushrooms, marjoram, and pepper. Stir to coat. Drizzle with the remaining 1 teaspoon of olive oil and the white wine. 3. Return to the air fryer and roast for 10 to 15 minutes more, or until the mushrooms and garlic cloves are tender. Serve.

Fried Artichoke Hearts

Prep time: 10 minutes | Cook time: 12 minutes | Serves 10

- Oil, for spraying
- 3 (14 ounces / 397 g) cans quartered artichokes, drained and patted dry
- ½ cup mayonnaise
- 1 cup panko bread crumbs
- ⅓ cup grated Parmesan cheese
- Salt and freshly ground black pepper, to taste

1. Line the air fryer basket with parchment and spray lightly with oil. 2. Place the artichokes on a plate. Put the mayonnaise and bread crumbs in separate bowls. 3. Working one at a time, dredge each artichoke piece in the mayonnaise, then in the bread crumbs to cover. 4. Place the artichokes in the prepared basket. You may need to work in batches, depending on the size of your air fryer. 5. Air fry at 370°F (188°C) for 10 to 12 minutes, or until crispy and golden brown. 6. Sprinkle with the Parmesan cheese and season with salt and black pepper. Serve immediately.

Lemony Endive in Curried Yogurt

Prep time: 5 minutes | Cook time: 10 minutes | Serves 6

- 6 heads endive
- ½ cup plain and fat-free yogurt
- 3 tablespoons lemon juice
- 1 teaspoon garlic powder
- ½ teaspoon curry powder
- Salt and ground black pepper, to taste

1. Wash the endives, and slice them in half lengthwise. 2. In a bowl, mix together the yogurt, lemon juice, garlic powder, curry powder, salt and pepper. 3. Brush the endive halves with the marinade, coating them completely. Allow to sit for at least 30 minutes or up to 24 hours. 4. Preheat the air fryer to 320°F (160°C). 5. Put the endives in the air fryer basket and air fry for 10 minutes. 6. Serve hot.

Cinnamon Apple Chips

Prep time: 5 minutes | Cook time: 7 to 8 hours | Serves 4

- 4 medium apples, any type, cored and cut into ⅓-inch-thick slices (thin slices yield crunchy chips)
- ¼ teaspoon ground cinnamon
- ¼ teaspoon ground nutmeg

1. Place the apple slices in a large bowl. Sprinkle the cinnamon and nutmeg onto the apple slices and toss to coat. 2. Insert the crisper plate into the basket and the basket into the unit. Preheat the unit by selecting DEHYDRATE, setting the temperature to 135°F (57°C), and setting the time to 3 minutes. Select START/STOP to begin. 3. Once the unit is preheated, place the apple chips into the basket. It is okay to stack them. 4. Select DEHYDRATE, set the temperature to 135°F (57°C), and set the time to 7 or 8 hours. Select START/STOP to begin. 5. When the cooking is complete, cool the apple chips. Serve or store at room temperature in an airtight container for up to 1 week.

Fried Peaches

Prep time: 15 minutes | Cook time: 6 to 8 minutes | Serves 4

- 2 egg whites
- 1 tablespoon water
- ¼ cup sliced almonds
- 2 tablespoons brown sugar
- ½ teaspoon almond extract
- 1 cup crisp rice cereal
- 2 medium, very firm peaches, peeled and pitted
- ¼ cup cornstarch
- Oil for misting or cooking spray

1. Preheat the air fryer to 390°F (199°C). 2. Beat together egg whites and water in a shallow dish. 3. In a food processor, combine the almonds, brown sugar, and almond extract. Process until ingredients combine well and the nuts are finely chopped. 4. Add cereal and pulse just until cereal crushes. Pour crumb mixture into a shallow dish or onto a plate. 5. Cut each peach into eighths and place in a plastic bag or container with lid. Add cornstarch, seal, and shake to coat. 6. Remove peach slices from bag or container, tapping them hard to shake off the excess cornstarch. Dip in egg wash and roll in crumbs. Spray with oil. 7. Place in air fryer basket and cook for 5 minutes. Shake basket, separate any that have stuck together, and spritz a little oil on any spots that aren't browning. 8. Cook for 1 to 3 minutes longer, until golden brown and crispy.

Cinnamon-Apple Chips

Prep time: 10 minutes | Cook time: 32 minutes | Serves 4

- Oil, for spraying
- 2 Red Delicious or Honeycrisp apples
- ¼ teaspoon ground cinnamon, divided

1. Line the air fryer basket with parchment and spray lightly with oil. 2. Trim the uneven ends off the apples. Using a mandoline on the thinnest setting or a sharp knife, cut the apples into very thin slices. Discard the cores. 3. Place half of the apple slices in a single layer in the prepared basket and sprinkle with half of the cinnamon. 4. Place a metal air fryer trivet on top of the apples to keep them from flying around while they are cooking. 5. Air fry at 300°F (149°C) for 16 minutes, flipping every 5 minutes to ensure even cooking. Repeat with the remaining apple slices and cinnamon. 6. Let cool to room temperature before serving. The chips will firm up as they cool.

Golden Onion Rings

Prep time: 15 minutes | Cook time: 14 minutes per batch | Serves 4

- 1 large white onion, peeled and cut into ½ to ¾-inch-thick slices (about 2 cups)
- ½ cup 2% milk
- 1 cup whole-wheat pastry flour, or all-purpose flour
- 2 tablespoons cornstarch
- ¾ teaspoon sea salt, divided
- ½ teaspoon freshly ground black pepper, divided
- ¾ teaspoon granulated garlic, divided
- 1½ cups whole-grain bread crumbs, or gluten-free bread crumbs
- Cooking oil spray (coconut, sunflower, or safflower)
- Ketchup, for serving (optional)

1. Carefully separate the onion slices into rings—a gentle touch is important here. 2. Place the milk in a shallow bowl and set aside. 3. Make the first breading: In a medium bowl, stir together the flour, cornstarch, ¼ teaspoon of salt, ¼ teaspoon of pepper, and ¼ teaspoon of granulated garlic. Set aside. 4. Make the second breading: In a separate medium bowl, stir together the bread crumbs with the remaining ½ teaspoon of salt, the remaining ½ teaspoon of garlic, and the remaining ½ teaspoon of pepper. Set aside. 5. Insert the crisper plate into the basket and the basket into the unit. Preheat the unit by selecting AIR FRY, setting the temperature to 390°F (199°C), and setting the time to 3 minutes. Select START/STOP to begin. 6. Once the unit is preheated, spray the crisper plate and the basket with cooking oil. 7. To make the onion rings, dip one ring into the milk and into the first breading mixture. Dip the ring into the milk again and back into the first breading mixture, coating thoroughly. Dip the ring into the milk one last time and then into the second breading mixture, coating thoroughly. Gently lay the onion ring in the basket. Repeat with additional rings and, as you place them into the basket, do not overlap them too much. Once all the onion rings are in the basket, generously spray the tops with cooking oil. 8. Select AIR FRY, set the temperature to 390°F (199°C), and set the time to 14 minutes. Insert the basket into the unit. Select START/STOP to begin. 9. After 4 minutes, open the unit and spray the rings generously with cooking oil. Close the unit to resume cooking. After 3 minutes, remove the basket and spray the onion rings again. Remove the rings, turn them over, and place them back into the basket. Generously spray them again with oil. Reinsert the basket to resume cooking. After 4 minutes, generously spray the rings with oil one last time. Resume cooking for the remaining 3 minutes, or until the onion rings are very crunchy and brown. 10. When the cooking is complete, serve the hot rings with ketchup, or other sauce of choice.

Carrot Chips

Prep time: 15 minutes | Cook time: 8 to 10 minutes | Serves 4

- 1 tablespoon olive oil, plus more for greasing the basket
- 4 to 5 medium carrots,
- trimmed and thinly sliced
- 1 teaspoon seasoned salt

1. Preheat the air fryer to 390°F (199°C). Grease the air fryer basket with the olive oil. 2. Toss the carrot slices with 1 tablespoon of olive oil and salt in a medium bowl until thoroughly coated. 3. Arrange the carrot slices in the greased basket. You may need to work in batches to avoid overcrowding. 4. Air fry for 8 to 10 minutes until the carrot slices are crisp-tender. Shake the basket once during cooking. 5. Transfer the carrot slices to a bowl and repeat with the remaining carrots. 6. Allow to cool for 5 minutes and serve.

Roasted Chickpeas

Prep time: 5 minutes | Cook time: 15 minutes | Makes about 1 cup

- 1 (15-ounce / 425-g) can chickpeas, drained
- 2 teaspoons curry powder
- ¼ teaspoon salt
- 1 tablespoon olive oil

1. Drain chickpeas thoroughly and spread in a single layer on paper towels. Cover with another paper towel and press gently to remove extra moisture. Don't press too hard or you'll crush the chickpeas. 2. Mix curry powder and salt together. 3. Place chickpeas in a medium bowl and sprinkle with seasonings. Stir well to coat. 4. Add olive oil and stir again to distribute oil. 5. Air fry at 390°F (199°C) for 15 minutes, stopping to shake basket about halfway through cooking time. 6. Cool completely and store in airtight container.

Italian Rice Balls

**Prep time: 20 minutes | Cook time: 10 minutes
| Makes 8 rice balls**

- 1½ cups cooked sticky rice
- ½ teaspoon Italian seasoning blend
- ¾ teaspoon salt, divided
- 8 black olives, pitted
- 1 ounce (28 g) Mozzarella cheese, cut into tiny pieces
- (small enough to stuff into olives)
- 2 eggs
- ⅓ cup Italian bread crumbs
- ¾ cup panko bread crumbs
- Cooking spray

1. Preheat air fryer to 390ºF (199ºC). 2. Stuff each black olive with a piece of Mozzarella cheese. Set aside. 3. In a bowl, combine the cooked sticky rice, Italian seasoning blend, and ½ teaspoon of salt and stir to mix well. Form the rice mixture into a log with your hands and divide it into 8 equal portions. Mold each portion around a black olive and roll into a ball. 4. Transfer to the freezer to chill for 10 to 15 minutes until firm. 5. In a shallow dish, place the Italian bread crumbs. In a separate shallow dish, whisk the eggs. In a third shallow dish, combine the panko bread crumbs and remaining salt. 6. One by one, roll the rice balls in the Italian bread crumbs, then dip in the whisked eggs, finally coat them with the panko bread crumbs. 7. Arrange the rice balls in the air fryer basket and spritz both sides with cooking spray. 8. Air fry for 10 minutes until the rice balls are golden brown. Flip the balls halfway through the cooking time. 9. Serve warm.

Hush Puppies

**Prep time: 45 minutes | Cook time: 10 minutes
| Serves 12**

- 1 cup self-rising yellow cornmeal
- ½ cup all-purpose flour
- 1 teaspoon sugar
- 1 teaspoon salt
- 1 teaspoon freshly ground black pepper
- 1 large egg
- ⅓ cup canned creamed corn
- 1 cup minced onion
- 2 teaspoons minced jalapeño pepper
- 2 tablespoons olive oil, divided

1. Thoroughly combine the cornmeal, flour, sugar, salt, and pepper in a large bowl. 2. Whisk together the egg and corn in a small bowl. Pour the egg mixture into the bowl of cornmeal mixture and stir to combine. Stir in the minced onion and jalapeño. Cover the bowl with plastic wrap and place in the refrigerator for 30 minutes. 3. Preheat the air fryer to 375ºF (191ºC). Line the air fryer basket with parchment paper and lightly brush it with 1 tablespoon of olive oil. 4. Scoop out the cornmeal mixture and form into 24 balls, about 1 inch. 5. Arrange the balls in the parchment paper-lined basket, leaving space between each ball. 6. Air fry in batches for 5 minutes. Shake the basket and brush the balls with the remaining

1 tablespoon of olive oil. Continue cooking for 5 minutes until golden brown. 7. Remove the balls (hush puppies) from the basket and serve on a plate.

Honey-Mustard Chicken Wings

**Prep time: 10 minutes | Cook time: 24 minutes
| Serves 2**

- 2 pounds (907 g) chicken wings
- Salt and freshly ground black pepper, to taste
- 2 tablespoons butter
- ¼ cup honey
- ¼ cup spicy brown mustard
- Pinch ground cayenne pepper
- 2 teaspoons Worcestershire sauce

1. Prepare the chicken wings by cutting off the wing tips and discarding (or freezing for chicken stock). Divide the drumettes from the wingettes by cutting through the joint. Place the chicken wing pieces in a large bowl. 2. Preheat the air fryer to 400ºF (204ºC). 3. Season the wings with salt and freshly ground black pepper and air fry the wings in two batches for 10 minutes per batch, shaking the basket half way through the cooking process. 4. While the wings are air frying, combine the remaining ingredients in a small saucepan over low heat. 5. When both batches are done, toss all the wings with the honey-mustard sauce and toss them all back into the basket for another 4 minutes to heat through and finish cooking. Give the basket a good shake part way through the cooking process to redistribute the wings. Remove the wings from the air fryer and serve.

Bacon-Wrapped Pickle Spears

**Prep time: 10 minutes | Cook time: 8 minutes |
Serves 4**

- 8 to 12 slices bacon
- ¼ cup (2 ounces / 57 g) cream cheese, softened
- ¼ cup shredded Mozzarella
- cheese
- 8 dill pickle spears
- ½ cup ranch dressing

1. Lay the bacon slices on a flat surface. In a medium bowl, combine the cream cheese and Mozzarella. Stir until well blended. Spread the cheese mixture over the bacon slices. 2. Place a pickle spear on a bacon slice and roll the bacon around the pickle in a spiral, ensuring the pickle is fully covered. (You may need to use more than one slice of bacon per pickle to fully cover the spear.) Tuck in the ends to ensure the bacon stays put. Repeat to wrap all the pickles. 3. Place the wrapped pickles in the air fryer basket in a single layer. Set the air fryer to 400ºF (204ºC) for 8 minutes, or until the bacon is cooked through and crisp on the edges. 4. Serve the pickle spears with ranch dressing on the side.

Eggplant Fries

Prep time: 10 minutes | Cook time: 7 to 8 minutes per batch | Serves 4

- 1 medium eggplant
- 1 teaspoon ground coriander
- 1 teaspoon cumin
- 1 teaspoon garlic powder
- ½ teaspoon salt
- 1 cup crushed panko bread crumbs
- 1 large egg
- 2 tablespoons water
- Oil for misting or cooking spray

1. Peel and cut the eggplant into fat fries, ⅜- to ½-inch thick. 2. Preheat the air fryer to 390°F (199°C). 3. In a small cup, mix together the coriander, cumin, garlic, and salt. 4. Combine 1 teaspoon of the seasoning mix and panko crumbs in a shallow dish. 5. Place eggplant fries in a large bowl, sprinkle with remaining seasoning, and stir well to combine. 6. Beat eggs and water together and pour over eggplant fries. Stir to coat. 7. Remove eggplant from egg wash, shaking off excess, and roll in panko crumbs. 8. Spray with oil. 9. Place half of the fries in air fryer basket. You should have only a single layer, but it's fine if they overlap a little. 10. Cook for 5 minutes. Shake basket, mist lightly with oil, and cook 2 to 3 minutes longer, until browned and crispy. 11. Repeat step 10 to cook remaining eggplant.

Apple Wedges

Prep time: 10 minutes | Cook time: 8 to 9 minutes | Serves 4

- ¼ cup panko bread crumbs
- ¼ cup pecans
- 1½ teaspoons cinnamon
- 1½ teaspoons brown sugar
- ¼ cup cornstarch
- 1 egg white
- 2 teaspoons water
- 1 medium apple
- Oil for misting or cooking spray

1. In a food processor, combine panko, pecans, cinnamon, and brown sugar. Process to make small crumbs. 2. Place cornstarch in a plastic bag or bowl with lid. In a shallow dish, beat together the egg white and water until slightly foamy. 3. Preheat the air fryer to 390°F (199°C). 4. Cut apple into small wedges. The thickest edge should be no more than ⅜- to ½-inch thick. Cut away the core, but do not peel. 5. Place apple wedges in cornstarch, reseal bag or bowl, and shake to coat. 6. Dip wedges in egg wash, shake off excess, and roll in crumb mixture. Spray with oil. 7. Place apples in air fryer basket in single layer and cook for 5 minutes. Shake basket and break apart any apples that have stuck together. Mist lightly with oil and cook 3 to 4 minutes longer, until crispy.

Crispy Cajun Dill Pickle Chips

Prep time: 5 minutes | Cook time: 10 minutes | Makes 16 slices

- ¼ cup all-purpose flour
- ½ cup panko bread crumbs
- 1 large egg, beaten
- 2 teaspoons Cajun seasoning
- 2 large dill pickles, sliced into 8 rounds each
- Cooking spray

1. Preheat the air fryer to 390°F (199°C). 2. Place the all-purpose flour, panko bread crumbs, and egg into 3 separate shallow bowls, then stir the Cajun seasoning into the flour. 3. Dredge each pickle chip in the flour mixture, then the egg, and finally the bread crumbs. Shake off any excess, then place each coated pickle chip on a plate. 4. Spritz the air fryer basket with cooking spray, then place 8 pickle chips in the basket and air fry for 5 minutes, or until crispy and golden brown. Repeat this process with the remaining pickle chips. 5. Remove the chips and allow to slightly cool on a wire rack before serving.

Lemon Shrimp with Garlic Olive Oil

Prep time: 5 minutes | Cook time: 6 minutes | Serves 4

- 1 pound (454 g) medium shrimp, cleaned and deveined
- ¼ cup plus 2 tablespoons olive oil, divided
- Juice of ½ lemon
- 3 garlic cloves, minced and divided
- ½ teaspoon salt
- ¼ teaspoon red pepper flakes
- Lemon wedges, for serving (optional)
- Marinara sauce, for dipping (optional)

1. Preheat the air fryer to 380°F(193°C). 2. In a large bowl, combine the shrimp with 2 tablespoons of the olive oil, as well as the lemon juice, ⅓ of the minced garlic, salt, and red pepper flakes. Toss to coat the shrimp well. 3. In a small ramekin, combine the remaining ¼ cup of olive oil and the remaining minced garlic. 4. Tear off a 12-by-12-inch sheet of aluminum foil. Pour the shrimp into the center of the foil, then fold the sides up and crimp the edges so that it forms an aluminum foil bowl that is open on top. Place this packet into the air fryer basket. 5. Roast the shrimp for 4 minutes, then open the air fryer and place the ramekin with oil and garlic in the basket beside the shrimp packet. Cook for 2 more minutes. 6. Transfer the shrimp on a serving plate or platter with the ramekin of garlic olive oil on the side for dipping. You may also serve with lemon wedges and marinara sauce, if desired.

Cheese-Stuffed Blooming Onion

Prep time: 10 minutes | Cook time: 15 minutes | Serves 2

- 1 large yellow onion (14 ounces / 397 g)
- 1 tablespoon olive oil
- Kosher salt and freshly ground black pepper, to taste
- ¼ cup plus 2 tablespoons panko bread crumbs
- ¼ cup grated Parmesan
- cheese
- 3 tablespoons mayonnaise
- 1 tablespoon fresh lemon juice
- 1 tablespoon chopped fresh flat-leaf parsley
- 2 teaspoons whole-grain Dijon mustard
- 1 garlic clove, minced

1. Place the onion on a cutting board and trim the top off and peel off the outer skin. Turn the onion upside down and use a paring knife, cut vertical slits halfway through the onion at ½-inch intervals around the onion, keeping the root intact. When you turn the onion right side up, it should open up like the petals of a flower. Drizzle the cut sides of the onion with the olive oil and season with salt and pepper. Place petal-side up in the air fryer and air fry at 350ºF (177ºC) for 10 minutes. 2. Meanwhile, in a bowl, stir together the panko, Parmesan, mayonnaise, lemon juice, parsley, mustard, and garlic until incorporated into a smooth paste. 3. Remove the onion from the fryer and stuff the paste all over and in between the onion "petals." Return the onion to the air fryer and air fry at 375ºF (191ºC) until the onion is tender in the center and the bread crumb mixture is golden brown, about 5 minutes. Remove the onion from the air fryer, transfer to a plate, and serve hot.

Shrimp Pirogues

Prep time: 15 minutes | Cook time: 4 to 5 minutes | Serves 8

- 12 ounces (340 g) small, peeled, and deveined raw shrimp
- 3 ounces (85 g) cream cheese, room temperature
- 2 tablespoons plain yogurt
- 1 teaspoon lemon juice
- 1 teaspoon dried dill weed, crushed
- Salt, to taste
- 4 small hothouse cucumbers, each approximately 6 inches long

1. Pour 4 tablespoons water in bottom of air fryer drawer. 2. Place shrimp in air fryer basket in single layer and air fry at 390ºF (199ºC) for 4 to 5 minutes, just until done. Watch carefully because shrimp cooks quickly, and overcooking makes it tough. 3. Chop shrimp into small pieces, no larger than ½ inch. Refrigerate while mixing the remaining ingredients. 4. With a fork, mash and whip the cream cheese until smooth. 5. Stir in the yogurt and beat until smooth. Stir in lemon juice, dill weed, and chopped shrimp. 6. Taste for seasoning. If needed, add ¼ to ½ teaspoon salt to suit your taste.

7. Store in refrigerator until serving time. 8. When ready to serve, wash and dry cucumbers and split them lengthwise. Scoop out the seeds and turn cucumbers upside down on paper towels to drain for 10 minutes. 9. Just before filling, wipe centers of cucumbers dry. Spoon the shrimp mixture into the pirogues and cut in half crosswise. Serve immediately.

Greek Street Tacos

Prep time: 10 minutes | Cook time: 3 minutes | Makes 8 small tacos

- 8 small flour tortillas (4-inch diameter)
- 8 tablespoons hummus
- 4 tablespoons crumbled feta cheese
- 4 tablespoons chopped kalamata or other olives (optional)
- Olive oil for misting

1. Place 1 tablespoon of hummus or tapenade in the center of each tortilla. Top with 1 teaspoon of feta crumbles and 1 teaspoon of chopped olives, if using. 2. Using your finger or a small spoon, moisten the edges of the tortilla all around with water. 3. Fold tortilla over to make a half-moon shape. Press center gently. Then press the edges firmly to seal in the filling. 4. Mist both sides with olive oil. 5. Place in air fryer basket very close but try not to overlap. 6. Air fry at 390ºF (199ºC) for 3 minutes, just until lightly browned and crispy.

Old Bay Chicken Wings

Prep time: 10 minutes | Cook time: 12 to 15 minutes | Serves 4

- 2 tablespoons Old Bay seasoning
- 2 teaspoons baking powder
- 2 teaspoons salt
- 2 pounds (907 g) chicken wings, patted dry
- Cooking spray

1. Preheat the air fryer to 400ºF (204ºC). Lightly spray the air fryer basket with cooking spray. 2. Combine the Old Bay seasoning, baking powder, and salt in a large zip-top plastic bag. Add the chicken wings, seal, and shake until the wings are thoroughly coated in the seasoning mixture. 3. Lay the chicken wings in the air fryer basket in a single layer and lightly mist with cooking spray. You may need to work in batches to avoid overcrowding. 4. Air fry for 12 to 15 minutes, flipping the wings halfway through, or until the wings are lightly browned and the internal temperature reaches at least 165ºF (74ºC) on a meat thermometer. 5. Remove from the basket to a plate and repeat with the remaining chicken wings. 6. Serve hot.

Cheese Wafers

Prep time: 30 minutes | Cook time: 5 to 6 minutes per batch | Makes 4 dozen

- ◄ 4 ounces (113 g) sharp Cheddar cheese, grated
- ◄ ¼ cup butter
- ◄ ½ cup flour
- ◄ ¼ teaspoon salt
- ◄ ½ cup crisp rice cereal
- ◄ Oil for misting or cooking spray

1. Cream the butter and grated cheese together. You can do it by hand, but using a stand mixer is faster and easier. 2. Sift flour and salt together. Add it to the cheese mixture and mix until well blended. 3. Stir in cereal. 4. Place dough on wax paper and shape into a long roll about 1 inch in diameter. Wrap well with the wax paper and chill for at least 4 hours. 5. When ready to cook, preheat the air fryer to 360°F (182°C). 6. Cut cheese roll into ¼-inch slices. 7. Spray the air fryer basket with oil or cooking spray and place slices in a single layer, close but not touching. 8. Cook for 5 to 6 minutes or until golden brown. When done, place them on paper towels to cool. 9. Repeat previous step to cook remaining cheese bites.

Mushroom Tarts

Prep time: 15 minutes | Cook time: 38 minutes | Makes 15 tarts

- ◄ 2 tablespoons extra-virgin olive oil, divided
- ◄ 1 small white onion, sliced
- ◄ 8 ounces (227 g) shiitake mushrooms, sliced
- ◄ ¼ teaspoon sea salt
- ◄ ¼ teaspoon freshly ground black pepper
- ◄ ¼ cup dry white wine
- ◄ 1 sheet frozen puff pastry, thawed
- ◄ 1 cup shredded Gruyère cheese
- ◄ Cooking oil spray
- ◄ 1 tablespoon thinly sliced fresh chives

1. Insert the crisper plate into the basket and the basket into the unit. Preheat the unit by selecting BAKE, setting the temperature to 300°F (149°C), and setting the time to 3 minutes. Select START/STOP to begin. 2. In a heatproof bowl that fits into the basket, stir together 1 tablespoon of olive oil, the onion, and the mushrooms. 3. Once the unit is preheated, place the bowl into the basket. 4. Select BAKE, set the temperature to 300°F (149°C), and set the time to 7 minutes. Select START/STOP to begin. 5. After about 2½ minutes, stir the vegetables. Resume cooking. After another 2½ minutes, the vegetables should be browned and tender. Season with the salt and pepper and add the wine. Resume cooking until the liquid evaporates, about 2 minutes. 6. When the cooking is complete, place the bowl on a heatproof surface. 7. Increase the air fryer temperature to 390°F (199°C) and set the time to 3 minutes. Select START/STOP to begin. 8. Unfold the puff pastry and cut it into 15 (3-by-3-inch) squares. Using a fork, pierce the dough and brush both sides with the remaining 1 tablespoon of olive oil. 9.

Evenly distribute half the cheese among the puff pastry squares, leaving a ½-inch border around the edges. Divide the mushroom-onion mixture among the pastry squares and top with the remaining cheese. 10. Once the unit is preheated, spray the crisper plate with cooking oil. Working in batches, place 5 tarts into the basket; do not stack or overlap. 11. Select BAKE, set the temperature to 390°F (199°C), and set the time to 8 minutes. Select START/STOP to begin. 12. After 6 minutes, check the tarts; if not yet golden brown, resume cooking for about 2 minutes more. 13. When the cooking is complete, remove the tarts and transfer to a wire rack to cool. Repeat steps 10, 11, and 12 with the remaining tarts. 14. Serve garnished with the chives.

Jalapeño Poppers

Prep time: 10 minutes | Cook time: 20 minutes | Serves 4

- ◄ Oil, for spraying
- ◄ 8 ounces (227 g) cream cheese
- ◄ ¾ cup gluten-free bread crumbs, divided
- ◄ 2 tablespoons chopped fresh
- parsley
- ◄ ½ teaspoon granulated garlic
- ◄ ½ teaspoon salt
- ◄ 10 jalapeño peppers, halved and seeded

1. Line the air fryer basket with parchment and spray lightly with oil. 2. In a medium bowl, mix together the cream cheese, half of the bread crumbs, the parsley, garlic, and salt. 3. Spoon the mixture into the jalapeño halves. Gently press the stuffed jalapeños in the remaining bread crumbs. 4. Place the stuffed jalapeños in the prepared basket. 5. Air fry at 370°F (188°C) for 20 minutes, or until the cheese is melted and the bread crumbs are crisp and golden brown.

Cream Cheese Wontons

Prep time: 15 minutes | Cook time: 6 minutes | Makes 20 wontons

- ◄ Oil, for spraying
- ◄ 20 wonton wrappers
- ◄ 4 ounces (113 g) cream cheese

1. Line the air fryer basket with parchment and spray lightly with oil. 2. Pour some water in a small bowl. 3. Lay out a wonton wrapper and place 1 teaspoon of cream cheese in the center. 4. Dip your finger in the water and moisten the edge of the wonton wrapper. Fold over the opposite corners to make a triangle and press the edges together. 5. Pinch the corners of the triangle together to form a classic wonton shape. Place the wonton in the prepared basket. Repeat with the remaining wrappers and cream cheese. You may need to work in batches, depending on the size of your air fryer. 6. Air fry at 400°F (204°C) for 6 minutes, or until golden brown around the edges.

Egg Roll Pizza Sticks

Prep time: 10 minutes | Cook time: 5 minutes | Serves 4

- Olive oil
- 8 pieces reduced-fat string cheese
- 8 egg roll wrappers
- 24 slices turkey pepperoni
- Marinara sauce, for dipping (optional)

1. Spray the air fryer basket lightly with olive oil. Fill a small bowl with water. 2. Place each egg roll wrapper diagonally on a work surface. It should look like a diamond. 3. Place 3 slices of turkey pepperoni in a vertical line down the center of the wrapper. 4. Place 1 Mozzarella cheese stick on top of the turkey pepperoni. 5. Fold the top and bottom corners of the egg roll wrapper over the cheese stick. 6. Fold the left corner over the cheese stick and roll the cheese stick up to resemble a spring roll. Dip a finger in the water and seal the edge of the roll 7. Repeat with the rest of the pizza sticks. 8. Place them in the air fryer basket in a single layer, making sure to leave a little space between each one. Lightly spray the pizza sticks with oil. You may need to cook these in batches. 9. Air fry at 375ºF (191ºC) until the pizza sticks are lightly browned and crispy, about 5 minutes. 10. These are best served hot while the cheese is melted. Accompany with a small bowl of marinara sauce, if desired.

Classic Spring Rolls

Prep time: 10 minutes | Cook time: 9 minutes | Makes 16 spring rolls

- 4 teaspoons toasted sesame oil
- 6 medium garlic cloves, minced or pressed
- 1 tablespoon grated peeled fresh ginger
- 2 cups thinly sliced shiitake mushrooms
- 4 cups chopped green cabbage
- 1 cup grated carrot
- ½ teaspoon sea salt
- 16 rice paper wrappers
- Cooking oil spray (sunflower, safflower, or refined coconut)
- Gluten-free sweet and sour sauce or Thai sweet chili sauce, for serving (optional)

1. Place a wok or sauté pan over medium heat until hot. 2. Add the sesame oil, garlic, ginger, mushrooms, cabbage, carrot, and salt. Cook for 3 to 4 minutes, stirring often, until the cabbage is lightly wilted. Remove the pan from the heat. 3. Gently run a rice paper under water. Lay it on a flat nonabsorbent surface. Place about ¼ cup of the cabbage filling in the middle. Once the wrapper is soft enough to roll, fold the bottom up over the filling, fold in the sides, and roll the wrapper all the way up. (Basically, make a tiny burrito.) 4. Repeat step 3 to make the remaining spring rolls until you have the number of spring rolls you want to cook right now (and the amount that will fit in the air fryer basket in a single layer without them touching each other). Refrigerate any leftover filling in an airtight container for about 1 week. 5. Insert the crisper plate into the basket and the basket into the unit. Preheat the unit by selecting AIR FRY, setting the temperature to 390ºF (199ºC), and setting the time to 3 minutes. Select START/STOP to begin. 6. Once the unit is preheated, spray the crisper plate and the basket with cooking oil. Place the spring rolls into the basket, leaving a little room between them so they don't stick to each other. Spray the top of each spring roll with cooking oil. 7. Select AIR FRY, set the temperature to 390ºF (199ºC), and set the time to 9 minutes. Select START/STOP to begin. 8. When the cooking is complete, the egg rolls should be crisp-ish and lightly browned. Serve immediately, plain or with a sauce of choice.

Shrimp Toasts with Sesame Seeds

Prep time: 15 minutes | Cook time: 6 to 8 minutes | Serves 4 to 6

- ½ pound (227 g) raw shrimp, peeled and deveined
- 1 egg, beaten
- 2 scallions, chopped, plus more for garnish
- 2 tablespoons chopped fresh cilantro
- 2 teaspoons grated fresh ginger
- 1 to 2 teaspoons sriracha
- sauce
- 1 teaspoon soy sauce
- ½ teaspoon toasted sesame oil
- 6 slices thinly sliced white sandwich bread
- ½ cup sesame seeds
- Cooking spray
- Thai chili sauce, for serving

1. Preheat the air fryer to 400ºF (204ºC). Spritz the air fryer basket with cooking spray. 2. In a food processor, add the shrimp, egg, scallions, cilantro, ginger, sriracha sauce, soy sauce and sesame oil, and pulse until chopped finely. You'll need to stop the food processor occasionally to scrape down the sides. Transfer the shrimp mixture to a bowl. 3. On a clean work surface, cut the crusts off the sandwich bread. Using a brush, generously brush one side of each slice of bread with shrimp mixture. 4. Place the sesame seeds on a plate. Press bread slices, shrimp-side down, into sesame seeds to coat evenly. Cut each slice diagonally into quarters. 5. Spread the coated slices in a single layer in the air fryer basket. 6. Air fry in batches for 6 to 8 minutes, or until golden and crispy. Flip the bread slices halfway through. Repeat with the remaining bread slices. 7. Transfer to a plate and let cool for 5 minutes. Top with the chopped scallions and serve warm with Thai chili sauce.

Tortellini with Spicy Dipping Sauce

Prep time: 5 minutes | Cook time: 20 minutes | Serves 4

◀ ¾ cup mayonnaise
◀ 2 tablespoons mustard
◀ 1 egg
◀ ½ cup flour

◀ ½ teaspoon dried oregano
◀ 1½ cups bread crumbs
◀ 2 tablespoons olive oil
◀ 2 cups frozen cheese tortellini

1. Preheat the air fryer to 380°F (193°C). 2. In a small bowl, combine the mayonnaise and mustard and mix well. Set aside. 3. In a shallow bowl, beat the egg. In a separate bowl, combine the flour and oregano. In another bowl, combine the bread crumbs and olive oil, and mix well. 4. Drop the tortellini, a few at a time, into the egg, then into the flour, then into the egg again, and then into the bread crumbs to coat. Put into the air fryer basket, cooking in batches. 5. Air fry for about 10 minutes, shaking halfway through the cooking time, or until the tortellini are crisp and golden brown on the outside. Serve with the mayonnaise mixture.

Air Fried Pot Stickers

Prep time: 10 minutes | Cook time: 18 to 20 minutes | Makes 30 pot stickers

◀ ½ cup finely chopped cabbage
◀ ¼ cup finely chopped red bell pepper
◀ 2 green onions, finely chopped
◀ 1 egg, beaten

◀ 2 tablespoons cocktail sauce
◀ 2 teaspoons low-sodium soy sauce
◀ 30 wonton wrappers
◀ 1 tablespoon water, for brushing the wrappers

1. Preheat the air fryer to 360°F (182°C). 2. In a small bowl, combine the cabbage, pepper, green onions, egg, cocktail sauce, and soy sauce, and mix well. 3. Put about 1 teaspoon of the mixture in the center of each wonton wrapper. Fold the wrapper in half, covering the filling; dampen the edges with water, and seal. You can crimp the edges of the wrapper with your fingers so they look like the pot stickers you get in restaurants. Brush them with water. 4. Place the pot stickers in the air fryer basket and air fry in 2 batches for 9 to 10 minutes, or until the pot stickers are hot and the bottoms are lightly browned. 5. Serve hot.

Crunchy Chickpeas

Prep time: 5 minutes | Cook time: 15 to 20 minutes | Serves 4

◀ ½ teaspoon chili powder
◀ ½ teaspoon ground cumin
◀ ¼ teaspoon cayenne pepper

◀ ¼ teaspoon salt
◀ 1 (19 ounces / 539 g) can chickpeas, drained and rinsed
◀ Cooking spray

1. Preheat the air fryer to 390°F (199°C). Lightly spritz the air fryer basket with cooking spray. 2. Mix the chili powder, cumin, cayenne pepper, and salt in a small bowl. 3. Place the chickpeas in a medium bowl and lightly mist with cooking spray. 4. Add the spice mixture to the chickpeas and toss until evenly coated. 5. Place the chickpeas in the air fryer basket and air fry for 15 to 20 minutes, or until the chickpeas are cooked to your preferred crunchiness. Shake the basket three or four times during cooking. 6. Let the chickpeas cool for 5 minutes before serving.

Chapter 4

Poultry

Chapter 4 Poultry

Smoky Chicken Leg Quarters

Prep time: 30 minutes | Cook time: 23 to 27 minutes | Serves 6

- ◄ ½ cup avocado oil
- ◄ 2 teaspoons smoked paprika
- ◄ 1 teaspoon sea salt
- ◄ 1 teaspoon garlic powder
- ◄ ½ teaspoon dried rosemary
- ◄ ½ teaspoon dried thyme
- ◄ ½ teaspoon freshly ground black pepper
- ◄ 2 pounds (907 g) bone-in, skin-on chicken leg quarters

1. In a blender or small bowl, combine the avocado oil, smoked paprika, salt, garlic powder, rosemary, thyme, and black pepper. 2. Place the chicken in a shallow dish or large zip-top bag. Pour the marinade over the chicken, making sure all the legs are coated. Cover and marinate for at least 2 hours or overnight. 3. Place the chicken in a single layer in the air fryer basket, working in batches if necessary. Set the air fryer to 400ºF (204ºC) and air fry for 15 minutes. Flip the chicken legs, then reduce the temperature to 350ºF (177ºC). Cook for 8 to 12 minutes more, until an instant-read thermometer reads 160ºF (71ºC) when inserted into the thickest piece of chicken. 4. Allow to rest for 5 to 10 minutes before serving.

Cobb Salad

Prep time: 15 minutes | Cook time: 8 minutes | Serves 4

- ◄ 8 slices reduced-sodium bacon
- ◄ 8 chicken breast tenders (about 1½ pounds / 680 g)
- ◄ 8 cups chopped romaine lettuce
- ◄ 1 cup cherry tomatoes, halved
- ◄ ¼ red onion, thinly sliced
- ◄ 2 hard-boiled eggs, peeled and sliced
- ◄ Avocado-Lime Dressing:
- ◄ ½ cup plain Greek yogurt
- ◄ ¼ cup almond milk
- ◄ ½ avocado
- ◄ Juice of ½ lime
- ◄ 3 scallions, coarsely chopped
- ◄ 1 clove garlic
- ◄ 2 tablespoons fresh cilantro
- ◄ ⅛ teaspoon ground cumin
- ◄ Salt and freshly ground black pepper, to taste

1. Preheat the air fryer to 400ºF (204ºC). 2. Wrap a piece of bacon around each piece of chicken and secure with a toothpick. Working in batches if necessary, arrange the bacon-wrapped chicken in a single layer in the air fryer basket. Air fry for 8 minutes until the bacon is browned and a thermometer inserted into the thickest piece of chicken register 165ºF (74ºC). Let cool for a few minutes, then slice into bite-size pieces. 3. To make the dressing: In a blender or food processor, combine the yogurt, milk, avocado, lime juice, scallions, garlic, cilantro, and cumin. Purée until smooth. Season to taste with salt and freshly ground pepper. 4. To assemble the salad, in a large bowl, combine the lettuce, tomatoes, and onion. Drizzle the dressing over the vegetables and toss gently until thoroughly combined. Arrange the chicken and eggs on top just before serving.

Teriyaki Chicken Thighs with Lemony Snow Peas

Prep time: 30 minutes | Cook time: 34 minutes | Serves 4

- ◄ ¼ cup chicken broth
- ◄ ½ teaspoon grated fresh ginger
- ◄ ⅛ teaspoon red pepper flakes
- ◄ 1½ tablespoons soy sauce
- ◄ 4 (5 ounces / 142 g) bone-in chicken thighs, trimmed
- ◄ 1 tablespoon mirin
- ◄ ½ teaspoon cornstarch
- ◄ 1 tablespoon sugar
- ◄ 6 ounces (170 g) snow peas, strings removed
- ◄ ⅛ teaspoon lemon zest
- ◄ 1 garlic clove, minced
- ◄ ¼ teaspoon salt
- ◄ Ground black pepper, to taste
- ◄ ½ teaspoon lemon juice

1. Combine the broth, ginger, pepper flakes, and soy sauce in a large bowl. Stir to mix well. 2. Pierce 10 to 15 holes into the chicken skin. Put the chicken in the broth mixture and toss to coat well. Let sit for 10 minutes to marinate. 3. Preheat the air fryer to 400ºF (205ºC). 4. Transfer the marinated chicken on a plate and pat dry with paper towels. 5. Scoop 2 tablespoons of marinade in a microwave-safe bowl and combine with mirin, cornstarch and sugar. Stir to mix well. Microwave for 1 minute or until frothy and has a thick consistency. Set aside. 6. Arrange the chicken in the preheated air fryer, skin side up, and air fry for 25 minutes or until the internal temperature of the chicken reaches at least 165ºF (74ºC). Gently turn the chicken over halfway through. 7. When the frying is complete, brush the chicken skin with marinade mixture. Air fryer the chicken for 5 more minutes or until glazed. 8. Remove the chicken from the air fryer and reserve ½ teaspoon of chicken fat remains in the air fryer. Allow the chicken to cool for 10 minutes. 9. Meanwhile, combine the reserved chicken fat, snow peas, lemon zest, garlic, salt, and ground black pepper in a small bowl. Toss to coat well. 10. Transfer the snow peas in the air fryer and air fry for 3 minutes or until soft. Remove the peas from the air fryer and toss with lemon juice. 11. Serve the chicken with lemony snow peas.

Thai-Style Cornish Game Hens

Prep time: 30 minutes | Cook time: 20 minutes | Serves 4

- 1 cup chopped fresh cilantro leaves and stems
- ¼ cup fish sauce
- 1 tablespoon soy sauce
- 1 serrano chile, seeded and chopped
- 8 garlic cloves, smashed
- 2 tablespoons sugar
- 2 tablespoons lemongrass
- paste
- 2 teaspoons black pepper
- 2 teaspoons ground coriander
- 1 teaspoon kosher salt
- 1 teaspoon ground turmeric
- 2 Cornish game hens, giblets removed, split in half lengthwise

1. In a blender, combine the cilantro, fish sauce, soy sauce, serrano, garlic, sugar, lemongrass, black pepper, coriander, salt, and turmeric. Blend until smooth. 2. Place the game hen halves in a large bowl. Pour the cilantro mixture over the hen halves and toss to coat. Marinate at room temperature for 30 minutes, or cover and refrigerate for up to 24 hours. 3. Arrange the hen halves in a single layer in the air fryer basket. Set the air fryer to 400ºF (204ºC) for 20 minutes. Use a meat thermometer to ensure the game hens have reached an internal temperature of 165ºF (74ºC).

Chicken and Broccoli Casserole

Prep time: 5 minutes | Cook time: 20 to 25 minutes | Serves 4

- ½ pound (227 g) broccoli, chopped into florets
- 2 cups shredded cooked chicken
- 4 ounces (113 g) cream cheese
- ⅓ cup heavy cream
- 1½ teaspoons Dijon mustard
- ½ teaspoon garlic powder
- Salt and freshly ground black pepper, to taste
- 2 tablespoons chopped fresh basil
- 1 cup shredded Cheddar cheese

1. Preheat the air fryer to 390ºF (199ºC). Lightly coat a casserole dish that will fit in air fryer, with olive oil and set aside. 2. Place the broccoli in a large glass bowl with 1 tablespoon of water and cover with a microwavable plate. Microwave on high for 2 to 3 minutes until the broccoli is bright green but not mushy. Drain if necessary and add to another large bowl along with the shredded chicken. 3. In the same glass bowl used to microwave the broccoli, combine the cream cheese and cream. Microwave for 30 seconds to 1 minute on high and stir until smooth. Add the mustard and garlic powder and season to taste with salt and freshly ground black pepper. Whisk until the sauce is smooth. 4. Pour the warm sauce over the broccoli and chicken mixture and then add the basil. Using a silicone spatula, gently fold the mixture until thoroughly combined. 5. Transfer the chicken mixture to the prepared casserole dish and top with the cheese. Air fry for 20 to 25 minutes until warmed through and the cheese has browned.

Potato-Crusted Chicken

Prep time: 15 minutes | Cook time: 22 to 25 minutes | Serves 4

- ¼ cup buttermilk
- 1 large egg, beaten
- 1 cup instant potato flakes
- ¼ cup grated Parmesan cheese
- 1 teaspoon salt
- ½ teaspoon freshly ground black pepper
- 2 whole boneless, skinless chicken breasts (about 1 pound / 454 g each), halved
- 1 to 2 tablespoons oil

1. In a shallow bowl, whisk the buttermilk and egg until blended. In another shallow bowl, stir together the potato flakes, cheese, salt, and pepper. 2. One at a time, dip the chicken pieces in the buttermilk mixture and the potato flake mixture, coating thoroughly. 3. Preheat the air fryer to 400ºF (204ºC). Line the air fryer basket with parchment paper. 4. Place the coated chicken on the parchment and spritz with oil. 5. Cook for 15 minutes. Flip the chicken, spritz it with oil, and cook for 7 to 10 minutes more until the outside is crispy and the inside is no longer pink.

French Garlic Chicken

Prep time: 30 minutes | Cook time: 27 minutes | Serves 4

- 2 tablespoon extra-virgin olive oil
- 1 tablespoon Dijon mustard
- 1 tablespoon apple cider vinegar
- 3 cloves garlic, minced
- 2 teaspoons herbes de Provence
- ½ teaspoon kosher salt
- 1 teaspoon black pepper
- 1 pound (454 g) boneless, skinless chicken thighs, halved crosswise
- 2 tablespoons butter
- 8 cloves garlic, chopped
- ¼ cup heavy whipping cream

1. In a small bowl, combine the olive oil, mustard, vinegar, minced garlic, herbes de Provence, salt, and pepper. Use a wire whisk to emulsify the mixture. 2. Pierce the chicken all over with a fork to allow the marinade to penetrate better. Place the chicken in a resealable plastic bag, pour the marinade over, and seal. Massage until the chicken is well coated. Marinate at room temperature for 30 minutes or in the refrigerator for up to 24 hours. 3. When you are ready to cook, place the butter and chopped garlic in a baking pan and place it in the air fryer basket. Set the air fryer to 400ºF (204ºC) for 5 minutes, or until the butter has melted and the garlic is sizzling. 4. Add the chicken and the marinade to the seasoned butter. Set the air fryer to 350ºF (177ºC) for 15 minutes. Use a meat thermometer to ensure the chicken has reached an internal temperature of 165ºF (74ºC). Transfer the chicken to a plate and cover lightly with foil to keep warm. 5. Add the cream to the pan, stirring to combine with the garlic, butter, and cooking juices. Place the pan in the air fryer basket. Set the air fryer to 350ºF (177ºC) for 7 minutes. 6. Pour the thickened sauce over the chicken and serve.

Jerk Chicken Thighs

Prep time: 30 minutes | Cook time: 15 to 20 minutes | Serves 6

- ◀ 2 teaspoons ground coriander
- ◀ 1 teaspoon ground allspice
- ◀ 1 teaspoon cayenne pepper
- ◀ 1 teaspoon ground ginger
- ◀ 1 teaspoon salt
- ◀ 1 teaspoon dried thyme
- ◀ ½ teaspoon ground cinnamon
- ◀ ½ teaspoon ground nutmeg
- ◀ 2 pounds (907 g) boneless chicken thighs, skin on
- ◀ 2 tablespoons olive oil

1. In a small bowl, combine the coriander, allspice, cayenne, ginger, salt, thyme, cinnamon, and nutmeg. Stir until thoroughly combined. 2. Place the chicken in a baking dish and use paper towels to pat dry. Thoroughly coat both sides of the chicken with the spice mixture. Cover and refrigerate for at least 2 hours, preferably overnight. 3. Preheat the air fryer to 360ºF (182ºC). 4. Working in batches if necessary, arrange the chicken in a single layer in the air fryer basket and lightly coat with the olive oil. Pausing halfway through the cooking time to flip the chicken, air fry for 15 to 20 minutes, until a thermometer inserted into the thickest part registers 165ºF (74ºC).

Hawaiian Huli Huli Chicken

Prep time: 30 minutes | Cook time: 15 minutes | Serves 4

- ◀ 4 boneless, skinless chicken thighs (about 1½ pounds / 680 g)
- ◀ 1 (8 ounces / 227 g) can pineapple chunks in juice, drained, ¼ cup juice reserved
- ◀ ¼ cup soy sauce
- ◀ ¼ cup sugar
- ◀ 2 tablespoons ketchup
- ◀ 1 tablespoon minced fresh ginger
- ◀ 1 tablespoon minced garlic
- ◀ ¼ cup chopped scallions

1. Use a fork to pierce the chicken all over to allow the marinade to penetrate better. Place the chicken in a large bowl or large resealable plastic bag. 2. Set the drained pineapple chunks aside. In a small microwave-safe bowl, combine the pineapple juice, soy sauce, sugar, ketchup, ginger, and garlic. Pour half the sauce over the chicken; toss to coat. Reserve the remaining sauce. Marinate the chicken at room temperature for 30 minutes, or cover and refrigerate for up to 24 hours. 3. Place the chicken in the air fryer basket. (Discard marinade.) Set the air fryer to 350ºF (177ºC) for 15 minutes, turning halfway through the cooking time. 4. Meanwhile, microwave the reserved sauce on high for 45 to 60 seconds, stirring every 15 seconds, until the sauce has the consistency of a thick glaze. 5. At the end of the cooking time, use a meat thermometer to ensure the chicken has reached an internal temperature of 165ºF (74ºC). 6. Transfer the chicken to a serving platter. Pour the sauce over the chicken. Garnish with the pineapple chunks and scallions.

South Indian Pepper Chicken

Prep time: 30 minutes | Cook time: 15 minutes | Serves 4

Spice Mix:
- ◀ 1 dried red chile, or ½ teaspoon dried red pepper flakes
- ◀ 1-inch piece cinnamon or cassia bark
- ◀ 1½ teaspoons coriander seeds

- ◀ 1 teaspoon fennel seeds
- ◀ 1 teaspoon cumin seeds
- ◀ 1 teaspoon black peppercorns
- ◀ ½ teaspoon cardamom seeds
- ◀ ¼ teaspoon ground turmeric
- ◀ 1 teaspoon kosher salt

Chicken:
- ◀ 1 pound (454 g) boneless, skinless chicken thighs, cut crosswise into thirds
- ◀ 2 medium onions, cut into ½-inch-thick slices

- ◀ ¼ cup olive oil
- ◀ Cauliflower rice, steamed rice, or naan bread, for serving

1. For the spice mix: Combine the dried chile, cinnamon, coriander, fennel, cumin, peppercorns, and cardamom in a clean coffee or spice grinder. Grind, shaking the grinder lightly so all the seeds and bits get into the blades, until the mixture is broken down to a fine powder. Stir in the turmeric and salt. 2. For the chicken: Place the chicken and onions in resealable plastic bag. Add the oil and 1½ tablespoons of the spice mix. Seal the bag and massage until the chicken is well coated. Marinate at room temperature for 30 minutes or in the refrigerator for up to 24 hours. 3. Place the chicken and onions in the air fryer basket. Set the air fryer to 350ºF (177ºC) for 10 minutes, stirring once halfway through the cooking time. Increase the temperature to 400ºF (204ºC) for 5 minutes. Use a meat thermometer to ensure the chicken has reached an internal temperature of 165ºF (74ºC). 4. Serve with steamed rice, cauliflower rice, or naan.

Blackened Chicken

Prep time: 10 minutes | Cook time: 20 minutes | Serves 4

- ◀ 1 large egg, beaten
- ◀ ¾ cup Blackened seasoning
- ◀ 2 whole boneless, skinless
- chicken breasts (about 1 pound / 454 g each), halved
- ◀ 1 to 2 tablespoons oil

1. Place the beaten egg in one shallow bowl and the Blackened seasoning in another shallow bowl. 2. One at a time, dip the chicken pieces in the beaten egg and the Blackened seasoning, coating thoroughly. 3. Preheat the air fryer to 360ºF (182ºC). Line the air fryer basket with parchment paper. 4. Place the chicken pieces on the parchment and spritz with oil. 5. Cook for 10 minutes. Flip the chicken, spritz it with oil, and cook for 10 minutes more until the internal temperature reaches 165ºF (74ºC) and the chicken is no longer pink inside. Let sit for 5 minutes before serving.

Yakitori

Prep time: 10 minutes | Cook time: 15 minutes | Serves 4

- ½ cup mirin
- ¼ cup dry white wine
- ½ cup soy sauce
- 1 tablespoon light brown sugar
- 1½ pounds (680 g) boneless, skinless chicken thighs, cut into 1½-inch pieces, fat trimmed
- 4 medium scallions, trimmed, cut into 1½-inch pieces
- Cooking spray
- Special Equipment:
- 4 (4-inch) bamboo skewers, soaked in water for at least 30 minutes

1. Combine the mirin, dry white wine, soy sauce, and brown sugar in a saucepan. Bring to a boil over medium heat. Keep stirring. 2. Boil for another 2 minutes or until it has a thick consistency. Turn off the heat. 3. Preheat the air fryer to 400°F (204°C). Spritz the air fryer basket with cooking spray. 4. Run the bamboo skewers through the chicken pieces and scallions alternatively. 5. Arrange the skewers in the preheated air fryer, then brush with mirin mixture on both sides. Spritz with cooking spray. 6. Air fry for 10 minutes or until the chicken and scallions are glossy. Flip the skewers halfway through. 7. Serve immediately.

Ranch Chicken Wings

Prep time: 10 minutes | Cook time: 40 minutes | Serves 4

- 2 tablespoons water
- 2 tablespoons hot pepper sauce
- 2 tablespoons unsalted butter, melted
- 2 tablespoons apple cider vinegar
- 1 (1-ounce / 28-g) envelope ranch salad dressing mix
- 1 teaspoon paprika
- 4 pounds (1.8 kg) chicken wings, tips removed
- Cooking oil spray

1. In a large bowl, whisk the water, hot pepper sauce, melted butter, vinegar, salad dressing mix, and paprika until combined. 2. Add the wings and toss to coat. At this point, you can cover the bowl and marinate the wings in the refrigerator for 4 to 24 hours for best results. However, you can just let the wings stand for 30 minutes in the refrigerator. 3. Insert the crisper plate into the basket and the basket into the unit. Preheat the unit by selecting AIR FRY, setting the temperature to 400°F (204°C), and setting the time to 3 minutes. Select START/STOP to begin. 4. Once the unit is preheated, spray the crisper plate with cooking oil. Working in batches, put half the wings into the basket; it is okay to stack them. Refrigerate the remaining wings. 5. Select AIR FRY, set the temperature to 400°F (204°C), and set the time to 20 minutes. Select START/STOP to begin. 6. After 5 minutes, remove the basket and shake it. Reinsert the basket to resume cooking. Remove and shake the basket every 5

minutes, three more times, until the chicken is browned and glazed and a food thermometer inserted into the wings registers 165°F (74°C). 7. Repeat steps 4, 5, and 6 with the remaining wings. 8. When the cooking is complete, serve warm.

Simply Terrific Turkey Meatballs

Prep time: 10 minutes | Cook time: 7 to 10 minutes | Serves 4

- 1 red bell pepper, seeded and coarsely chopped
- 2 cloves garlic, coarsely chopped
- ¼ cup chopped fresh parsley
- 1½ pounds (680 g) 85% lean ground turkey
- 1 egg, lightly beaten
- ½ cup grated Parmesan cheese
- 1 teaspoon salt
- ½ teaspoon freshly ground black pepper

1. Preheat the air fryer to 400°F (204°C). 2. In a food processor fitted with a metal blade, combine the bell pepper, garlic, and parsley. Pulse until finely chopped. Transfer the vegetables to a large mixing bowl. 3. Add the turkey, egg, Parmesan, salt, and black pepper. Mix gently until thoroughly combined. Shape the mixture into 1¼-inch meatballs. 4. Working in batches if necessary, arrange the meatballs in a single layer in the air fryer basket; coat lightly with olive oil spray. Pausing halfway through the cooking time to shake the basket, air fry for 7 to 10 minutes, until lightly browned and a thermometer inserted into the center of a meatball registers 165°F (74°C).

One-Dish Chicken and Rice

Prep time: 10 minutes | Cook time: 40 minutes | Serves 4

- 1 cup long-grain white rice, rinsed and drained
- 1 cup cut frozen green beans (do not thaw)
- 1 tablespoon minced fresh ginger
- 3 cloves garlic, minced
- 1 tablespoon toasted sesame oil
- 1 teaspoon kosher salt
- 1 teaspoon black pepper
- 1 pound (454 g) chicken wings, preferably drumettes

1. In a baking pan, combine the rice, green beans, ginger, garlic, sesame oil, salt, and pepper. Stir to combine. Place the chicken wings on top of the rice mixture. 2. Cover the pan with foil. Make a long slash in the foil to allow the pan to vent steam. Place the pan in the air fryer basket. Set the air fryer to 375°F (191°C) for 30 minutes. 3. Remove the foil. Set the air fryer to 400°F (204°C) for 10 minutes, or until the wings have browned and rendered fat into the rice and vegetables, turning the wings halfway through the cooking time.

Chicken Legs with Leeks

Prep time: 30 minutes | Cook time: 18 minutes | Serves 6

- 2 leeks, sliced
- 2 large-sized tomatoes, chopped
- 3 cloves garlic, minced
- ½ teaspoon dried oregano
- 6 chicken legs, boneless and
- skinless
- ½ teaspoon smoked cayenne pepper
- 2 tablespoons olive oil
- A freshly ground nutmeg

1. In a mixing dish, thoroughly combine all ingredients, minus the leeks. Place in the refrigerator and let it marinate overnight. 2. Lay the leeks onto the bottom of the air fryer basket. Top with the chicken legs. 3. Roast chicken legs at 375ºF (191ºC) for 18 minutes, turning halfway through. Serve with hoisin sauce.

Lemon-Basil Turkey Breasts

Prep time: 30 minutes | Cook time: 58 minutes | Serves 4

- 2 tablespoons olive oil
- 2 pounds (907 g) turkey breasts, bone-in, skin-on
- Coarse sea salt and ground black pepper, to taste
- 1 teaspoon fresh basil leaves, chopped
- 2 tablespoons lemon zest, grated

1. Rub olive oil on all sides of the turkey breasts; sprinkle with salt, pepper, basil, and lemon zest. 2. Place the turkey breasts skin side up on the parchment-lined air fryer basket. 3. Cook in the preheated air fryer at 330ºF (166ºC) for 30 minutes. Now, turn them over and cook an additional 28 minutes. 4. Serve with lemon wedges, if desired. Bon appétit!

Broccoli Cheese Chicken

Prep time: 10 minutes | Cook time: 19 to 24 minutes | Serves 6

- 1 tablespoon avocado oil
- ¼ cup chopped onion
- ½ cup finely chopped broccoli
- 4 ounces (113 g) cream cheese, at room temperature
- 2 ounces (57 g) Cheddar cheese, shredded
- 1 teaspoon garlic powder
- ½ teaspoon sea salt, plus additional for seasoning, divided
- ¼ freshly ground black pepper, plus additional for seasoning, divided
- 2 pounds (907 g) boneless, skinless chicken breasts
- 1 teaspoon smoked paprika

1. Heat a medium skillet over medium-high heat and pour in the avocado oil. Add the onion and broccoli and cook, stirring occasionally, for 5 to 8 minutes, until the onion is tender. 2. Transfer to a large bowl and stir in the cream cheese, Cheddar cheese, and garlic powder, and season to taste with salt and pepper. 3. Hold a sharp knife parallel to the chicken breast and cut a long pocket into one side. Stuff the chicken pockets with the broccoli mixture, using toothpicks to secure the pockets around the filling. 4. In a small dish, combine the paprika, ½ teaspoon salt, and ¼ teaspoon pepper. Sprinkle this over the outside of the chicken. 5. Set the air fryer to 400ºF (204ºC). Place the chicken in a single layer in the air fryer basket, cooking in batches if necessary, and cook for 14 to 16 minutes, until an instant-read thermometer reads 160ºF (71ºC). Place the chicken on a plate and tent a piece of aluminum foil over the chicken. Allow to rest for 5 to 10 minutes before serving.

Teriyaki Chicken Legs

Prep time: 12 minutes | Cook time: 18 to 20 minutes | Serves 2

- 4 tablespoons teriyaki sauce
- 1 tablespoon orange juice
- 1 teaspoon smoked paprika
- 4 chicken legs
- Cooking spray

1. Mix together the teriyaki sauce, orange juice, and smoked paprika. Brush on all sides of chicken legs. 2. Spray the air fryer basket with nonstick cooking spray and place chicken in basket. 3. Air fry at 360ºF (182ºC) for 6 minutes. Turn and baste with sauce. Cook for 6 more minutes, turn and baste. Cook for 6 to 8 minutes more, until juices run clear when chicken is pierced with a fork.

Hawaiian Chicken Bites

Prep time: 1 hour 15 minutes | Cook time: 15 minutes | Serves 4

- ½ cup pineapple juice
- 2 tablespoons apple cider vinegar
- ½ tablespoon minced ginger
- ½ cup ketchup
- 2 garlic cloves, minced
- ½ cup brown sugar
- 2 tablespoons sherry
- ½ cup soy sauce
- 4 chicken breasts, cubed
- Cooking spray

1. Combine the pineapple juice, cider vinegar, ginger, ketchup, garlic, and sugar in a saucepan. Stir to mix well. Heat over low heat for 5 minutes or until thickened. Fold in the sherry and soy sauce. 2. Dunk the chicken cubes in the mixture. Press to submerge. Wrap the bowl in plastic and refrigerate to marinate for at least an hour. 3. Preheat the air fryer to 360ºF (182ºC). Spritz the air fryer basket with cooking spray. 4. Remove the chicken cubes from the marinade. Shake the excess off and put in the preheated air fryer. Spritz with cooking spray. 5. Air fry for 15 minutes or until the chicken cubes are glazed and well browned. Shake the basket at least three times during the frying. 6. Serve immediately.

Buffalo Chicken Wings

Prep time: 10 minutes | Cook time: 20 to 25 minutes | Serves 4

- ◄ 2 tablespoons baking powder
- ◄ 1 teaspoon smoked paprika
- ◄ Sea salt and freshly ground black pepper, to taste
- ◄ 2 pounds (907 g) chicken wings or chicken drumettes
- ◄ Avocado oil spray
- ◄ ⅓ cup avocado oil
- ◄ ½ cup Buffalo hot sauce, such as Frank's RedHot
- ◄ ¼ cup (4 tablespoons) unsalted butter
- ◄ 2 tablespoons apple cider vinegar
- ◄ 1 teaspoon minced garlic

1. In a large bowl, stir together the baking powder, smoked paprika, and salt and pepper to taste. Add the chicken wings and toss to coat. 2. Set the air fryer to 400°F (204°C). Spray the wings with oil. 3. Place the wings in the basket in a single layer, working in batches, and air fry for 20 to 25 minutes. Check with an instant-read thermometer and remove when they reach 155°F (68°C). Let rest until they reach 165°F (74°C). 4. While the wings are cooking, whisk together the avocado oil, hot sauce, butter, vinegar, and garlic in a small saucepan over medium-low heat until warm. 5. When the wings are done cooking, toss them with the Buffalo sauce. Serve warm.

General Tso's Chicken

Prep time: 10 minutes | Cook time: 14 minutes | Serves 4

- ◄ 1 tablespoon sesame oil
- ◄ 1 teaspoon minced garlic
- ◄ ½ teaspoon ground ginger
- ◄ 1 cup chicken broth
- ◄ 4 tablespoons soy sauce, divided
- ◄ ½ teaspoon sriracha, plus more for serving
- ◄ 2 tablespoons hoisin sauce
- ◄ 4 tablespoons cornstarch, divided
- ◄ 4 boneless, skinless chicken breasts, cut into 1-inch pieces
- ◄ Olive oil spray
- ◄ 2 medium scallions, sliced, green parts only
- ◄ Sesame seeds, for garnish

1. In a small saucepan over low heat, combine the sesame oil, garlic, and ginger and cook for 1 minute. 2. Add the chicken broth, 2 tablespoons of soy sauce, the sriracha, and hoisin. Whisk to combine. 3. Whisk in 2 tablespoons of cornstarch and continue cooking over low heat until the sauce starts to thicken, about 5 minutes. Remove the pan from the heat, cover it, and set aside. 4. Insert the crisper plate into the basket and the basket into the unit. Preheat the unit by selecting BAKE, setting the temperature to 400°F (204°C), and setting the time to 3 minutes. Select START/STOP to begin. 5. In a medium bowl, toss together the chicken, remaining 2 tablespoons of soy sauce, and remaining 2 tablespoons of cornstarch. 6. Once the unit is preheated, spray the crisper plate

with olive oil. Place the chicken into the basket and spray it with olive oil. 7. Select BAKE, set the temperature to 400°F (204°C), and set the time to 9 minutes. Select START/STOP to begin. 8. After 5 minutes, remove the basket, shake, and spray the chicken with more olive oil. Reinsert the basket to resume cooking. 9. When the cooking is complete, a food thermometer inserted into the chicken should register at least 165°F (74°C). Transfer the chicken to a large bowl and toss it with the sauce. Garnish with the scallions and sesame seeds and serve.

Fajita Chicken Strips

Prep time: 10 minutes | Cook time: 15 minutes | Serves 4

- ◄ 1 pound (454 g) boneless, skinless chicken tenderloins, cut into strips
- ◄ 3 bell peppers, any color, cut into chunks
- ◄ 1 onion, cut into chunks
- ◄ 1 tablespoon olive oil
- ◄ 1 tablespoon fajita seasoning mix
- ◄ Cooking spray

1. Preheat the air fryer to 370°F (188°C). 2. In a large bowl, mix together the chicken, bell peppers, onion, olive oil, and fajita seasoning mix until completely coated. 3. Spray the air fryer basket lightly with cooking spray. 4. Place the chicken and vegetables in the air fryer basket and lightly spray with cooking spray. 5. Air fry for 7 minutes. Shake the basket and air fry for an additional 5 to 8 minutes, until the chicken is cooked through and the veggies are starting to char. 6. Serve warm.

Thai Curry Meatballs

Prep time: 10 minutes | Cook time: 10 minutes | Serves 4

- ◄ 1 pound (454 g) ground chicken
- ◄ ¼ cup chopped fresh cilantro
- ◄ 1 teaspoon chopped fresh mint
- ◄ 1 tablespoon fresh lime juice
- ◄ 1 tablespoon Thai red, green, or yellow curry paste
- ◄ 1 tablespoon fish sauce
- ◄ 2 garlic cloves, minced
- ◄ 2 teaspoons minced fresh ginger
- ◄ ½ teaspoon kosher salt
- ◄ ½ teaspoon black pepper
- ◄ ¼ teaspoon red pepper flakes

1. Preheat the air fryer to 400°F (204°C). 2. In a large bowl, gently mix the ground chicken, cilantro, mint, lime juice, curry paste, fish sauce, garlic, ginger, salt, black pepper, and red pepper flakes until thoroughly combined. 3. Form the mixture into 16 meatballs. Place the meatballs in a single layer in the air fryer basket. Air fry for 10 minutes, turning the meatballs halfway through the cooking time. Use a meat thermometer to ensure the meatballs have reached an internal temperature of 165°F (74°C). Serve immediately.

Tex-Mex Chicken Roll-Ups

Prep time: 10 minutes | Cook time: 14 to 17 minutes | Serves 8

- 2 pounds (907 g) boneless, skinless chicken breasts or thighs
- 1 teaspoon chili powder
- ½ teaspoon smoked paprika
- ½ teaspoon ground cumin
- Sea salt and freshly ground
- black pepper, to taste
- 6 ounces (170 g) Monterey Jack cheese, shredded
- 4 ounces (113 g) canned diced green chiles
- Avocado oil spray

1. Place the chicken in a large zip-top bag or between two pieces of plastic wrap. Using a meat mallet or heavy skillet, pound the chicken until it is about ¼ inch thick. 2. In a small bowl, combine the chili powder, smoked paprika, cumin, and salt and pepper to taste. Sprinkle both sides of the chicken with the seasonings. 3. Sprinkle the chicken with the Monterey Jack cheese, then the diced green chiles. 4. Roll up each piece of chicken from the long side, tucking in the ends as you go. Secure the roll-up with a toothpick. 5. Set the air fryer to 350ºF (177ºC). Spray the outside of the chicken with avocado oil. Place the chicken in a single layer in the basket, working in batches if necessary, and roast for 7 minutes. Flip and cook for another 7 to 10 minutes, until an instant-read thermometer reads 160ºF (71ºC). 6. Remove the chicken from the air fryer and allow it to rest for about 5 minutes before serving.

Bacon Lovers' Stuffed Chicken

Prep time: 10 minutes | Cook time: 20 minutes | Serves 4

- 4 (5-ounce / 142-g) boneless, skinless chicken breasts, pounded to ¼ inch thick
- 2 (5.2-ounce / 147-g) packages Boursin cheese (or Kite Hill brand chive
- cream cheese style spread, softened, for dairy-free)
- 8 slices thin-cut bacon or beef bacon
- Sprig of fresh cilantro, for garnish (optional)

1. Spray the air fryer basket with avocado oil. Preheat the air fryer to 400ºF (204ºC). 2. Place one of the chicken breasts on a cutting board. With a sharp knife held parallel to the cutting board, make a 1-inch-wide incision at the top of the breast. Carefully cut into the breast to form a large pocket, leaving a ½-inch border along the sides and bottom. Repeat with the other 3 chicken breasts. 3. Snip the corner of a large resealable plastic bag to form a ¾-inch hole. Place the Boursin cheese in the bag and pipe the cheese into the pockets in the chicken breasts, dividing the cheese evenly among them. 4. Wrap 2 slices of bacon around each chicken breast and secure the ends with toothpicks. Place the bacon-wrapped chicken in the air fryer basket and air fry until the bacon is crisp and the chicken's internal temperature reaches 165ºF (74ºC), about 18 to 20

minutes, flipping after 10 minutes. Garnish with a sprig of cilantro before serving, if desired. 5. Store leftovers in an airtight container in the refrigerator for up to 4 days. Reheat in a preheated 400ºF (204ºC) air fryer for 5 minutes, or until warmed through.

Ham Chicken with Cheese

Prep time: 15 minutes | Cook time: 25 minutes | Serves 4

- ¼ cup unsalted butter, softened
- 4 ounces (113 g) cream cheese, softened
- 1½ teaspoons Dijon mustard
- 2 tablespoons white wine vinegar
- ¼ cup water
- 2 cups shredded cooked chicken
- ¼ pound (113 g) ham, chopped
- 4 ounces (113 g) sliced Swiss or Provolone cheese

1. Preheat the air fryer to 380ºF (193ºC). Lightly coat a casserole dish that will fit in the air fryer, such as an 8-inch round pan, with olive oil and set aside. 2. In a large bowl and using an electric mixer, combine the butter, cream cheese, Dijon mustard, and vinegar. With the motor running at low speed, slowly add the water and beat until smooth. Set aside. 3. Arrange an even layer of chicken in the bottom of the prepared pan, followed by the ham. Spread the butter and cream cheese mixture on top of the ham, followed by the cheese slices on the top layer. Air fry for 20 to 25 minutes until warmed through and the cheese has browned.

Quick Chicken Fajitas

Prep time: 10 minutes | Cook time: 15 minutes | Serves 2

- 10 ounces (283 g) boneless, skinless chicken breast, sliced into ¼-inch strips
- 2 tablespoons coconut oil, melted
- 1 tablespoon chili powder
- ½ teaspoon cumin
- ½ teaspoon paprika
- ½ teaspoon garlic powder
- ¼ medium onion, peeled and sliced
- ½ medium green bell pepper, seeded and sliced
- ½ medium red bell pepper, seeded and sliced

1. Place chicken and coconut oil into a large bowl and sprinkle with chili powder, cumin, paprika, and garlic powder. Toss chicken until well coated with seasoning. Place chicken into the air fryer basket. 2. Adjust the temperature to 350ºF (177ºC) and air fry for 15 minutes. 3. Add onion and peppers into the basket when the cooking time has 7 minutes remaining. 4. Toss the chicken two or three times during cooking. Vegetables should be tender and chicken fully cooked to at least 165ºF (74ºC) internal temperature when finished. Serve warm.

Korean Flavor Glazed Chicken Wings

Prep time: 10 minutes | Cook time: 25 minutes | Serves 4

Wings:
- ◀ 2 pounds (907 g) chicken wings
- ◀ 1 teaspoon salt

Sauce:
- ◀ 2 tablespoons gochujang
- ◀ 1 tablespoon mayonnaise
- ◀ 1 tablespoon minced ginger
- ◀ 1 tablespoon minced garlic

For Garnish:
- ◀ 2 teaspoons sesame seeds

- ◀ 1 teaspoon ground black pepper

- ◀ 1 teaspoon agave nectar
- ◀ 2 packets Splenda
- ◀ 1 tablespoon sesame oil

- ◀ ¼ cup chopped green onions

1. Preheat the air fryer to 400°F (204°C). Line a baking pan with aluminum foil, then arrange the rack on the pan. 2. On a clean work surface, rub the chicken wings with salt and ground black pepper, then arrange the seasoned wings on the rack. 3. Air fry for 20 minutes or until the wings are well browned. Flip the wings halfway through. You may need to work in batches to avoid overcrowding. 4. Meanwhile, combine the ingredients for the sauce in a small bowl. Stir to mix well. Reserve half of the sauce in a separate bowl until ready to serve. 5. Remove the air fried chicken wings from the air fryer and toss with remaining half of the sauce to coat well. 6. Place the wings back to the air fryer and air fry for 5 more minutes or until the internal temperature of the wings reaches at least 165°F (74°C). 7. Remove the wings from the air fryer and place on a large plate. Sprinkle with sesame seeds and green onions. Serve with reserved sauce.

Mediterranean Stuffed Chicken Breasts

Prep time: 5 minutes | Cook time: 20 to 25 minutes | Serves 4

- ◀ 4 small boneless, skinless chicken breast halves (about 1½ pounds / 680 g)
- ◀ Salt and freshly ground black pepper, to taste
- ◀ 4 ounces (113 g) goat cheese
- ◀ 6 pitted Kalamata olives, coarsely chopped

- ◀ Zest of ½ lemon
- ◀ 1 teaspoon minced fresh rosemary or ½ teaspoon ground dried rosemary
- ◀ ½ cup almond meal
- ◀ ¼ cup balsamic vinegar
- ◀ 6 tablespoons unsalted butter

1. Preheat the air fryer to 360°F (182°C). 2. With a boning knife, cut a wide pocket into the thickest part of each chicken breast half, taking care not to cut all the way through. Season the chicken evenly on both sides with salt and freshly ground black pepper. 3. In a small bowl, mix the cheese, olives, lemon zest, and rosemary. Stuff the pockets with the cheese mixture and secure with toothpicks. 4. Place the almond meal in a shallow bowl and dredge the chicken, shaking off the excess. Coat lightly with olive oil spray. 5. Working in batches if necessary, arrange the chicken breasts in a single layer in the air fryer basket. Pausing halfway through the cooking time to flip the chicken, air fry for 20 to 25 minutes, until a thermometer inserted into the thickest part registers 165°F (74°C). 6. While the chicken is baking, prepare the sauce. In a small pan over medium heat, simmer the balsamic vinegar until thick and syrupy, about 5 minutes. Set aside until the chicken is done. When ready to serve, warm the sauce over medium heat and whisk in the butter, 1 tablespoon at a time, until melted and smooth. Season to taste with salt and pepper. 7. Serve the chicken breasts with the sauce drizzled on top.

Peruvian Chicken with Green Herb Sauce

Prep time: 30 minutes | Cook time: 15 minutes | Serves 4

Chicken:
- ◀ 4 boneless, skinless chicken thighs (about 1½ pounds / 680 g)
- ◀ 2 teaspoons grated lemon zest
- ◀ 2 tablespoons fresh lemon juice
- ◀ 1 tablespoon extra-virgin

Sauce:
- ◀ 1 cup fresh cilantro leaves
- ◀ 1 jalapeño, seeded and coarsely chopped
- ◀ 1 garlic clove, minced
- ◀ 1 tablespoon extra-virgin

- olive oil
- ◀ 1 serrano chile, seeded and minced
- ◀ 1 teaspoon ground cumin
- ◀ ½ teaspoon dried oregano, crushed
- ◀ ½ teaspoon kosher salt

- olive oil
- ◀ 2½ teaspoons fresh lime juice
- ◀ ¼ teaspoon kosher salt
- ◀ ⅓ cup mayonnaise

1. For the chicken: Use a fork to pierce the chicken all over to allow the marinade to penetrate better. In a small bowl, combine the lemon zest, lemon juice, olive oil, serrano, cumin, oregano, and salt. Place the chicken in a large bowl or large resealable plastic bag. Pour the marinade over the chicken. Toss to coat. Marinate at room temperature for 30 minutes, or cover and refrigerate for up to 24 hours. 2. Place the chicken in the air fryer basket. (Discard remaining marinade.) Set the air fryer to 350°F (177°C) for 15 minutes, turning halfway through the cooking time. 3. Meanwhile, for the sauce: Combine the cilantro, jalapeño, garlic, olive oil, lime juice, and salt in a blender. Blend until combined. Add the mayonnaise and blend until puréed. Transfer to a small bowl. Cover and chill until ready to serve. 4. At the end of the cooking time, use a meat thermometer to ensure the chicken has reached an internal temperature of 165°F (74°C). Serve the chicken with the sauce.

Chicken and Vegetable Fajitas

Prep time: 15 minutes | Cook time: 23 minutes | Serves 6

Chicken:
- ◀ 1 pound (454 g) boneless, skinless chicken thighs, cut crosswise into thirds
- ◀ 1 tablespoon vegetable oil
- ◀ 4½ teaspoons taco seasoning

Vegetables:
- ◀ 1 cup sliced onion
- ◀ 1 cup sliced bell pepper
- ◀ 1 or 2 jalapeños, quartered lengthwise
- ◀ 1 tablespoon vegetable oil
- ◀ ½ teaspoon kosher salt
- ◀ ½ teaspoon ground cumin

For Serving:
- ◀ Tortillas
- ◀ Sour cream
- ◀ Shredded cheese
- ◀ Guacamole
- ◀ Salsa

1. For the chicken: In a medium bowl, toss together the chicken, vegetable oil, and taco seasoning to coat. 2. For the vegetables: In a separate bowl, toss together the onion, bell pepper, jalapeño(s), vegetable oil, salt, and cumin to coat. 3. Place the chicken in the air fryer basket. Set the air fryer to 375ºF (191ºC) for 10 minutes. Add the vegetables to the basket, toss everything together to blend the seasonings, and set the air fryer for 13 minutes more. Use a meat thermometer to ensure the chicken has reached an internal temperature of 165ºF (74ºC). 4. Transfer the chicken and vegetables to a serving platter. Serve with tortillas and the desired fajita fixings.

Chicken Wellington

Prep time: 30 minutes | Cook time: 31 minutes | Serves 2

- ◀ 2 (5 ounces / 142 g) boneless, skinless chicken breasts
- ◀ ½ cup White Worcestershire sauce
- ◀ 3 tablespoons butter
- ◀ ½ cup finely diced onion (about ½ onion)
- ◀ 8 ounces (227 g) button mushrooms, finely chopped
- ◀ ¼ cup chicken stock
- ◀ 2 tablespoons White Worcestershire sauce (or white wine)
- ◀ Salt and freshly ground black pepper, to taste
- ◀ 1 tablespoon chopped fresh tarragon
- ◀ 2 sheets puff pastry, thawed
- ◀ 1 egg, beaten
- ◀ Vegetable oil

1. Place the chicken breasts in a shallow dish. Pour the White Worcestershire sauce over the chicken coating both sides and marinate for 30 minutes. 2. While the chicken is marinating, melt the butter in a large skillet over medium-high heat on the stovetop. Add the onion and sauté for a few minutes, until it starts to soften. Add the mushrooms and sauté for 3 to 5 minutes until the vegetables are brown and soft. Deglaze the skillet with the chicken stock, scraping up any bits from the bottom of the pan. Add the White Worcestershire sauce and simmer for 2 to 3 minutes until the mixture reduces and starts to thicken. Season with salt and freshly ground black pepper. Remove the mushroom mixture from the heat and stir in the fresh tarragon. Let the mushroom mixture cool. 3. Preheat the air fryer to 360ºF (182ºC). 4. Remove the chicken from the marinade and transfer it to the air fryer basket. Tuck the small end of the chicken breast under the thicker part to shape it into a circle rather than an oval. Pour the marinade over the chicken and air fry for 10 minutes. 5. Roll out the puff pastry and cut out two 6-inch squares. Brush the perimeter of each square with the egg wash. Place half of the mushroom mixture in the center of each puff pastry square. Place the chicken breasts, top side down on the mushroom mixture. Starting with one corner of puff pastry and working in one direction, pull the pastry up over the chicken to enclose it and press the ends of the pastry together in the middle. Brush the pastry with the egg wash to seal the edges. Turn the Wellingtons over and set aside. 6. Make a decorative design with the remaining puff pastry, cut out four 10-inch strips. For each Wellington, twist two of the strips together, place them over the chicken breast wrapped in puff pastry, and tuck the ends underneath to seal it. Brush the entire top and sides of the Wellingtons with the egg wash. 7. Preheat the air fryer to 350ºF (177ºC). 8. Spray or brush the air fryer basket with vegetable oil. Air fry the chicken Wellingtons for 13 minutes. Carefully turn the Wellingtons over. Air fry for another 8 minutes. Transfer to serving plates, light a candle and enjoy!

Golden Chicken Cutlets

Prep time: 15 minutes | Cook time: 15 minutes | Serves 4

- ◀ 2 tablespoons panko breadcrumbs
- ◀ ¼ cup grated Parmesan cheese
- ◀ ⅛ tablespoon paprika
- ◀ ½ tablespoon garlic powder
- ◀ 2 large eggs
- ◀ 4 chicken cutlets
- ◀ 1 tablespoon parsley
- ◀ Salt and ground black pepper, to taste
- ◀ Cooking spray

1. Preheat air fryer to 400ºF (204ºC). Spritz the air fryer basket with cooking spray. 2. Combine the breadcrumbs, Parmesan, paprika, garlic powder, salt, and ground black pepper in a large bowl. Stir to mix well. Beat the eggs in a separate bowl. 3. Dredge the chicken cutlets in the beaten eggs, then roll over the breadcrumbs mixture to coat well. Shake the excess off. 4. Transfer the chicken cutlets in the preheated air fryer and spritz with cooking spray. 5. Air fry for 15 minutes or until crispy and golden brown. Flip the cutlets halfway through. 6. Serve with parsley on top.

Juicy Paprika Chicken Breast

Prep time: 5 minutes | Cook time: 30 minutes | Serves 4

- Oil, for spraying
- 4 (6-ounce / 170-g) boneless, skinless chicken breasts
- 1 tablespoon olive oil
- 1 tablespoon paprika
- 1 tablespoon packed light brown sugar
- ½ teaspoon cayenne pepper
- ½ teaspoon onion powder
- ½ teaspoon granulated garlic

1. Line the air fryer basket with parchment and spray lightly with oil. 2. Brush the chicken with the olive oil. 3. In a small bowl, mix together the paprika, brown sugar, cayenne pepper, onion powder, and garlic and sprinkle it over the chicken. 4. Place the chicken in the prepared basket. You may need to work in batches, depending on the size of your air fryer. 5. Air fry at 360°F (182°C) for 15 minutes, flip, and cook for another 15 minutes, or until the internal temperature reaches 165°F (74°C). Serve immediately.

Chicken Paillard

Prep time: 10 minutes | Cook time: 10 minutes | Serves 2

- 2 large eggs, room temperature
- 1 tablespoon water
- ½ cup powdered Parmesan cheese (about 1½ ounces / 43 g) or pork dust
- 2 teaspoons dried thyme leaves
- 1 teaspoon ground black pepper
- 2 (5 ounces / 142 g) boneless, skinless chicken
- breasts, pounded to ½ inch thick
- Lemon Butter Sauce:
- 2 tablespoons unsalted butter, melted
- 2 teaspoons lemon juice
- ¼ teaspoon finely chopped fresh thyme leaves, plus more for garnish
- ⅛ teaspoon fine sea salt
- Lemon slices, for serving

1. Spray the air fryer basket with avocado oil. Preheat the air fryer to 390°F (199°C). 2. Beat the eggs in a shallow dish, then add the water and stir well. 3. In a separate shallow dish, mix together the Parmesan, thyme, and pepper until well combined. 4. One at a time, dip the chicken breasts in the eggs and let any excess drip off, then dredge both sides of the chicken in the Parmesan mixture. As you finish, set the coated chicken in the air fryer basket. 5. Roast the chicken in the air fryer for 5 minutes, then flip the chicken and cook for another 5 minutes, or until cooked through and the internal temperature reaches 165°F (74°C). 6. While the chicken cooks, make the lemon butter sauce: In a small bowl, mix together all the sauce ingredients until well combined. 7. Plate the chicken and pour the sauce over it. Garnish with chopped fresh thyme and serve with lemon slices. 8. Store leftovers in an airtight container in the refrigerator for up to 4 days. Reheat in a preheated 390°F (199°C) air fryer for 5 minutes, or until heated through.

Chicken Drumsticks with Barbecue-Honey Sauce

Prep time: 5 minutes | Cook time: 40 minutes | Serves 5

- 1 tablespoon olive oil
- 10 chicken drumsticks
- Chicken seasoning or rub, to taste
- Salt and ground black pepper, to taste
- 1 cup barbecue sauce
- ¼ cup honey

1. Preheat the air fryer to 390°F (199°C). Grease the air fryer basket with olive oil. 2. Rub the chicken drumsticks with chicken seasoning or rub, salt and ground black pepper on a clean work surface. 3. Arrange the chicken drumsticks in a single layer in the air fryer, then air fry for 18 minutes or until lightly browned. Flip the drumsticks halfway through. You may need to work in batches to avoid overcrowding. 4. Meanwhile, combine the barbecue sauce and honey in a small bowl. Stir to mix well. 5. Remove the drumsticks from the air fryer and baste with the sauce mixture to serve.

Buttermilk Breaded Chicken

Prep time: 7 minutes | Cook time: 20 to 25 minutes | Serves 4

- 1 cup all-purpose flour
- 2 teaspoons paprika
- Pinch salt
- Freshly ground black pepper, to taste
- ⅓ cup buttermilk
- 2 eggs
- 2 tablespoons extra-virgin olive oil
- 1½ cups bread crumbs
- 6 chicken pieces, drumsticks, breasts, and thighs, patted dry
- Cooking oil spray

1. In a shallow bowl, stir together the flour, paprika, salt, and pepper. 2. In another bowl, beat the buttermilk and eggs until smooth. 3. In a third bowl, stir together the olive oil and bread crumbs until mixed. 4. Dredge the chicken in the flour, dip in the eggs to coat, and finally press into the bread crumbs, patting the crumbs firmly onto the chicken skin. 5. Insert the crisper plate into the basket and the basket into the unit. Preheat the unit by selecting AIR FRY, setting the temperature to 375°F (191°C), and setting the time to 3 minutes. Select START/STOP to begin. 6. Once the unit is preheated, spray the crisper plate with cooking oil. Place the chicken into the basket. 7. Select AIR FRY, set the temperature to 375°F (191°C), and set the time to 25 minutes. Select START/STOP to begin. 8. After 10 minutes, flip the chicken. Resume cooking. After 10 minutes more, check the chicken. If a food thermometer inserted into the chicken registers 165°F (74°C) and the chicken is brown and crisp, it is done. Otherwise, resume cooking for up to 5 minutes longer. 9. When the cooking is complete, let cool for 5 minutes, then serve.

Buffalo Crispy Chicken Strips

Prep time: 15 minutes | Cook time: 13 to 17 minutes per batch | Serves 4

- ¾ cup all-purpose flour
- 2 eggs
- 2 tablespoons water
- 1 cup seasoned panko bread crumbs
- 2 teaspoons granulated garlic
- 1 teaspoon salt
- 1 teaspoon freshly ground black pepper
- 16 chicken breast strips, or 3 large boneless, skinless chicken breasts, cut into 1-inch strips
- Olive oil spray
- ¼ cup Buffalo sauce, plus more as needed

1. Put the flour in a small bowl. 2. In another small bowl, whisk the eggs and the water. 3. In a third bowl, stir together the panko, granulated garlic, salt, and pepper. 4. Dip each chicken strip in the flour, in the egg, and in the panko mixture to coat. Press the crumbs onto the chicken with your fingers. 5. Insert the crisper plate into the basket and the basket into the unit. Preheat the unit by selecting AIR FRY, setting the temperature to 375°F (191°C), and setting the time to 3 minutes. Select START/STOP to begin. 6. Once the unit is preheated, place a parchment paper liner into the basket. Working in batches if needed, place the chicken strips into the basket. Do not stack unless using a wire rack for the second layer. Spray the top of the chicken with olive oil. 7. Select AIR FRY, set the temperature to 375°F (191°C), and set the time to 17 minutes. Select START/STOP to begin. 8. After 10 or 12 minutes, remove the basket, flip the chicken, and spray again with olive oil. Reinsert the basket to resume cooking. 9. When the cooking is complete, the chicken should be golden brown and crispy and a food thermometer inserted into the chicken should register 165°F (74°C). 10. Repeat steps 6, 7, and 8 with any remaining chicken. 11. Transfer the chicken to a large bowl. Drizzle the Buffalo sauce over the top of the cooked chicken, toss to coat, and serve.

Easy Turkey Tenderloin

Prep time: 20 minutes | Cook time: 30 minutes | Serves 4

- Olive oil
- ½ teaspoon paprika
- ½ teaspoon garlic powder
- ½ teaspoon salt
- ½ teaspoon freshly ground black pepper
- Pinch cayenne pepper
- 1½ pounds (680 g) turkey breast tenderloin

1. Spray the air fryer basket lightly with olive oil. 2. In a small bowl, combine the paprika, garlic powder, salt, black pepper, and cayenne pepper. Rub the mixture all over the turkey. 3. Place the turkey in the air fryer basket and lightly spray with olive oil. 4. Air fry at 370°F (188°C) for 15 minutes. Flip the turkey over and lightly spray with olive oil. Air fry until the internal temperature reaches at least 170°F (77°C) for an additional 10 to 15 minutes. 5. Let the turkey rest for 10 minutes before slicing and serving.

Chapter 5

Beef, Pork, and Lamb

Chapter 5 Beef, Pork, and Lamb

Stuffed Beef Tenderloin with Feta Cheese

Prep time: 10 minutes | Cook time: 10 minutes | Serves 4

- 1½ pounds (680 g) beef tenderloin, pounded to ¼ inch thick
- 3 teaspoons sea salt
- 1 teaspoon ground black pepper
- 2 ounces (57 g) creamy goat cheese
- ½ cup crumbled feta cheese
- ¼ cup finely chopped onions
- 2 cloves garlic, minced
- Cooking spray

1. Preheat the air fryer to 400ºF (204ºC). Spritz the air fryer basket with cooking spray. 2. Unfold the beef tenderloin on a clean work surface. Rub the salt and pepper all over the beef tenderloin to season. 3. Make the filling for the stuffed beef tenderloins: Combine the goat cheese, feta, onions, and garlic in a medium bowl. Stir until well blended. 4. Spoon the mixture in the center of the tenderloin. Roll the tenderloin up tightly like rolling a burrito and use some kitchen twine to tie the tenderloin. 5. Arrange the tenderloin in the air fryer basket and air fry for 10 minutes, flipping the tenderloin halfway through to ensure even cooking, or until an instant-read thermometer inserted in the center of the tenderloin registers 135ºF (57ºC) for medium-rare. 6. Transfer to a platter and serve immediately.

Cheeseburger Casserole

Prep time: 5 minutes | Cook time: 50 minutes | Serves 4

- ¼ pound (113 g) reduced-sodium bacon
- 1 pound (454 g) 85% lean ground beef
- 1 clove garlic, minced
- ¼ teaspoon onion powder
- 4 eggs
- ¼ cup heavy cream
- ¼ cup tomato paste
- 2 tablespoons dill pickle relish
- ¼ teaspoon salt
- ¼ teaspoon freshly ground black pepper
- 1½ cups grated Cheddar cheese, divided

1. Lightly coat a casserole dish that will fit in air fryer, with olive oil and set aside. 2. Arrange the bacon in a single layer in the air fryer basket (it's OK if the bacon sits a bit on the sides). Set the air fryer to 350ºF (177ºC) and air fry for 10 minutes. Check for crispiness and air fry for 2 to 3 minutes longer if needed. Transfer the bacon to a plate lined with paper towels and let cool. Drain the grease. 3. Set the air fryer to 400ºF (204ºC). Crumble the beef into a single layer in the air fryer basket. Scatter the garlic on top and sprinkle with the onion powder. Air fry for 15 to 20 minutes until the beef is browned and cooked through. 4. While the beef is baking, in a bowl whisk together the eggs, cream, tomato paste, pickle relish, salt, and pepper. Stir in 1 cup of the cheese. Set aside. 5. When the beef is done, transfer it to the prepared pan. Use the side of a spoon to break up any large pieces of beef. 6. Drain the grease and, when cool enough to handle, wash the air fryer basket. Set the air fryer to 350ºF (177ºC). 7. Crumble the bacon and add it to the beef, spreading the meats into an even layer. Pour the egg mixture over the beef mixture and top with the remaining ½ cup of cheese. Air fry for 20 to 25 minutes until the eggs are set and the top is golden brown.

Poblano Pepper Cheeseburgers

Prep time: 5 minutes | Cook time: 30 minutes | Serves 4

- 2 poblano chile peppers
- 1½ pounds (680 g) 85% lean ground beef
- 1 clove garlic, minced
- 1 teaspoon salt
- ½ teaspoon freshly ground black pepper
- 4 slices Cheddar cheese (about 3 ounces / 85 g)
- 4 large lettuce leaves

1. Preheat the air fryer to 400ºF (204ºC). 2. Arrange the poblano peppers in the basket of the air fryer. Pausing halfway through the cooking time to turn the peppers, air fry for 20 minutes, or until they are softened and beginning to char. Transfer the peppers to a large bowl and cover with a plate. When cool enough to handle, peel off the skin, remove the seeds and stems, and slice into strips. Set aside. 3. Meanwhile, in a large bowl, combine the ground beef with the garlic, salt, and pepper. Shape the beef into 4 patties. 4. Lower the heat on the air fryer to 360ºF (182ºC). Arrange the burgers in a single layer in the basket of the air fryer. Pausing halfway through the cooking time to turn the burgers, air fry for 10 minutes, or until a thermometer inserted into the thickest part registers 160ºF (71ºC). 5. Top the burgers with the cheese slices and continue baking for a minute or two, just until the cheese has melted. Serve the burgers on a lettuce leaf topped with the roasted poblano peppers.

Carne Asada

Prep time: 5 minutes | Cook time: 15 minutes | Serves 4

- 3 chipotle peppers in adobo, chopped
- ⅓ cup chopped fresh oregano
- ⅓ cup chopped fresh parsley
- 4 cloves garlic, minced
- Juice of 2 limes
- 1 teaspoon ground cumin seeds
- ⅓ cup olive oil
- 1 to 1½ pounds (454 g to 680 g) flank steak
- Salt, to taste

1. Combine the chipotle, oregano, parsley, garlic, lime juice, cumin, and olive oil in a large bowl. Stir to mix well. 2. Dunk the flank steak in the mixture and press to coat well. Wrap the bowl in plastic and marinate under room temperature for at least 30 minutes. 3. Preheat the air fryer to 390ºF (199ºC). 4. Discard the marinade and place the steak in the preheated air fryer. Sprinkle with salt. 5. Air fry for 15 minutes or until the steak is medium-rare or it reaches your desired doneness. Flip the steak halfway through the cooking time. 6. Remove the steak from the air fryer and slice to serve.

Pork Cutlets with Aloha Salsa

Prep time: 20 minutes | Cook time: 7 to 9 minutes | Serves 4

Aloha Salsa:
- 1 cup fresh pineapple, chopped in small pieces
- ¼ cup red onion, finely chopped
- ¼ cup green or red bell pepper, chopped
- ½ teaspoon ground cinnamon
- 1 teaspoon low-sodium soy sauce
- ⅛ teaspoon crushed red pepper
- ⅛ teaspoon ground black
- pepper
- 2 eggs
- 2 tablespoons milk
- ¼ cup flour
- ¼ cup panko bread crumbs
- 4 teaspoons sesame seeds
- 1 pound (454 g) boneless, thin pork cutlets (⅜- to ½-inch thick)
- lemon pepper and salt
- ¼ cup cornstarch
- Oil for misting or cooking spray

1. In a medium bowl, stir together all ingredients for salsa. Cover and refrigerate while cooking pork. 2. Preheat the air fryer to 390ºF (199ºC). 3. Beat together eggs and milk in shallow dish. 4. In another shallow dish, mix together the flour, panko, and sesame seeds. 5. Sprinkle pork cutlets with lemon pepper and salt to taste. Most lemon pepper seasoning contains salt, so go easy adding extra. 6. Dip pork cutlets in cornstarch, egg mixture, and then panko coating. Spray both sides with oil or cooking spray. 7. Cook cutlets for 3 minutes. Turn cutlets over, spraying both sides, and continue cooking for 4 to 6 minutes or until well done. 8. Serve fried cutlets with salsa on the side.

Tomato and Bacon Zoodles

Prep time: 10 minutes | Cook time: 15 to 22 minutes | Serves 2

- 8 ounces (227 g) sliced bacon
- ½ cup grape tomatoes
- 1 large zucchini, spiralized
- ½ cup ricotta cheese
- ¼ cup heavy (whipping)
- cream
- ⅓ cup finely grated Parmesan cheese, plus more for serving
- Sea salt and freshly ground black pepper, to taste

1. Set the air fryer to 400ºF (204ºC). Arrange the bacon strips in a single layer in the air fryer basket—some overlapping is okay because the bacon will shrink, but cook in batches if needed. Air fry for 8 minutes. Flip the bacon strips and air fry for 2 to 5 minutes more, until the bacon is crisp. Remove the bacon from the air fryer. 2. Put the tomatoes in the air fryer basket and air fry for 3 to 5 minutes, until they are just starting to burst. Remove the tomatoes from the air fryer. 3. Put the zucchini noodles in the air fryer and air fry for 2 to 4 minutes, to the desired doneness. 4. Meanwhile, combine the ricotta, heavy cream, and Parmesan in a saucepan over medium-low heat. Cook, stirring often, until warm and combined. 5. Crumble the bacon. Place the zucchini, bacon, and tomatoes in a bowl. Toss with the ricotta sauce. Season with salt and pepper, and sprinkle with additional Parmesan.

Easy Beef Satay

Prep time: 30 minutes | Cook time: 8 minutes | Serves 4

- 1 pound (454 g) beef flank steak, thinly sliced into long strips
- 2 tablespoons vegetable oil
- 1 tablespoon fish sauce
- 1 tablespoon soy sauce
- 1 tablespoon minced fresh ginger
- 1 tablespoon minced garlic
- 1 tablespoon sugar
- 1 teaspoon Sriracha or other hot sauce
- 1 teaspoon ground coriander
- ½ cup chopped fresh cilantro
- ¼ cup chopped roasted peanuts

1. Place the beef strips in a large bowl or resealable plastic bag. Add the vegetable oil, fish sauce, soy sauce, ginger, garlic, sugar, Sriracha, coriander, and ¼ cup of the cilantro to the bag. Seal and massage the bag to thoroughly coat and combine. Marinate at room temperature for 30 minutes, or cover and refrigerate for up to 24 hours. 2. Using tongs, remove the beef strips from the bag and lay them flat in the air fryer basket, minimizing overlap as much as possible; discard the marinade. Set the air fryer to 400ºF (204ºC) for 8 minutes, turning the beef strips halfway through the cooking time. 3. Transfer the meat to a serving platter. Sprinkle with the remaining ¼ cup cilantro and the peanuts. Serve.

Greek Stuffed Tenderloin

Prep time: 10 minutes | Cook time: 10 minutes | Serves 4

- 1½ pounds (680 g) venison or beef tenderloin, pounded to ¼ inch thick
- 3 teaspoons fine sea salt
- 1 teaspoon ground black pepper

For Garnish/Serving (Optional):
- Prepared yellow mustard
- Halved cherry tomatoes
- Extra-virgin olive oil
- 2 ounces (57 g) creamy goat cheese
- ½ cup crumbled feta cheese (about 2 ounces / 57 g)
- ¼ cup finely chopped onions
- 2 cloves garlic, minced

- Sprigs of fresh rosemary
- Lavender flowers

1. Spray the air fryer basket with avocado oil. Preheat the air fryer to 400°F (204°C). 2. Season the tenderloin on all sides with the salt and pepper. 3. In a medium-sized mixing bowl, combine the goat cheese, feta, onions, and garlic. Place the mixture in the center of the tenderloin. Starting at the end closest to you, tightly roll the tenderloin like a jelly roll. Tie the rolled tenderloin tightly with kitchen twine. 4. Place the meat in the air fryer basket and air fry for 5 minutes. Flip the meat over and cook for another 5 minutes, or until the internal temperature reaches 135°F (57°C) for medium-rare. 5. To serve, smear a line of prepared yellow mustard on a platter, then place the meat next to it and add halved cherry tomatoes on the side, if desired. Drizzle with olive oil and garnish with rosemary sprigs and lavender flowers, if desired. 6. Best served fresh. Store leftovers in an airtight container in the fridge for 3 days. Reheat in a preheated 350°F (177°C) air fryer for 4 minutes, or until heated through.

Italian Lamb Chops with Avocado Mayo

Prep time: 5 minutes | Cook time: 12 minutes | Serves 2

- 2 lamp chops
- 2 teaspoons Italian herbs
- 2 avocados
- ½ cup mayonnaise
- 1 tablespoon lemon juice

1. Season the lamb chops with the Italian herbs, then set aside for 5 minutes. 2. Preheat the air fryer to 400°F (204°C) and place the rack inside. 3. Put the chops on the rack and air fry for 12 minutes. 4. In the meantime, halve the avocados and open to remove the pits. Spoon the flesh into a blender. 5. Add the mayonnaise and lemon juice and pulse until a smooth consistency is achieved. 6. Take care when removing the chops from the air fryer, then plate up and serve with the avocado mayo.

Beef Whirls

Prep time: 30 minutes | Cook time: 18 minutes | Serves 6

- 3 cube steaks (6 ounces / 170 g each)
- 1 (16-ounce / 454-g) bottle Italian dressing
- 1 cup Italian-style bread crumbs
- ½ cup grated Parmesan
- cheese
- 1 teaspoon dried basil
- 1 teaspoon dried oregano
- 1 teaspoon dried parsley
- ¼ cup beef broth
- 1 to 2 tablespoons oil

1. In a large resealable bag, combine the steaks and Italian dressing. Seal the bag and refrigerate to marinate for 2 hours. 2. In a medium bowl, whisk the bread crumbs, cheese, basil, oregano, and parsley until blended. Stir in the beef broth. 3. Place the steaks on a cutting board and cut each in half so you have 6 equal pieces. Sprinkle with the bread crumb mixture. Roll up the steaks, jelly roll-style, and secure with toothpicks. 4. Preheat the air fryer to 400°F (204°C). 5. Place 3 roll-ups in the air fryer basket. 6. Cook for 5 minutes. Flip the roll-ups and spritz with oil. Cook for 4 minutes more until the internal temperature reaches 145°F (63°C). Repeat with the remaining roll-ups. Let rest for 5 to 10 minutes before serving.

Air Fried Beef Satay with Peanut Dipping Sauce

Prep time: 30 minutes | Cook time: 5 to 7 minutes | Serves 4

- 8 ounces (227 g) London broil, sliced into 8 strips
- 2 teaspoons curry powder

Peanut Dipping sauce:
- 2 tablespoons creamy peanut butter
- 1 tablespoon reduced-sodium soy sauce

Special Equipment:
- 4 bamboo skewers, cut into halves and soaked in water
- ½ teaspoon kosher salt
- Cooking spray

- 2 teaspoons rice vinegar
- 1 teaspoon honey
- 1 teaspoon grated ginger

for 20 minutes to keep them from burning while cooking

1. Preheat the air fryer to 360°F (182°C). Spritz the air fryer basket with cooking spray. 2. In a bowl, place the London broil strips and sprinkle with the curry powder and kosher salt to season. Thread the strips onto the soaked skewers. 3. Arrange the skewers in the prepared air fryer basket and spritz with cooking spray. Air fry for 5 to 7 minutes, or until the beef is well browned, turning halfway through. 4. In the meantime, stir together the peanut butter, soy sauce, rice vinegar, honey, and ginger in a bowl to make the dipping sauce. 5. Transfer the beef to the serving dishes and let rest for 5 minutes. Serve with the peanut dipping sauce on the side.

Kheema Burgers

Prep time: 15 minutes | Cook time: 12 minutes | Serves 4

Burgers:
- ◄ 1 pound (454 g) 85% lean ground beef or ground lamb
- ◄ 2 large eggs, lightly beaten
- ◄ 1 medium yellow onion, diced
- ◄ ¼ cup chopped fresh cilantro
- ◄ 1 tablespoon minced fresh ginger
- ◄ 3 cloves garlic, minced

- ◄ 2 teaspoons garam masala
- ◄ 1 teaspoon ground turmeric
- ◄ ½ teaspoon ground cinnamon
- ◄ ⅛ teaspoon ground cardamom
- ◄ 1 teaspoon kosher salt
- ◄ 1 teaspoon cayenne pepper

Raita Sauce:
- ◄ 1 cup grated cucumber
- ◄ ½ cup sour cream

- ◄ ¼ teaspoon kosher salt
- ◄ ¼ teaspoon black pepper

For Serving:
- ◄ 4 lettuce leaves, hamburger buns, or naan breads

1. For the burgers: In a large bowl, combine the ground beef, eggs, onion, cilantro, ginger, garlic, garam masala, turmeric, cinnamon, cardamom, salt, and cayenne. Gently mix until ingredients are thoroughly combined. 2. Divide the meat into four portions and form into round patties. Make a slight depression in the middle of each patty with your thumb to prevent them from puffing up into a dome shape while cooking. 3. Place the patties in the air fryer basket. Set the air fryer to 350°F (177°C) for 12 minutes. Use a meat thermometer to ensure the burgers have reached an internal temperature of 160°F / 71°C (for medium). 4. Meanwhile, for the sauce: In a small bowl, combine the cucumber, sour cream, salt, and pepper. 5. To serve: Place the burgers on the lettuce, buns, or naan and top with the sauce.

Parmesan-Crusted Steak

Prep time: 30 minutes | Cook time: 12 minutes | Serves 6

- ◄ ½ cup (1 stick) unsalted butter, at room temperature
- ◄ 1 cup finely grated Parmesan cheese
- ◄ ¼ cup finely ground

blanched almond flour
- ◄ 1½ pounds (680 g) New York strip steak
- ◄ Sea salt and freshly ground black pepper, to taste

1. Place the butter, Parmesan cheese, and almond flour in a food processor. Process until smooth. Transfer to a sheet of parchment paper and form into a log. Wrap tightly in plastic wrap. Freeze for 45 minutes or refrigerate for at least 4 hours. 2. While the butter is chilling, season the steak liberally with salt and pepper. Let the steak rest at room temperature for about 45 minutes. 3. Place the grill pan or basket in your air fryer, set it to 400°F (204°C), and let it preheat for 5 minutes. 4. Working in batches, if necessary, place the steak on the grill pan and air fry for 4 minutes. Flip and

cook for 3 minutes more, until the steak is brown on both sides. 5. Remove the steak from the air fryer and arrange an equal amount of the Parmesan butter on top of each steak. Return the steak to the air fryer and continue cooking for another 5 minutes, until an instant-read thermometer reads 120°F (49°C) for medium-rare and the crust is golden brown (or to your desired doneness). 6. Transfer the cooked steak to a plate; let rest for 10 minutes before serving.

Kheema Meatloaf

Prep time: 10 minutes | Cook time: 15 minutes | Serves 4

- ◄ 1 pound (454 g) 85% lean ground beef
- ◄ 2 large eggs, lightly beaten
- ◄ 1 cup diced yellow onion
- ◄ ¼ cup chopped fresh cilantro
- ◄ 1 tablespoon minced fresh ginger
- ◄ 1 tablespoon minced garlic

- ◄ 2 teaspoons garam masala
- ◄ 1 teaspoon kosher salt
- ◄ 1 teaspoon ground turmeric
- ◄ 1 teaspoon cayenne pepper
- ◄ ½ teaspoon ground cinnamon
- ◄ ⅛ teaspoon ground cardamom

1. In a large bowl, gently mix the ground beef, eggs, onion, cilantro, ginger, garlic, garam masala, salt, turmeric, cayenne, cinnamon, and cardamom until thoroughly combined. 2. Place the seasoned meat in a baking pan. Place the pan in the air fryer basket. Set the air fryer to 350°F (177°C) for 15 minutes. Use a meat thermometer to ensure the meat loaf has reached an internal temperature of 160°F / 71°C (medium). 3. Drain the fat and liquid from the pan and let stand for 5 minutes before slicing. 4. Slice and serve hot.

Southern Chili

Prep time: 20 minutes | Cook time: 25 minutes | Serves 4

- ◄ 1 pound (454 g) ground beef (85% lean)
- ◄ 1 cup minced onion
- ◄ 1 (28-ounce / 794-g) can tomato purée
- ◄ 1 (15-ounce / 425-g) can

diced tomatoes with green chilies
- ◄ 1 (15-ounce / 425-g) can light red kidney beans, rinsed and drained
- ◄ ¼ cup Chili seasoning

1. Preheat the air fryer to 400°F (204°C). 2. In a baking pan, mix the ground beef and onion. Place the pan in the air fryer. 3. Cook for 4 minutes. Stir and cook for 4 minutes more until browned. Remove the pan from the fryer. Drain the meat and transfer to a large bowl. 4. Reduce the air fryer temperature to 350°F (177°C). 5. To the bowl with the meat, add in the tomato purée, diced tomatoes and green chilies, kidney beans, and Chili seasoning. Mix well. Pour the mixture into the baking pan. 6. Cook for 25 minutes, stirring every 10 minutes, until thickened.

Italian Sausages with Peppers and Onions

Prep time: 5 minutes | Cook time: 28 minutes | Serves 3

- ◄ 1 medium onion, thinly sliced
- ◄ 1 yellow or orange bell pepper, thinly sliced
- ◄ 1 red bell pepper, thinly sliced
- ◄ ¼ cup avocado oil or melted coconut oil
- ◄ 1 teaspoon fine sea salt
- ◄ 6 Italian sausages
- ◄ Dijon mustard, for serving (optional)

1. Preheat the air fryer to 400ºF (204ºC). 2. Place the onion and peppers in a large bowl. Drizzle with the oil and toss well to coat the veggies. Season with the salt. 3. Place the onion and peppers in a pie pan and cook in the air fryer for 8 minutes, stirring halfway through. Remove from the air fryer and set aside. 4. Spray the air fryer basket with avocado oil. Place the sausages in the air fryer basket and air fry for 20 minutes, or until crispy and golden brown. During the last minute or two of cooking, add the onion and peppers to the basket with the sausages to warm them through. 5. Place the onion and peppers on a serving platter and arrange the sausages on top. Serve Dijon mustard on the side, if desired. 6. Store leftovers in an airtight container in the fridge for up to 7 days or in the freezer for up to a month. Reheat in a preheated 390ºF (199ºC) air fryer for 3 minutes, or until heated through.

Five-Spice Pork Belly

Prep time: 10 minutes | Cook time: 17 minutes | Serves 4

- ◄ 1 pound (454 g) unsalted pork belly
- ◄ 2 teaspoons Chinese five-spice powder
- ◄ Sauce:
- ◄ 1 tablespoon coconut oil
- ◄ 1 (1-inch) piece fresh ginger, peeled and grated
- ◄ 2 cloves garlic, minced
- ◄ ½ cup beef or chicken broth
- ◄ ¼ to ½ cup Swerve confectioners'-style sweetener or equivalent amount of liquid or powdered sweetener
- ◄ 3 tablespoons wheat-free tamari, or ½ cup coconut aminos
- ◄ 1 green onion, sliced, plus more for garnish

1. Spray the air fryer basket with avocado oil. Preheat the air fryer to 400ºF (204ºC). 2. Cut the pork belly into ½-inch-thick slices and season well on all sides with the five-spice powder. Place the slices in a single layer in the air fryer basket (if you're using a smaller air fryer, work in batches if necessary) and cook for 8 minutes, or until cooked to your liking, flipping halfway through. 3. While the pork belly cooks, make the sauce: Heat the coconut oil in a small saucepan over medium heat. Add the ginger and garlic and sauté for 1 minute, or until fragrant. Add the broth, sweetener, and tamari and simmer for 10 to 15 minutes, until thickened. Add the green onion

and cook for another minute, until the green onion is softened. Taste and adjust the seasoning to your liking. 4. Transfer the pork belly to a large bowl. Pour the sauce over the pork belly and coat well. Place the pork belly slices on a serving platter and garnish with sliced green onions. 5. Best served fresh. Store leftovers in an airtight container in the fridge for up to 4 days. Reheat in a preheated 400ºF (204ºC) air fryer for 3 minutes, or until heated through.

Italian Sausage Links

Prep time: 10 minutes | Cook time: 24 minutes | Serves 4

- ◄ 1 bell pepper (any color), sliced
- ◄ 1 medium onion, sliced
- ◄ 1 tablespoon avocado oil
- ◄ 1 teaspoon Italian seasoning
- ◄ Sea salt and freshly ground black pepper, to taste
- ◄ 1 pound (454 g) Italian sausage links

1. Place the bell pepper and onion in a medium bowl, and toss with the avocado oil, Italian seasoning, and salt and pepper to taste. 2. Set the air fryer to 400ºF (204ºC). Put the vegetables in the air fryer basket and cook for 12 minutes. 3. Push the vegetables to the side of the basket and arrange the sausage links in the bottom of the basket in a single layer. Spoon the vegetables over the sausages. Cook for 12 minutes, tossing halfway through, until an instant-read thermometer inserted into the sausage reads 160ºF (71ºC).

Filipino Crispy Pork Belly

Prep time: 20 minutes | Cook time: 30 minutes | Serves 4

- ◄ 1 pound (454 g) pork belly
- ◄ 3 cups water
- ◄ 6 garlic cloves
- ◄ 2 tablespoons soy sauce
- ◄ 1 teaspoon kosher salt
- ◄ 1 teaspoon black pepper
- ◄ 2 bay leaves

1. Cut the pork belly into three thick chunks so it will cook more evenly. 2. Place the pork, water, garlic, soy sauce, salt, pepper, and bay leaves in the inner pot of an Instant Pot or other electric pressure cooker. Seal and cook at high pressure for 15 minutes. Let the pressure release naturally for 10 minutes, then manually release the remaining pressure. (If you do not have a pressure cooker, place all the ingredients in a large saucepan. Cover and cook over low heat until a knife can be easily inserted into the skin side of pork belly, about 1 hour.) Using tongs, very carefully transfer the meat to a wire rack over a rimmed baking sheet to drain and dry for 10 minutes. 3. Cut each chunk of pork belly into two long slices. Arrange the slices in the air fryer basket. Set the air fryer to 400ºF (204ºC) for 15 minutes, or until the fat has crisped. 4. Serve immediately.

London Broil with Herb Butter

Prep time: 30 minutes | Cook time: 20 to 25 minutes | Serves 4

- ◄ 1½ pounds (680 g) London broil top round steak
- ◄ ¼ cup olive oil
- ◄ 2 tablespoons balsamic vinegar
- ◄ 1 tablespoon Worcestershire sauce
- ◄ 4 cloves garlic, minced
- ◄ Herb Butter:
- ◄ 6 tablespoons unsalted butter, softened
- ◄ 1 tablespoon chopped fresh parsley
- ◄ ¼ teaspoon salt
- ◄ ¼ teaspoon dried ground rosemary or thyme
- ◄ ¼ teaspoon garlic powder
- ◄ Pinch of red pepper flakes

1. Place the beef in a gallon-size resealable bag. In a small bowl, whisk together the olive oil, balsamic vinegar, Worcestershire sauce, and garlic. Pour the marinade over the beef, massaging gently to coat, and seal the bag. Let sit at room temperature for an hour or refrigerate overnight. 2. To make the herb butter: In a small bowl, mix the butter with the parsley, salt, rosemary, garlic powder, and red pepper flakes until smooth. Cover and refrigerate until ready to use. 3. Preheat the air fryer to 400°F (204°C). 4. Remove the beef from the marinade (discard the marinade) and place the beef in the air fryer basket. Pausing halfway through the cooking time to turn the meat, air fry for 20 to 25 minutes, until a thermometer inserted into the thickest part indicates the desired doneness, 125°F / 52°C (rare) to 150°F / 66°C (medium). Let the beef rest for 10 minutes before slicing. Serve topped with the herb butter.

Pork and Beef Egg Rolls

Prep time: 30 minutes | Cook time: 7 to 8 minutes per batch | Makes 8 egg rolls

- ◄ ¼ pound (113 g) very lean ground beef
- ◄ ¼ pound (113 g) lean ground pork
- ◄ 1 tablespoon soy sauce
- ◄ 1 teaspoon olive oil
- ◄ ½ cup grated carrots
- ◄ 2 green onions, chopped
- ◄ 2 cups grated Napa cabbage
- ◄ ¼ cup chopped water
- chestnuts
- ◄ ¼ teaspoon salt
- ◄ ¼ teaspoon garlic powder
- ◄ ¼ teaspoon black pepper
- ◄ 1 egg
- ◄ 1 tablespoon water
- ◄ 8 egg roll wraps
- ◄ Oil for misting or cooking spray

1. In a large skillet, brown beef and pork with soy sauce. Remove cooked meat from skillet, drain, and set aside. 2. Pour off any excess grease from skillet. Add olive oil, carrots, and onions. Sauté until barely tender, about 1 minute. 3. Stir in cabbage, cover, and cook for 1 minute or just until cabbage slightly wilts. Remove from heat. 4. In a large bowl, combine the cooked meats and vegetables, water chestnuts, salt, garlic powder, and pepper. Stir well. If needed, add more salt to taste. 5. Beat together egg and water in a small bowl. 6. Fill egg roll wrappers, using about ¼ cup of filling

for each wrap. Roll up and brush all over with egg wash to seal. Spray very lightly with olive oil or cooking spray. 7. Place 4 egg rolls in air fryer basket and air fry at 390°F (199°C) for 4 minutes. Turn over and cook 3 to 4 more minutes, until golden brown and crispy. 8. Repeat to cook remaining egg rolls.

Fajita Meatball Lettuce Wraps

Prep time: 10 minutes | Cook time: 10 minutes | Serves 4

- ◄ 1 pound (454 g) ground beef (85% lean)
- ◄ ½ cup salsa, plus more for serving if desired
- ◄ ¼ cup chopped onions
- ◄ ¼ cup diced green or red
- For Serving (Optional):
- ◄ 8 leaves Boston lettuce
- ◄ Pico de gallo or salsa
- bell peppers
- ◄ 1 large egg, beaten
- ◄ 1 teaspoon fine sea salt
- ◄ ½ teaspoon chili powder
- ◄ ½ teaspoon ground cumin
- ◄ 1 clove garlic, minced
- ◄ Lime slices

1. Spray the air fryer basket with avocado oil. Preheat the air fryer to 350°F (177°C). 2. In a large bowl, mix together all the ingredients until well combined. 3. Shape the meat mixture into eight 1-inch balls. Place the meatballs in the air fryer basket, leaving a little space between them. Air fry for 10 minutes, or until cooked through and no longer pink inside and the internal temperature reaches 145°F (63°C). 4. Serve each meatball on a lettuce leaf, topped with pico de gallo or salsa, if desired. Serve with lime slices if desired. 5. Store leftovers in an airtight container in the fridge for 3 days or in the freezer for up to a month. Reheat in a preheated 350°F (177°C) air fryer for 4 minutes, or until heated through.

Spinach and Provolone Steak Rolls

Prep time: 10 minutes | Cook time: 12 minutes | Makes 8 rolls

- ◄ 1 (1 pound / 454 g) flank steak, butterflied
- ◄ 8 (1 ounce / 28 g, ¼-inch-thick) deli slices provolone cheese
- ◄ 1 cup fresh spinach leaves
- ◄ ½ teaspoon salt
- ◄ ¼ teaspoon ground black pepper

1. Place steak on a large plate. Place provolone slices to cover steak, leaving 1-inch at the edges. Lay spinach leaves over cheese. Gently roll steak and tie with kitchen twine or secure with toothpicks. Carefully slice into eight pieces. Sprinkle each with salt and pepper. 2. Place rolls into ungreased air fryer basket, cut side up. Adjust the temperature to 400°F (204°C) and air fry for 12 minutes. Steak rolls will be browned and cheese will be melted when done and have an internal temperature of at least 150°F (66°C) for medium steak and 180°F (82°C) for well-done steak. Serve warm.

Cheese Crusted Chops

Prep time: 10 minutes | Cook time: 12 minutes | Serves 4 to 6

- ◄ ¼ teaspoon pepper
- ◄ ½ teaspoons salt
- ◄ 4 to 6 thick boneless pork chops
- ◄ 1 cup pork rind crumbs
- ◄ ¼ teaspoon chili powder
- ◄ ½ teaspoons onion powder
- ◄ 1 teaspoon smoked paprika
- ◄ 2 beaten eggs
- ◄ 3 tablespoons grated Parmesan cheese
- ◄ Cooking spray

1. Preheat the air fryer to 400ºF (205ºC). 2. Rub the pepper and salt on both sides of pork chops. 3. In a food processor, pulse pork rinds into crumbs. Mix crumbs with chili powder, onion powder, and paprika in a bowl. 4. Beat eggs in another bowl. 5. Dip pork chops into eggs then into pork rind crumb mixture. 6. Spritz the air fryer basket with cooking spray and add pork chops to the basket. 7. Air fry for 12 minutes. 8. Serve garnished with the Parmesan cheese.

BBQ Pork Steaks

Prep time: 5 minutes | Cook time: 15 minutes | Serves 4

- ◄ 4 pork steaks
- ◄ 1 tablespoon Cajun seasoning
- ◄ 2 tablespoons BBQ sauce
- ◄ 1 tablespoon vinegar
- ◄ 1 teaspoon soy sauce
- ◄ ½ cup brown sugar
- ◄ ½ cup ketchup

1. Preheat the air fryer to 290ºF (143ºC). 2. Sprinkle pork steaks with Cajun seasoning. 3. Combine remaining ingredients and brush onto steaks. 4. Add coated steaks to air fryer. Air fry 15 minutes until just browned. 5. Serve immediately.

Lemony Pork Loin Chop Schnitzel

Prep time: 15 minutes | Cook time: 15 minutes | Serves 4

- ◄ 4 thin boneless pork loin chops
- ◄ 2 tablespoons lemon juice
- ◄ ½ cup flour
- ◄ ¼ teaspoon marjoram
- ◄ 1 teaspoon salt
- ◄ 1 cup panko breadcrumbs
- ◄ 2 eggs
- ◄ Lemon wedges, for serving
- ◄ Cooking spray

1. Preheat the air fryer to 390ºF (199ºC) and spritz with cooking spray. 2. On a clean work surface, drizzle the pork chops with lemon juice on both sides. 3. Combine the flour with marjoram and salt on a shallow plate. Pour the breadcrumbs on a separate shallow dish. Beat the eggs in a large bowl. 4. Dredge the pork chops in the flour, then dunk in the beaten eggs to coat well. Shake the excess off and roll over the breadcrumbs. 5. Arrange the chops in the preheated air fryer and spritz with cooking spray. Air fry for 15 minutes or until the chops are golden and crispy. Flip the chops halfway through. Squeeze the lemon wedges over the fried chops and serve immediately.

Baby Back Ribs

Prep time: 5 minutes | Cook time: 25 minutes | Serves 4

- ◄ 2 pounds (907 g) baby back ribs
- ◄ 2 teaspoons chili powder
- ◄ 1 teaspoon paprika
- ◄ ½ teaspoon onion powder
- ◄ ½ teaspoon garlic powder
- ◄ ¼ teaspoon ground cayenne pepper
- ◄ ½ cup low-carb, sugar-free barbecue sauce

1. Rub ribs with all ingredients except barbecue sauce. Place into the air fryer basket. 2. Adjust the temperature to 400ºF (204ºC) and roast for 25 minutes. 3. When done, ribs will be dark and charred with an internal temperature of at least 185ºF (85ºC). Brush ribs with barbecue sauce and serve warm.

Pork Butt with Garlicky Coriander-Parsley Sauce

Prep time: 1 hour 15 minutes | Cook time: 30 minutes | Serves 4

- ◄ 1 teaspoon golden flaxseed meal
- ◄ 1 egg white, well whisked
- ◄ 1 tablespoon soy sauce
- ◄ 1 teaspoon lemon juice, preferably freshly squeezed

Garlicky Coriander-Parsley Sauce:
- ◄ 3 garlic cloves, minced
- ◄ ⅓ cup fresh coriander leaves
- ◄ ⅓ cup fresh parsley leaves
- ◄ 1 tablespoon olive oil
- ◄ 1 pound (454 g) pork butt, cut into pieces 2-inches long
- ◄ Salt and ground black pepper, to taste

- ◄ 1 teaspoon lemon juice
- ◄ ½ tablespoon salt
- ◄ ⅓ cup extra-virgin olive oil

1. Combine the flaxseed meal, egg white, soy sauce, lemon juice, salt, black pepper, and olive oil in a large bowl. Dunk the pork strips in and press to submerge. 2. Wrap the bowl in plastic and refrigerate to marinate for at least an hour. 3. Preheat the air fryer to 380ºF (193ºC). 4. Arrange the marinated pork strips in the preheated air fryer and air fry for 30 minutes or until cooked through and well browned. Flip the strips halfway through. 5. Meanwhile, combine the ingredients for the sauce in a small bowl. Stir to mix well. Arrange the bowl in the refrigerator to chill until ready to serve. 6. Serve the air fried pork strips with the chilled sauce.

Simple Ground Beef with Zucchini

Prep time: 5 minutes | Cook time: 12 minutes | Serves 4

- 1½ pounds (680 g) ground beef
- 1 pound (454 g) chopped zucchini
- 2 tablespoons extra-virgin olive oil
- 1 teaspoon dried oregano
- 1 teaspoon dried basil
- 1 teaspoon dried rosemary
- 2 tablespoons fresh chives, chopped

1. Preheat the air fryer to 400°F (204°C). 2. In a large bowl, combine all the ingredients, except for the chives, until well blended. 3. Place the beef and zucchini mixture in the baking pan. Air fry for 12 minutes, or until the beef is browned and the zucchini is tender. 4. Divide the beef and zucchini mixture among four serving dishes. Top with fresh chives and serve hot.

Herb-Roasted Beef Tips with Onions

Prep time: 5 minutes | Cook time: 10 minutes | Serves 4

- 1 pound (454 g) rib eye steak, cubed
- 2 garlic cloves, minced
- 2 tablespoons olive oil
- 1 tablespoon fresh oregano
- 1 teaspoon salt
- ½ teaspoon black pepper
- 1 yellow onion, thinly sliced

1. Preheat the air fryer to 380°F(193°C). 2. In a medium bowl, combine the steak, garlic, olive oil, oregano, salt, pepper, and onion. Mix until all of the beef and onion are well coated. 3. Put the seasoned steak mixture into the air fryer basket. Roast for 5 minutes. Stir and roast for 5 minutes more. 4. Let rest for 5 minutes before serving with some favorite sides.

Peppercorn-Crusted Beef Tenderloin

Prep time: 10 minutes | Cook time: 25 minutes | Serves 6

- 2 tablespoons salted butter, melted
- 2 teaspoons minced roasted garlic
- 3 tablespoons ground
- 4-peppercorn blend
- 1 (2 pounds / 907 g) beef tenderloin, trimmed of visible fat

1. In a small bowl, mix the butter and roasted garlic. Brush it over the beef tenderloin. 2. Place the ground peppercorns onto a plate and roll the tenderloin through them, creating a crust. Place

tenderloin into the air fryer basket. 3. Adjust the temperature to 400°F (204°C) and roast for 25 minutes. 4. Turn the tenderloin halfway through the cooking time. 5. Allow meat to rest 10 minutes before slicing.

Pork Milanese

Prep time: 10 minutes | Cook time: 12 minutes | Serves 4

- 4 (1-inch) boneless pork chops
- Fine sea salt and ground black pepper, to taste
- 2 large eggs
- ¾ cup powdered Parmesan cheese
- Chopped fresh parsley, for garnish
- Lemon slices, for serving

1. Spray the air fryer basket with avocado oil. Preheat the air fryer to 400°F (204°C). 2. Place the pork chops between 2 sheets of plastic wrap and pound them with the flat side of a meat tenderizer until they're ¼ inch thick. Lightly season both sides of the chops with salt and pepper. 3. Lightly beat the eggs in a shallow bowl. Divide the Parmesan cheese evenly between 2 bowls and set the bowls in this order: Parmesan, eggs, Parmesan. Dredge a chop in the first bowl of Parmesan, then dip it in the eggs, and then dredge it again in the second bowl of Parmesan, making sure both sides and all edges are well coated. Repeat with the remaining chops. 4. Place the chops in the air fryer basket and air fry for 12 minutes, or until the internal temperature reaches 145°F (63°C), flipping halfway through. 5. Garnish with fresh parsley and serve immediately with lemon slices. Store leftovers in an airtight container in the refrigerator for up to 3 days. Reheat in a preheated 390°F (199°C) air fryer for 5 minutes, or until warmed through.

Mustard Lamb Chops

Prep time: 5 minutes | Cook time: 14 minutes | Serves 4

- Oil, for spraying
- 1 tablespoon Dijon mustard
- 2 teaspoons lemon juice
- ½ teaspoon dried tarragon
- ¼ teaspoon salt
- ¼ teaspoon freshly ground black pepper
- 4 (1¼-inch-thick) loin lamb chops

1. Preheat the air fryer to 390°F (199°C). Line the air fryer basket with parchment and spray lightly with oil. 2. In a small bowl, mix together the mustard, lemon juice, tarragon, salt, and black pepper. 3. Pat dry the lamb chops with a paper towel. Brush the chops on both sides with the mustard mixture. 4. Place the chops in the prepared basket. You may need to work in batches, depending on the size of your air fryer. 5. Cook for 8 minutes, flip, and cook for another 6 minutes, or until the internal temperature reaches 125°F (52°C) for rare, 145°F (63°C) for medium-rare, or 155°F (68°C) for medium.

Spice-Rubbed Pork Loin

Prep time: 5 minutes | Cook time: 20 minutes | Serves 6

◄ 1 teaspoon paprika
◄ ½ teaspoon ground cumin
◄ ½ teaspoon chili powder
◄ ½ teaspoon garlic powder
◄ 2 tablespoons coconut oil

◄ 1 (1½ pounds / 680 g) boneless pork loin
◄ ½ teaspoon salt
◄ ¼ teaspoon ground black pepper

1. In a small bowl, mix paprika, cumin, chili powder, and garlic powder. 2. Drizzle coconut oil over pork. Sprinkle pork loin with salt and pepper, then rub spice mixture evenly on all sides. 3. Place pork loin into ungreased air fryer basket. Adjust the temperature to 400ºF (204ºC) and air fry for 20 minutes, turning pork halfway through cooking. Pork loin will be browned and have an internal temperature of at least 145ºF (63ºC) when done. Serve warm.

Bo Luc Lac

Prep time: 50 minutes | Cook time: 8 minutes | Serves 4

For the Meat:
◄ 2 teaspoons soy sauce
◄ 4 garlic cloves, minced
◄ 1 teaspoon kosher salt
◄ 2 teaspoons sugar
◄ ¼ teaspoon ground black pepper
For the Salad:
◄ 1 head Bibb lettuce, leaves separated and torn into large pieces
◄ ¼ cup fresh mint leaves
◄ ½ cup halved grape tomatoes
◄ ½ red onion, halved and thinly sliced
◄ 2 tablespoons apple cider vinegar
◄ 1 garlic clove, minced

◄ 1 teaspoon toasted sesame oil
◄ 1½ pounds (680 g) top sirloin steak, cut into 1-inch cubes
◄ Cooking spray

◄ 2 teaspoons sugar
◄ ¼ teaspoon kosher salt
◄ ¼ teaspoon ground black pepper
◄ 2 tablespoons vegetable oil
◄ For Serving:
◄ Lime wedges, for garnish
◄ Coarse salt and freshly cracked black pepper, to taste

1. Combine the ingredients for the meat, except for the steak, in a large bowl. Stir to mix well. 2. Dunk the steak cubes in the bowl and press to coat. Wrap the bowl in plastic and marinate under room temperature for at least 30 minutes. 3. Preheat the air fryer to 450ºF (232ºC). Spritz the air fryer basket with cooking spray. 4. Discard the marinade and transfer the steak cubes in the preheated air fryer basket. You need to air fry in batches to avoid overcrowding. 5. Air fry for 4 minutes or until the steak cubes are lightly browned but still have a little pink. Shake the basket halfway through the cooking time. 6. Meanwhile, combine the ingredients for the salad in a separate large bowl. Toss to mix well. 7. Pour the salad in a large serving bowl and top with the steak cubes. Squeeze the lime wedges over and sprinkle with salt and black pepper before serving.

Cheesy Low-Carb Lasagna

Prep time: 10 minutes | Cook time: 10 minutes | Serves 4

Meat Layer:
◄ Extra-virgin olive oil
◄ 1 pound (454 g) 85% lean ground beef
◄ 1 cup prepared marinara sauce
Cheese Layer:
◄ 8 ounces (227 g) ricotta cheese
◄ 1 cup shredded Mozzarella cheese
◄ ½ cup grated Parmesan cheese

◄ ¼ cup diced celery
◄ ¼ cup diced red onion
◄ ½ teaspoon minced garlic
◄ Kosher salt and black pepper, to taste

◄ 2 large eggs
◄ 1 teaspoon dried Italian seasoning, crushed
◄ ½ teaspoon each minced garlic, garlic powder, and black pepper

1. For the meat layer: Grease a cake pan with 1 teaspoon olive oil. 2. In a large bowl, combine the ground beef, marinara, celery, onion, garlic, salt, and pepper. Place the seasoned meat in the pan. 3. Place the pan in the air fryer basket. Set the air fryer to 375ºF (191ºC) for 10 minutes. 4. Meanwhile, for the cheese layer: In a medium bowl, combine the ricotta, half the Mozzarella, the Parmesan, lightly beaten eggs, Italian seasoning, minced garlic, garlic powder, and pepper. Stir until well blended. 5. At the end of the cooking time, spread the cheese mixture over the meat mixture. Sprinkle with the remaining ½ cup Mozzarella. Set the air fryer to 375ºF (191ºC) for 10 minutes, or until the cheese is browned and bubbling. 6. At the end of the cooking time, use a meat thermometer to ensure the meat has reached an internal temperature of 160ºF (71ºC). 7. Drain the fat and liquid from the pan. Let stand for 5 minutes before serving.

Easy Lamb Chops with Asparagus

Prep time: 10 minutes | Cook time: 15 minutes | Serves 4

◄ 4 asparagus spears, trimmed
◄ 2 tablespoons olive oil, divided
◄ 1 pound (454 g) lamb chops
◄ 1 garlic clove, minced

◄ 2 teaspoons chopped fresh thyme, for serving
◄ Salt and ground black pepper, to taste

1. Preheat the air fryer to 400ºF (204ºC). Spritz the air fryer basket with cooking spray. 2. On a large plate, brush the asparagus with 1 tablespoon olive oil, then sprinkle with salt. Set aside. 3. On a separate plate, brush the lamb chops with remaining olive oil and sprinkle with salt and ground black pepper. 4. Arrange the lamb chops in the preheated air fryer. Air fry for 10 minutes. 5. Flip the lamb chops and add the asparagus and garlic. Air fry for 5 more minutes or until the lamb is well browned and the asparagus is tender. 6. Serve them on a plate with thyme on top.

Bacon and Cheese Stuffed Pork Chops

Prep time: 10 minutes | Cook time: 12 minutes | Serves 4

◄ ½ ounce (14 g) plain pork rinds, finely crushed
◄ ½ cup shredded sharp Cheddar cheese
◄ 4 slices cooked sugar-free bacon, crumbled

◄ 4 (4-ounce / 113-g) boneless pork chops
◄ ½ teaspoon salt
◄ ¼ teaspoon ground black pepper

1. In a small bowl, mix pork rinds, Cheddar, and bacon. 2. Make a 3-inch slit in the side of each pork chop and stuff with ¼ pork rind mixture. Sprinkle each side of pork chops with salt and pepper. 3. Place pork chops into ungreased air fryer basket, stuffed side up. Adjust the temperature to 400°F (204°C) and air fry for 12 minutes. Pork chops will be browned and have an internal temperature of at least 145°F (63°C) when done. Serve warm.

Mongolian-Style Beef

Prep time: 10 minutes | Cook time: 10 minutes | Serves 4

◄ Oil, for spraying
◄ ¼ cup cornstarch
◄ 1 pound (454 g) flank steak, thinly sliced
◄ ¾ cup packed light brown sugar
◄ ½ cup soy sauce

◄ 2 teaspoons toasted sesame oil
◄ 1 tablespoon minced garlic
◄ ½ teaspoon ground ginger
◄ ½ cup water
◄ Cooked white rice or ramen noodles, for serving

1. Line the air fryer basket with parchment and spray lightly with oil. 2. Place the cornstarch in a bowl and dredge the steak until evenly coated. Shake off any excess cornstarch. 3. Place the steak in the prepared basket and spray lightly with oil. 4. Roast at 390°F (199°C) for 5 minutes, flip, and cook for another 5 minutes. 5. In a small saucepan, combine the brown sugar, soy sauce, sesame oil, garlic, ginger, and water and bring to a boil over medium-high heat, stirring frequently. Remove from the heat. 6. Transfer the meat to the sauce and toss until evenly coated. Let sit for about 5 minutes so the steak absorbs the flavors. Serve with white rice or ramen noodles.

Kielbasa Sausage with Pineapple and Bell Peppers

Prep time: 15 minutes | Cook time: 10 minutes | Serves 2 to 4

◄ ¾ pound (340 g) kielbasa sausage, cut into ½-inch slices
◄ 1 (8-ounce / 227-g) can pineapple chunks in juice, drained
◄ 1 cup bell pepper chunks

◄ 1 tablespoon barbecue seasoning
◄ 1 tablespoon soy sauce
◄ Cooking spray

1. Preheat the air fryer to 390°F (199°C). Spritz the air fryer basket with cooking spray. 2. Combine all the ingredients in a large bowl. Toss to mix well. 3. Pour the sausage mixture in the preheated air fryer. 4. Air fry for 10 minutes or until the sausage is lightly browned and the bell pepper and pineapple are soft. Shake the basket halfway through. Serve immediately.

Chapter 6

Fish and Seafood

Chapter 6 Fish and Seafood

Bacon-Wrapped Scallops

Prep time: 5 minutes | Cook time: 10 minutes | Serves 4

- 8 (1-ounce / 28-g) sea scallops, cleaned and patted dry
- 8 slices sugar-free bacon
- ¼ teaspoon salt
- ¼ teaspoon ground black pepper

1. Wrap each scallop in 1 slice bacon and secure with a toothpick. Sprinkle with salt and pepper. 2. Place scallops into ungreased air fryer basket. Adjust the temperature to 360°F (182°C) and air fry for 10 minutes. Scallops will be opaque and firm, and have an internal temperature of 135°F (57°C) when done. Serve warm.

Crab Cakes with Sriracha Mayonnaise

Prep time: 15 minutes | Cook time: 10 minutes | Serves 4

Sriracha Mayonnaise:
- 1 cup mayonnaise
- 1 tablespoon sriracha
- 1½ teaspoons freshly squeezed lemon juice

Crab Cakes:
- 1 teaspoon extra-virgin olive oil
- ¼ cup finely diced red bell pepper
- ¼ cup diced onion
- ¼ cup diced celery
- 1 pound (454 g) lump crab meat
- 1 teaspoon Old Bay seasoning
- 1 egg
- 1½ teaspoons freshly squeezed lemon juice
- 1¾ cups panko bread crumbs, divided
- Vegetable oil, for spraying

1. Mix the mayonnaise, sriracha, and lemon juice in a small bowl. Place ⅔ cup of the mixture in a separate bowl to form the base of the crab cakes. Cover the remaining sriracha mayonnaise and refrigerate. (This will become dipping sauce for the crab cakes once they are cooked.) 2. Heat the olive oil in a heavy-bottomed, medium skillet over medium-high heat. Add the bell pepper, onion, and celery and sauté for 3 minutes. Transfer the vegetables to the bowl with the reserved ⅔ cup of sriracha mayonnaise. Mix in the crab, Old Bay seasoning, egg, and lemon juice. Add 1 cup of the panko. Form the crab mixture into 8 cakes. Dredge the cakes in the remaining ¾ cup of panko, turning to coat. Place on a baking sheet. Cover and refrigerate for at least 1 hour and up to 8 hours. 3. Preheat the air fryer to 375°F (191°C). Spray the air fryer basket with oil. Working in batches as needed so as not to overcrowd the basket, place the chilled crab cakes in a single layer in the basket. Spray the crab cakes with oil. Bake until golden brown, 8 to 10 minutes, carefully turning halfway through cooking. Remove to a platter and keep warm. Repeat with the remaining crab cakes as needed. Serve the crab cakes immediately with sriracha mayonnaise dipping sauce.

Tortilla Shrimp Tacos

Prep time: 10 minutes | Cook time: 6 minutes | Serves 4

Spicy Mayo:
- 3 tablespoons mayonnaise
- 1 tablespoon Louisiana-style hot pepper sauce

Cilantro-Lime Slaw:
- 2 cups shredded green cabbage
- ½ small red onion, thinly sliced
- 1 small jalapeño, thinly sliced
- 2 tablespoons chopped fresh cilantro
- Juice of 1 lime
- ¼ teaspoon kosher salt

Shrimp:
- 1 large egg, beaten
- 1 cup crushed tortilla chips
- 24 jumbo shrimp (about 1 pound / 454 g), peeled and deveined
- ⅛ teaspoon kosher salt
- Cooking spray
- 8 corn tortillas, for serving

1. For the spicy mayo: In a small bowl, mix the mayonnaise and hot pepper sauce. 2. For the cilantro-lime slaw: In a large bowl, toss together the cabbage, onion, jalapeño, cilantro, lime juice, and salt to combine. Cover and refrigerate to chill. 3. For the shrimp: Place the egg in a shallow bowl and the crushed tortilla chips in another. Season the shrimp with the salt. Dip the shrimp in the egg, then in the crumbs, pressing gently to adhere. Place on a work surface and spray both sides with oil. 4. Preheat the air fryer to 360°F (182°C). 5. Working in batches, arrange a single layer of the shrimp in the air fryer basket. Air fry for 6 minutes, flipping halfway, until golden and cooked through in the center. 6. To serve, place 2 tortillas on each plate and top each with 3 shrimp. Top each taco with ¼ cup slaw, then drizzle with spicy mayo.

Classic Fish Sticks with Tartar Sauce

Prep time: 10 minutes | Cook time: 12 to 15 minutes | Serves 4

◄ 1½ pounds (680 g) cod fillets, cut into 1-inch strips
◄ 1 teaspoon salt
◄ ½ teaspoon freshly ground black pepper

Tartar Sauce:
◄ ½ cup sour cream
◄ ½ cup mayonnaise
◄ 3 tablespoons chopped dill pickle
◄ 2 tablespoons capers,

◄ 2 eggs
◄ ¾ cup almond flour
◄ ¼ cup grated Parmesan cheese

drained and chopped
◄ ½ teaspoon dried dill
◄ 1 tablespoon dill pickle liquid (optional)

1. Preheat the air fryer to 400°F (204°C). 2. Season the cod with the salt and black pepper; set aside. 3. In a shallow bowl, lightly beat the eggs. In a second shallow bowl, combine the almond flour and Parmesan cheese. Stir until thoroughly combined. 4. Working with a few pieces at a time, dip the fish into the egg mixture followed by the flour mixture. Press lightly to ensure an even coating. 5. Working in batches if necessary, arrange the fish in a single layer in the air fryer basket and spray lightly with olive oil. Pausing halfway through the cooking time to turn the fish, air fry for 12 to 15 minutes, until the fish flakes easily with a fork. Let sit in the basket for a few minutes before serving with the tartar sauce. 6. To make the tartar sauce: In a small bowl, combine the sour cream, mayonnaise, pickle, capers, and dill. If you prefer a thinner sauce, stir in the pickle liquid.

Cornmeal-Crusted Trout Fingers

Prep time: 15 minutes | Cook time: 6 minutes | Serves 2

◄ ½ cup yellow cornmeal, medium or finely ground (not coarse)
◄ ⅓ cup all-purpose flour
◄ 1½ teaspoons baking powder
◄ 1 teaspoon kosher salt, plus more as needed
◄ ½ teaspoon freshly ground black pepper, plus more as needed
◄ ⅛ teaspoon cayenne pepper
◄ ¾ pound (340 g) skinless

trout fillets, cut into strips 1 inch wide and 3 inches long
◄ 3 large eggs, lightly beaten
◄ Cooking spray
◄ ½ cup mayonnaise
◄ 2 tablespoons capers, rinsed and finely chopped
◄ 1 tablespoon fresh tarragon
◄ 1 teaspoon fresh lemon juice, plus lemon wedges, for serving

1. Preheat the air fryer to 400°F (204°C). 2. In a large bowl, whisk together the cornmeal, flour, baking powder, salt, black pepper, and cayenne. Dip the trout strips in the egg, then toss them in the cornmeal mixture until fully coated. Transfer the trout to a rack set over a baking sheet and liberally spray all over with cooking spray. 3. Transfer half the fish to the air fryer and air fry until the fish is cooked through and golden brown, about 6 minutes. Transfer the fish sticks to a plate and repeat with the remaining fish. 4. Meanwhile, in a bowl, whisk together the mayonnaise, capers, tarragon, and lemon juice. Season the tartar sauce with salt and black pepper. 5. Serve the trout fingers hot along with the tartar sauce and lemon wedges.

Pecan-Crusted Catfish

Prep time: 5 minutes | Cook time: 12 minutes | Serves 4

◄ ½ cup pecan meal
◄ 1 teaspoon fine sea salt
◄ ¼ teaspoon ground black pepper
◄ 4 (4 ounces / 113 g) catfish

fillets
◄ For Garnish (Optional):
◄ Fresh oregano
◄ Pecan halves

1. Spray the air fryer basket with avocado oil. Preheat the air fryer to 375°F (191°C). 2. In a large bowl, mix the pecan meal, salt, and pepper. One at a time, dredge the catfish fillets in the mixture, coating them well. Use your hands to press the pecan meal into the fillets. Spray the fish with avocado oil and place them in the air fryer basket. 3. Air fry the coated catfish for 12 minutes, or until it flakes easily and is no longer translucent in the center, flipping halfway through. 4. Garnish with oregano sprigs and pecan halves, if desired. 5. Store leftovers in an airtight container in the fridge for up to 3 days. Reheat in a preheated 350°F (177°C) air fryer for 4 minutes, or until heated through.

Tilapia with Pecans

Prep time: 20 minutes | Cook time: 16 minutes | Serves 5

◄ 2 tablespoons ground flaxseeds
◄ 1 teaspoon paprika
◄ Sea salt and white pepper, to taste
◄ 1 teaspoon garlic paste

◄ 2 tablespoons extra-virgin olive oil
◄ ½ cup pecans, ground
◄ 5 tilapia fillets, sliced into halves

1. Combine the ground flaxseeds, paprika, salt, white pepper, garlic paste, olive oil, and ground pecans in a Ziploc bag. Add the fish fillets and shake to coat well. 2. Spritz the air fryer basket with cooking spray. Cook in the preheated air fryer at 400°F (204°C) for 10 minutes; turn them over and cook for 6 minutes more. Work in batches. 3. Serve with lemon wedges, if desired. Enjoy!

Blackened Salmon

Prep time: 10 minutes | Cook time: 8 minutes | Serves 2

- ◁ 10 ounces (283 g) salmon fillet
- ◁ ½ teaspoon ground coriander
- ◁ 1 teaspoon ground cumin
- ◁ 1 teaspoon dried basil
- ◁ 1 tablespoon avocado oil

1. In the shallow bowl, mix ground coriander, ground cumin, and dried basil. 2. Then coat the salmon fillet in the spices and sprinkle with avocado oil. 3. Put the fish in the air fryer basket and cook at 395ºF (202ºC) for 4 minutes per side.

Lemony Shrimp

Prep time: 10 minutes | Cook time: 7 to 8 minutes | Serves 4

- ◁ 1 pound (454 g) shrimp, deveined
- ◁ 4 tablespoons olive oil
- ◁ 1½ tablespoons lemon juice
- ◁ 1½ tablespoons fresh parsley, roughly chopped
- ◁ 2 cloves garlic, finely
- minced
- ◁ 1 teaspoon crushed red pepper flakes, or more to taste
- ◁ Garlic pepper, to taste
- ◁ Sea salt flakes, to taste

1. Preheat the air fryer to 385ºF (196ºC). 2. Toss all the ingredients in a large bowl until the shrimp are coated on all sides. 3. Arrange the shrimp in the air fryer basket and air fry for 7 to 8 minutes, or until the shrimp are pink and cooked through. 4. Serve warm.

Roasted Fish with Almond-Lemon Crumbs

Prep time: 10 minutes | Cook time: 7 to 8 minutes | Serves 4

- ◁ ½ cup raw whole almonds
- ◁ 1 scallion, finely chopped
- ◁ Grated zest and juice of 1 lemon
- ◁ ½ tablespoon extra-virgin olive oil
- ◁ ¾ teaspoon kosher salt,
- divided
- ◁ Freshly ground black pepper, to taste
- ◁ 4 (6 ounces / 170 g each) skinless fish fillets
- ◁ Cooking spray
- ◁ 1 teaspoon Dijon mustard

1. In a food processor, pulse the almonds to coarsely chop. Transfer to a small bowl and add the scallion, lemon zest, and olive oil. Season with ¼ teaspoon of the salt and pepper to taste and mix to combine. 2. Spray the top of the fish with oil and squeeze the lemon juice over the fish. Season with the remaining ½ teaspoon salt and pepper to taste. Spread the mustard on top of the fish. Dividing evenly, press the almond mixture onto the top of the fillets

to adhere. 3. Preheat the air fryer to 375ºF (191ºC). 4. Working in batches, place the fillets in the air fryer basket in a single layer. Air fry for 7 to 8 minutes, until the crumbs start to brown and the fish is cooked through. 5. Serve immediately.

Fish Taco Bowl

Prep time: 10 minutes | Cook time: 12 minutes | Serves 4

- ◁ ½ teaspoon salt
- ◁ ¼ teaspoon garlic powder
- ◁ ¼ teaspoon ground cumin
- ◁ 4 (4-ounce / 113-g) cod fillets
- ◁ 4 cups finely shredded green
- cabbage
- ◁ ⅓ cup mayonnaise
- ◁ ¼ teaspoon ground black pepper
- ◁ ¼ cup chopped pickled jalapeños

1. Sprinkle salt, garlic powder, and cumin over cod and place into ungreased air fryer basket. Adjust the temperature to 350ºF (177ºC) and air fry for 12 minutes, turning fillets halfway through cooking. Cod will flake easily and have an internal temperature of at least 145ºF (63ºC) when done. 2. In a large bowl, toss cabbage with mayonnaise, pepper, and jalapeños until fully coated. Serve cod warm over cabbage slaw on four medium plates.

Steamed Tuna with Lemongrass

Prep time: 10 minutes | Cook time: 10 minutes | Serves 4

- ◁ 4 small tuna steaks
- ◁ 2 tablespoons low-sodium soy sauce
- ◁ 2 teaspoons sesame oil
- ◁ 2 teaspoons rice wine vinegar
- ◁ 1 teaspoon grated peeled
- fresh ginger
- ◁ ⅛ teaspoon freshly ground black pepper
- ◁ 1 stalk lemongrass, bent in half
- ◁ 3 tablespoons freshly squeezed lemon juice

1. Place the tuna steaks on a plate. 2. In a small bowl, whisk the soy sauce, sesame oil, vinegar, and ginger until combined. Pour this mixture over the tuna and gently rub it into both sides. Sprinkle the fish with the pepper. Let marinate for 10 minutes. 3. Insert the crisper plate into the basket and the basket into the unit. Preheat the unit by selecting BAKE, setting the temperature to 390ºF (199ºC), and setting the time to 3 minutes. Select START/STOP to begin. 4. Once the unit is preheated, place the lemongrass into the basket and top it with the tuna steaks. Drizzle the tuna with the lemon juice and 1 tablespoon of water. 5. Select BAKE, set the temperature to 390ºF (199ºC), and set the time to 10 minutes. Select START/STOP to begin. 6. When the cooking is complete, a food thermometer inserted into the tuna should register at least 145ºF (63ºC). Discard the lemongrass and serve the tuna.

Crab Legs

Prep time: 5 minutes | Cook time: 15 minutes | Serves 4

- ¼ cup salted butter, melted and divided
- 3 pounds (1.4 kg) crab legs
- ¼ teaspoon garlic powder
- Juice of ½ medium lemon

1. In a large bowl, drizzle 2 tablespoons butter over crab legs. Place crab legs into the air fryer basket. 2. Adjust the temperature to 400ºF (204ºC) and air fry for 15 minutes. 3. Shake the air fryer basket to toss the crab legs halfway through the cooking time. 4. In a small bowl, mix remaining butter, garlic powder, and lemon juice. 5. To serve, crack open crab legs and remove meat. Dip in lemon butter.

Fish Croquettes with Lemon-Dill Aioli

Prep time: 15 minutes | Cook time: 10 minutes | Serves 4

Croquettes:
- 3 large eggs, divided
- 12 ounces (340 g) raw cod fillet, flaked apart with two forks
- ¼ cup 1% milk
- ½ cup boxed instant mashed potatoes
- 2 teaspoons olive oil
- ⅓ cup chopped fresh dill
- 1 shallot, minced

Lemon-Dill Aioli:
- 5 tablespoons mayonnaise
- Juice of ½ lemon

- 1 large garlic clove, minced
- ¾ cup plus 2 tablespoons bread crumbs, divided
- 1 teaspoon fresh lemon juice
- 1 teaspoon kosher salt
- ½ teaspoon dried thyme
- ¼ teaspoon freshly ground black pepper
- Cooking spray

- 1 tablespoon chopped fresh dill

1. For the croquettes: In a medium bowl, lightly beat 2 of the eggs. Add the fish, milk, instant mashed potatoes, olive oil, dill, shallot, garlic, 2 tablespoons of the bread crumbs, lemon juice, salt, thyme, and pepper. Mix to thoroughly combine. Place in the refrigerator for 30 minutes. 2. For the lemon-dill aioli: In a small bowl, combine the mayonnaise, lemon juice, and dill. Set aside. 3. Measure out about 3½ tablespoons of the fish mixture and gently roll in your hands to form a log about 3 inches long. Repeat to make a total of 12 logs. 4. Beat the remaining egg in a small bowl. Place the remaining ¾ cup bread crumbs in a separate bowl. Dip the croquettes in the egg, then coat in the bread crumbs, gently pressing to adhere. Place on a work surface and spray both sides with cooking spray. 5. Preheat the air fryer to 350ºF (177ºC). 6. Working in batches, arrange a single layer of the croquettes in the air fryer basket. Air fry for about 10 minutes, flipping halfway, until golden. 7. Serve with the aioli for dipping.

Browned Shrimp Patties

Prep time: 15 minutes | Cook time: 10 to 12 minutes | Serves 4

- ½ pound (227 g) raw shrimp, shelled, deveined, and chopped finely
- 2 cups cooked sushi rice
- ¼ cup chopped red bell pepper
- ¼ cup chopped celery
- ¼ cup chopped green onion
- 2 teaspoons Worcestershire sauce
- ½ teaspoon salt
- ½ teaspoon garlic powder
- ½ teaspoon Old Bay seasoning
- ½ cup plain bread crumbs
- Cooking spray

1. Preheat the air fryer to 390ºF (199ºC). 2. Put all the ingredients except the bread crumbs and oil in a large bowl and stir to incorporate. 3. Scoop out the shrimp mixture and shape into 8 equal-sized patties with your hands, no more than ½-inch thick. Roll the patties in the bread crumbs on a plate and spray both sides with cooking spray. 4. Place the patties in the air fryer basket. You may need to work in batches to avoid overcrowding. 5. Air fry for 10 to 12 minutes, flipping the patties halfway through, or until the outside is crispy brown. 6. Divide the patties among four plates and serve warm.

Fish Cakes

Prep time: 30 minutes | Cook time: 10 to 12 minutes | Serves 4

- ¾ cup mashed potatoes (about 1 large russet potato)
- 12 ounces (340 g) cod or other white fish
- Salt and pepper, to taste
- Oil for misting or cooking spray
- 1 large egg
- ¼ cup potato starch
- ½ cup panko bread crumbs
- 1 tablespoon fresh chopped chives
- 2 tablespoons minced onion

1. Peel potatoes, cut into cubes, and cook on stovetop till soft. 2. Salt and pepper raw fish to taste. Mist with oil or cooking spray, and air fry at 360ºF (182ºC) for 6 to 8 minutes, until fish flakes easily. If fish is crowded, rearrange halfway through cooking to ensure all pieces cook evenly. 3. Transfer fish to a plate and break apart to cool. 4. Beat egg in a shallow dish. 5. Place potato starch in another shallow dish, and panko crumbs in a third dish. 6. When potatoes are done, drain in colander and rinse with cold water. 7. In a large bowl, mash the potatoes and stir in the chives and onion. Add salt and pepper to taste, then stir in the fish. 8. If needed, stir in a tablespoon of the beaten egg to help bind the mixture. 9. Shape into 8 small, fat patties. Dust lightly with potato starch, dip in egg, and roll in panko crumbs. Spray both sides with oil or cooking spray. 10. Air fry at 360ºF (182ºC) for 10 to 12 minutes, until golden brown and crispy.

Salmon with Cauliflower

Prep time: 10 minutes | Cook time: 25 minutes | Serves 4

◄ 1 pound (454 g) salmon fillet, diced
◄ 1 cup cauliflower, shredded
◄ 1 tablespoon dried cilantro
◄ 1 tablespoon coconut oil, melted
◄ 1 teaspoon ground turmeric
◄ ¼ cup coconut cream

1. Mix salmon with cauliflower, dried cilantro, ground turmeric, coconut cream, and coconut oil. 2. Transfer the salmon mixture into the air fryer and cook the meal at 350ºF (177ºC) for 25 minutes. Stir the meal every 5 minutes to avoid the burning.

Paprika Crab Burgers

Prep time: 30 minutes | Cook time: 14 minutes | Serves 3

◄ 2 eggs, beaten
◄ 1 shallot, chopped
◄ 2 garlic cloves, crushed
◄ 1 tablespoon olive oil
◄ 1 teaspoon yellow mustard
◄ 1 teaspoon fresh cilantro, chopped
◄ 10 ounces (283 g) crab meat
◄ 1 teaspoon smoked paprika
◄ ½ teaspoon ground black pepper
◄ Sea salt, to taste
◄ ¾ cup Parmesan cheese

1. In a mixing bowl, thoroughly combine the eggs, shallot, garlic, olive oil, mustard, cilantro, crab meat, paprika, black pepper, and salt. Mix until well combined. 2. Shape the mixture into 6 patties. Roll the crab patties over grated Parmesan cheese, coating well on all sides. Place in your refrigerator for 2 hours. 3. Spritz the crab patties with cooking oil on both sides. Cook in the preheated air fryer at 360ºF (182ºC) for 14 minutes. Serve on dinner rolls if desired. Bon appétit!

Sole and Cauliflower Fritters

Prep time: 5 minutes | Cook time: 24 minutes | Serves 2

◄ ½ pound (227 g) sole fillets
◄ ½ pound (227 g) mashed cauliflower
◄ ½ cup red onion, chopped
◄ 1 bell pepper, finely chopped
◄ 1 egg, beaten
◄ 2 garlic cloves, minced
◄ 2 tablespoons fresh parsley, chopped
◄ 1 tablespoon olive oil
◄ 1 tablespoon coconut aminos
◄ ½ teaspoon scotch bonnet pepper, minced
◄ ½ teaspoon paprika
◄ Salt and white pepper, to taste
◄ Cooking spray

1. Preheat the air fryer to 395ºF (202ºC). Spray the air fryer basket with cooking spray. 2. Place the sole fillets in the basket and air fry for 10 minutes, flipping them halfway through. 3. When the fillets are done, transfer them to a large bowl. Mash the fillets into flakes. Add the remaining ingredients and stir to combine. 4. Make the fritters: Scoop out 2 tablespoons of the fish mixture and shape into a patty about ½ inch thick with your hands. Repeat with the remaining fish mixture. 5. Arrange the patties in the air fryer basket and bake for 14 minutes, flipping the patties halfway through, or until they are golden brown and cooked through. 6. Cool for 5 minutes and serve on a plate.

Parmesan-Crusted Halibut Fillets

Prep time: 5 minutes | Cook time: 10 minutes | Serves 4

◄ 2 medium-sized halibut fillets
◄ Dash of tabasco sauce
◄ 1 teaspoon curry powder
◄ ½ teaspoon ground coriander
◄ ½ teaspoon hot paprika
◄ Kosher salt and freshly
  cracked mixed peppercorns, to taste
◄ 2 eggs
◄ 1½ tablespoons olive oil
◄ ½ cup grated Parmesan cheese

1. Preheat the air fryer to 365ºF (185ºC). 2. On a clean work surface, drizzle the halibut fillets with the tabasco sauce. Sprinkle with the curry powder, coriander, hot paprika, salt, and cracked mixed peppercorns. Set aside. 3. In a shallow bowl, beat the eggs until frothy. In another shallow bowl, combine the olive oil and Parmesan cheese. 4. One at a time, dredge the halibut fillets in the beaten eggs, shaking off any excess, then roll them over the Parmesan cheese until evenly coated. 5. Arrange the halibut fillets in the air fryer basket in a single layer and air fry for 10 minutes, or until the fish is golden brown and crisp. 6. Cool for 5 minutes before serving.

Golden Shrimp

Prep time: 20 minutes | Cook time: 7 minutes | Serves 4

◄ 2 egg whites
◄ ½ cup coconut flour
◄ 1 cup Parmigiano-Reggiano, grated
◄ ½ teaspoon celery seeds
◄ ½ teaspoon porcini powder
◄ ½ teaspoon onion powder
◄ 1 teaspoon garlic powder
◄ ½ teaspoon dried rosemary
◄ ½ teaspoon sea salt
◄ ½ teaspoon ground black pepper
◄ 1½ pounds (680 g) shrimp, deveined

1. Whisk the egg with coconut flour and Parmigiano-Reggiano. Add in seasonings and mix to combine well. 2. Dip your shrimp in the batter. Roll until they are covered on all sides. 3. Cook in the preheated air fryer at 390ºF (199ºC) for 5 to 7 minutes or until golden brown. Work in batches. Serve with lemon wedges if desired.

Roasted Salmon Fillets

Prep time: 5 minutes | Cook time: 10 minutes | Serves 2

- 2 (8-ounce / 227 -g) skin-on salmon fillets, 1½ inches thick
- 1 teaspoon vegetable oil
- Salt and pepper, to taste
- Vegetable oil spray

1. Preheat the air fryer to 400°F (204°C). 2. Make foil sling for air fryer basket by folding 1 long sheet of aluminum foil so it is 4 inches wide. Lay sheet of foil widthwise across basket, pressing foil into and up sides of basket. Fold excess foil as needed so that edges of foil are flush with top of basket. Lightly spray foil and basket with vegetable oil spray. 3. Pat salmon dry with paper towels, rub with oil, and season with salt and pepper. Arrange fillets skin side down on sling in prepared basket, spaced evenly apart. Air fry salmon until center is still translucent when checked with the tip of a paring knife and registers 125°F (52°C) (for medium-rare), 10 to 14 minutes, using sling to rotate fillets halfway through cooking. 4. Using the sling, carefully remove salmon from air fryer. Slide fish spatula along underside of fillets and transfer to individual serving plates, leaving skin behind. Serve.

Cod Tacos with Mango Salsa

Prep time: 15 minutes | Cook time: 17 minutes | Serves 4

- 1 mango, peeled and diced
- 1 small jalapeño pepper, diced
- ½ red bell pepper, diced
- ½ red onion, minced
- Pinch chopped fresh cilantro
- Juice of ½ lime
- ¼ teaspoon salt
- ¼ teaspoon ground black pepper
- ½ cup Mexican beer
- 1 egg
- ¾ cup cornstarch
- ¾ cup all-purpose flour
- ½ teaspoon ground cumin
- ¼ teaspoon chili powder
- 1 pound (454 g) cod, cut into 4 pieces
- Olive oil spray
- 4 corn tortillas, or flour tortillas, at room temperature

1. In a small bowl, stir together the mango, jalapeño, red bell pepper, red onion, cilantro, lime juice, salt, and pepper. Set aside. 2. In a medium bowl, whisk the beer and egg. 3. In another medium bowl, stir together the cornstarch, flour, cumin, and chili powder. 4. Insert the crisper plate into the basket and the basket into the unit. Preheat the unit by selecting AIR FRY, setting the temperature to 375°F (191°C), and setting the time to 3 minutes. Select START/ STOP to begin. 5. Dip the fish pieces into the egg mixture and in the flour mixture to coat completely. 6. Once the unit is preheated, place a parchment paper liner into the basket. Place the fish on the liner in a single layer. 7. Select AIR FRY, set the temperature to 375°F (191°C), and set the time to 17 minutes. Select START/ STOP to begin. 8. After about 9 minutes, spray the fish with olive oil. Reinsert the basket to resume cooking. 9. When the cooking is complete, the fish should be golden and crispy. Place the pieces in the tortillas, top with the mango salsa, and serve.

Italian Baked Cod

Prep time: 5 minutes | Cook time: 12 minutes | Serves 4

- 4 (6-ounce / 170-g) cod fillets
- 2 tablespoons salted butter, melted
- 1 teaspoon Italian seasoning
- ¼ teaspoon salt
- ½ cup low-carb marinara sauce

1. Place cod into an ungreased round nonstick baking dish. Pour butter over cod and sprinkle with Italian seasoning and salt. Top with marinara. 2. Place dish into air fryer basket. Adjust the temperature to 350°F (177°C) and bake for 12 minutes. Fillets will be lightly browned, easily flake, and have an internal temperature of at least 145°F (63°C) when done. Serve warm.

Cripsy Shrimp with Cilantro

Prep time: 40 minutes | Cook time: 10 minutes | Serves 4

- 1 pound (454 g) raw large shrimp, peeled and deveined with tails on or off
- ½ cup chopped fresh cilantro
- Juice of 1 lime
- ½ cup all-purpose flour
- 1 egg
- ¾ cup bread crumbs
- Salt and freshly ground black pepper, to taste
- Cooking oil spray
- 1 cup cocktail sauce

1. Place the shrimp in a resealable plastic bag and add the cilantro and lime juice. Seal the bag. Shake it to combine. Marinate the shrimp in the refrigerator for 30 minutes. 2. Place the flour in a small bowl. 3. In another small bowl, beat the egg. 4. Place the bread crumbs in a third small bowl, season with salt and pepper, and stir to combine. 5. Insert the crisper plate into the basket and the basket into the unit. Preheat the unit by selecting AIR FRY, setting the temperature to 400°F (204°C), and setting the time to 3 minutes. Select START/STOP to begin. 6. Remove the shrimp from the plastic bag. Dip each in the flour, the egg, and the bread crumbs to coat. Gently press the crumbs onto the shrimp. 7. Once the unit is preheated, spray the crisper plate and the basket with cooking oil. Place the shrimp in the basket. It is okay to stack them. Spray the shrimp with the cooking oil. 8. Select AIR FRY, set the temperature to 400°F (204°C), and set the time to 8 minutes. Select START/ STOP to begin. 9. After 4 minutes, remove the basket and flip the shrimp one at a time. Reinsert the basket to resume cooking. 10. When the cooking is complete, the shrimp should be crisp. Let cool for 5 minutes. Serve with cocktail sauce.

Tuna Patty Sliders

Prep time: 15 minutes | Cook time: 10 to 15 minutes | Serves 4

- 3 (5-ounce / 142-g) cans tuna, packed in water
- ⅔ cup whole-wheat panko bread crumbs
- ⅓ cup shredded Parmesan
- cheese
- 1 tablespoon sriracha
- ¾ teaspoon black pepper
- 10 whole-wheat slider buns
- Cooking spray

1. Preheat the air fryer to 350ºF (177ºC). 2. Spray the air fryer basket lightly with cooking spray. 3. In a medium bowl combine the tuna, bread crumbs, Parmesan cheese, sriracha, and black pepper and stir to combine. 4. Form the mixture into 10 patties. 5. Place the patties in the air fryer basket in a single layer. Spray the patties lightly with cooking spray. You may need to cook them in batches. 6. Air fry for 6 to 8 minutes. Turn the patties over and lightly spray with cooking spray. Air fry until golden brown and crisp, another 4 to 7 more minutes. Serve warm.

Crunchy Air Fried Cod Fillets

Prep time: 10 minutes | Cook time: 12 minutes | Serves 2

- ⅓ cup panko bread crumbs
- 1 teaspoon vegetable oil
- 1 small shallot, minced
- 1 small garlic clove, minced
- ½ teaspoon minced fresh thyme
- Salt and pepper, to taste
- 1 tablespoon minced fresh parsley
- 1 tablespoon mayonnaise
- 1 large egg yolk
- ¼ teaspoon grated lemon zest, plus lemon wedges for serving
- 2 (8 ounces / 227 g) skinless cod fillets, 1¼ inches thick
- Vegetable oil spray

1. Preheat the air fryer to 300ºF (149ºC). 2. Make foil sling for air fryer basket by folding 1 long sheet of aluminum foil so it is 4 inches wide. Lay sheet of foil widthwise across basket, pressing foil into and up sides of basket. Fold excess foil as needed so that edges of foil are flush with top of basket. Lightly spray the foil and basket with vegetable oil spray. 3. Toss the panko with the oil in a bowl until evenly coated. Stir in the shallot, garlic, thyme, ¼ teaspoon salt, and ⅛ teaspoon pepper. Microwave, stirring frequently, until the panko is light golden brown, about 2 minutes. Transfer to a shallow dish and let cool slightly; stir in the parsley. Whisk the mayonnaise, egg yolk, lemon zest, and ⅛ teaspoon pepper together in another bowl. 4. Pat the cod dry with paper towels and season with salt and pepper. Arrange the fillets, skinned-side down, on plate and brush tops evenly with mayonnaise mixture. (Tuck thinner tail ends of fillets under themselves as needed to create uniform pieces.) Working with 1 fillet at a time, dredge the coated side in panko mixture, pressing gently to adhere. Arrange the fillets, crumb-side up, on sling in the prepared basket, spaced evenly apart.

5. Bake for 12 to 16 minutes, using a sling to rotate fillets halfway through cooking. Using a sling, carefully remove cod from air fryer. Serve with the lemon wedges.

Lemony Shrimp and Zucchini

Prep time: 15 minutes | Cook time: 7 to 8 minutes | Serves 4

- 1¼ pounds (567 g) extra-large raw shrimp, peeled and deveined
- 2 medium zucchini (about 8 ounces / 227 g each), halved lengthwise and cut into ½-inch-thick slices
- 1½ tablespoons olive oil
- ½ teaspoon garlic salt
- 1½ teaspoons dried oregano
- ⅛ teaspoon crushed red pepper flakes (optional)
- Juice of ½ lemon
- 1 tablespoon chopped fresh mint
- 1 tablespoon chopped fresh dill

1. Preheat the air fryer to 350ºF (177ºC). 2. In a large bowl, combine the shrimp, zucchini, oil, garlic salt, oregano, and pepper flakes (if using) and toss to coat. 3. Working in batches, arrange a single layer of the shrimp and zucchini in the air fryer basket. Air fry for 7 to 8 minutes, shaking the basket halfway, until the zucchini is golden and the shrimp are cooked through. 4. Transfer to a serving dish and tent with foil while you air fry the remaining shrimp and zucchini. 5. Top with the lemon juice, mint, and dill and serve.

Lemon-Dill Salmon Burgers

Prep time: 10 minutes | Cook time: 8 minutes | Serves 4

- 2 (6 ounces / 170 g) fillets of salmon, finely chopped by hand or in a food processor
- 1 cup fine bread crumbs
- 1 teaspoon freshly grated lemon zest
- 2 tablespoons chopped fresh dill weed
- 1 teaspoon salt
- Freshly ground black pepper, to taste
- 2 eggs, lightly beaten
- 4 brioche or hamburger buns
- Lettuce, tomato, red onion, avocado, mayonnaise or mustard, for serving

1. Preheat the air fryer to 400ºF (204ºC). 2. Combine all the ingredients in a bowl. Mix together well and divide into four balls. Flatten the balls into patties, making an indentation in the center of each patty with your thumb (this will help the burger stay flat as it cooks) and flattening the sides of the burgers so that they fit nicely into the air fryer basket. 3. Transfer the burgers to the air fryer basket and air fry for 4 minutes. Flip the burgers over and air fry for another 3 to 4 minutes, until nicely browned and firm to the touch. 4. Serve on soft brioche buns with your choice of topping: lettuce, tomato, red onion, avocado, mayonnaise or mustard

Calamari with Hot Sauce

Prep time: 10 minutes | Cook time: 6 minutes | Serves 2

◄ 10 ounces (283 g) calamari, trimmed
◄ 2 tablespoons keto hot sauce
◄ 1 tablespoon avocado oil

1. Slice the calamari and sprinkle with avocado oil. 2. Put the calamari in the air fryer and cook at 400ºF (204ºC) for 3 minutes per side. 3. Then transfer the calamari in the serving plate and sprinkle with hot sauce.

Cod with Jalapeño

Prep time: 5 minutes | Cook time: 14 minutes | Serves 4

◄ 4 cod fillets, boneless
◄ 1 jalapeño, minced
◄ 1 tablespoon avocado oil
◄ ½ teaspoon minced garlic

1. In the shallow bowl, mix minced jalapeño, avocado oil, and minced garlic. 2. Put the cod fillets in the air fryer basket in one layer and top with minced jalapeño mixture. 3. Cook the fish at 365ºF (185ºC) for 7 minutes per side.

Mouthwatering Cod over Creamy Leek Noodles

Prep time: 10 minutes | Cook time: 24 minutes | Serves 4

◄ 1 small leek, sliced into long thin noodles (about 2 cups)
◄ ½ cup heavy cream
◄ 2 cloves garlic, minced
◄ 1 teaspoon fine sea salt,
Coating:
◄ ¼ cup grated Parmesan cheese
◄ 2 tablespoons mayonnaise
◄ 2 tablespoons unsalted butter, softened

divided
◄ 4 (4-ounce / 113-g) cod fillets (about 1 inch thick)
◄ ½ teaspoon ground black pepper

◄ 1 tablespoon chopped fresh thyme, or ½ teaspoon dried thyme leaves, plus more for garnish

1. Preheat the air fryer to 350ºF (177ºC). 2. Place the leek noodles in a casserole dish or a pan that will fit in your air fryer. 3. In a small bowl, stir together the cream, garlic, and ½ teaspoon of the salt. Pour the mixture over the leeks and cook in the air fryer for 10 minutes, or until the leeks are very tender. 4. Pat the fish dry and season with the remaining ½ teaspoon of salt and the pepper. When the leeks are ready, open the air fryer and place the fish fillets on top of the leeks. Air fry for 8 to 10 minutes, until the fish flakes easily with a fork (the thicker the fillets, the longer this will

take). 5. While the fish cooks, make the coating: In a small bowl, combine the Parmesan, mayo, butter, and thyme. 6. When the fish is ready, remove it from the air fryer and increase the heat to 425ºF (218ºC) (or as high as your air fryer can go). Spread the fillets with a ½-inch-thick to ¾-inch-thick layer of the coating. 7. Place the fish back in the air fryer and air fry for 3 to 4 minutes, until the coating browns. 8. Garnish with fresh or dried thyme, if desired. Store leftovers in an airtight container in the refrigerator for up to 3 days. Reheat in a casserole dish in a preheated 350ºF (177ºC) air fryer for 6 minutes, or until heated through.

Herbed Shrimp Pita

Prep time: 5 minutes | Cook time: 8 minutes | Serves 4

◄ 1 pound (454 g) medium shrimp, peeled and deveined
◄ 2 tablespoons olive oil
◄ 1 teaspoon dried oregano
◄ ½ teaspoon dried thyme
◄ ½ teaspoon garlic powder
◄ ¼ teaspoon onion powder
◄ ½ teaspoon salt
◄ ¼ teaspoon black pepper
◄ 4 whole wheat pitas
◄ 4 ounces (113 g) feta cheese, crumbled
◄ 1 cup shredded lettuce
◄ 1 tomato, diced
◄ ¼ cup black olives, sliced
◄ 1 lemon

1. Preheat the oven to 380°F(193ºC). 2. In a medium bowl, combine the shrimp with the olive oil, oregano, thyme, garlic powder, onion powder, salt, and black pepper. 3. Pour shrimp in a single layer in the air fryer basket and roast for 6 to 8 minutes, or until cooked through. 4. Remove from the air fryer and divide into warmed pitas with feta, lettuce, tomato, olives, and a squeeze of lemon.

Crab Cakes with Bell Peppers

Prep time: 5 minutes | Cook time: 10 minutes | Serves 4

◄ 8 ounces (227 g) jumbo lump crab meat
◄ 1 egg, beaten
◄ Juice of ½ lemon
◄ ⅓ cup bread crumbs
◄ ¼ cup diced green bell pepper
◄ ¼ cup diced red bell pepper
◄ ¼ cup mayonnaise
◄ 1 tablespoon Old Bay seasoning
◄ 1 teaspoon flour
◄ Cooking spray

1. Preheat the air fryer to 375ºF (190ºC). 2. Make the crab cakes: Place all the ingredients except the flour and oil in a large bowl and stir until well incorporated. 3. Divide the crab mixture into four equal portions and shape each portion into a patty with your hands. Top each patty with a sprinkle of ¼ teaspoon of flour. 4. Arrange the crab cakes in the air fryer basket and spritz them with cooking spray. 5. Air fry for 10 minutes, flipping the crab cakes halfway through, or until they are cooked through. 6. Divide the crab cakes among four plates and serve.

Sweet Tilapia Fillets

Prep time: 5 minutes | Cook time: 14 minutes | Serves 4

- 2 tablespoons erythritol
- 1 tablespoon apple cider vinegar
- 4 tilapia fillets, boneless
- 1 teaspoon olive oil

1. Mix apple cider vinegar with olive oil and erythritol. 2. Then rub the tilapia fillets with the sweet mixture and put in the air fryer basket in one layer. 3. Cook the fish at 360°F (182°C) for 7 minutes per side.

Cayenne Flounder Cutlets

Prep time: 15 minutes | Cook time: 10 minutes | Serves 2

- 1 egg
- 1 cup Pecorino Romano cheese, grated
- Sea salt and white pepper, to taste
- ½ teaspoon cayenne pepper
- 1 teaspoon dried parsley flakes
- 2 flounder fillets

1. To make a breading station, whisk the egg until frothy. 2. In another bowl, mix Pecorino Romano cheese, and spices. 3. Dip the fish in the egg mixture and turn to coat evenly; then, dredge in the cracker crumb mixture, turning a couple of times to coat evenly. 4. Cook in the preheated air fryer at 390°F (199°C) for 5 minutes; turn them over and cook another 5 minutes. Enjoy!

Panko Catfish Nuggets

Prep time: 10 minutes | Cook time: 7 to 8 minutes | Serves 4

- 2 medium catfish fillets, cut into chunks (approximately 1 × 2 inch)
- Salt and pepper, to taste
- 2 eggs
- 2 tablespoons skim milk
- ½ cup cornstarch
- 1 cup panko bread crumbs
- Cooking spray

1. Preheat the air fryer to 390°F (199°C). 2. In a medium bowl, season the fish chunks with salt and pepper to taste. 3. In a small bowl, beat together the eggs with milk until well combined. 4. Place the cornstarch and bread crumbs into separate shallow dishes. 5. Dredge the fish chunks one at a time in the cornstarch, coating well on both sides, then dip in the egg mixture, shaking off any excess, finally press well into the bread crumbs. Spritz the fish chunks with cooking spray. 6. Arrange the fish chunks in the air fryer basket in a single layer. You may need to cook in batches depending on the size of your air fryer basket. 7. Fry the fish chunks for 7 to 8 minutes until they are no longer translucent in the center and golden brown. Shake the basket once during cooking. 8. Remove the fish chunks from the basket to a plate. Repeat with the remaining fish chunks. 9. Serve warm.

Swordfish Skewers with Caponata

Prep time: 15 minutes | Cook time: 20 minutes | Serves 2

- 1 (10-ounce / 283-g) small Italian eggplant, cut into 1-inch pieces
- 6 ounces (170 g) cherry tomatoes
- 3 scallions, cut into 2 inches long
- 2 tablespoons extra-virgin olive oil, divided
- Salt and pepper, to taste
- 12 ounces (340 g) skinless swordfish steaks, 1¼ inches
- thick, cut into 1-inch pieces
- 2 teaspoons honey, divided
- 2 teaspoons ground coriander, divided
- 1 teaspoon grated lemon zest, divided
- 1 teaspoon juice
- 4 (6-inch) wooden skewers
- 1 garlic clove, minced
- ½ teaspoon ground cumin
- 1 tablespoon chopped fresh basil

1. Preheat the air fryer to 400°F (204°C). 2. Toss eggplant, tomatoes, and scallions with 1 tablespoon oil, ¼ teaspoon salt, and ⅛ teaspoon pepper in bowl; transfer to air fryer basket. Air fry until eggplant is softened and browned and tomatoes have begun to burst, about 14 minutes, tossing halfway through cooking. Transfer vegetables to cutting board and set aside to cool slightly. 3. Pat swordfish dry with paper towels. Combine 1 teaspoon oil, 1 teaspoon honey, 1 teaspoon coriander, ½ teaspoon lemon zest, ⅛ teaspoon salt, and pinch pepper in a clean bowl. Add swordfish and toss to coat. Thread swordfish onto skewers, leaving about ¼ inch between each piece (3 or 4 pieces per skewer). 4. Arrange skewers in air fryer basket, spaced evenly apart. (Skewers may overlap slightly.) Return basket to air fryer and air fry until swordfish is browned and registers 140°F (60°C), 6 to 8 minutes, flipping and rotating skewers halfway through cooking. 5. Meanwhile, combine remaining 2 teaspoons oil, remaining 1 teaspoon honey, remaining 1 teaspoon coriander, remaining ½ teaspoon lemon zest, lemon juice, garlic, cumin, ¼ teaspoon salt, and ⅛ teaspoon pepper in large bowl. Microwave, stirring once, until fragrant, about 30 seconds. Coarsely chop the cooked vegetables, transfer to bowl with dressing, along with any accumulated juices, and gently toss to combine. Stir in basil and season with salt and pepper to taste. Serve skewers with caponata.

Shrimp Caesar Salad

Prep time: 30 minutes | Cook time: 4 to 6 minutes | Serves 4

- 12 ounces (340 g) fresh large shrimp, peeled and deveined
- 1 tablespoon plus 1 teaspoon freshly squeezed lemon juice, divided
- 4 tablespoons olive oil or avocado oil, divided
- 2 garlic cloves, minced, divided
- ¼ teaspoon sea salt, plus additional to season the marinade
- ¼ teaspoon freshly ground black pepper, plus additional to season the marinade
- ⅓ cup sugar-free mayonnaise
- 2 tablespoons freshly grated Parmesan cheese
- 1 teaspoon Dijon mustard
- 1 tinned anchovy, mashed
- 12 ounces (340 g) romaine hearts, torn

1. Place the shrimp in a large bowl. Add 1 tablespoon of lemon juice, 1 tablespoon of olive oil, and 1 minced garlic clove. Season with salt and pepper. Toss well and refrigerate for 15 minutes. 2. While the shrimp marinates, make the dressing: In a blender, combine the mayonnaise, Parmesan cheese, Dijon mustard, the remaining 1 teaspoon of lemon juice, the anchovy, the remaining minced garlic clove, ¼ teaspoon of salt, and ¼ teaspoon of pepper. Process until smooth. With the blender running, slowly stream in the remaining 3 tablespoons of oil. Transfer the mixture to a jar; seal and refrigerate until ready to serve. 3. Remove the shrimp from its marinade and place it in the air fryer basket in a single layer. Set the air fryer to 400°F (204°C) and air fry for 2 minutes. Flip the shrimp and cook for 2 to 4 minutes more, until the flesh turns opaque. 4. Place the romaine in a large bowl and toss with the desired amount of dressing. Top with the shrimp and serve immediately.

Maple Balsamic Glazed Salmon

Prep time: 5 minutes | Cook time: 10 minutes | Serves 4

- 4 (6-ounce / 170-g) fillets of salmon
- Salt and freshly ground black pepper, to taste
- Vegetable oil
- ¼ cup pure maple syrup
- 3 tablespoons balsamic vinegar
- 1 teaspoon Dijon mustard

1. Preheat the air fryer to 400°F (204°C). 2. Season the salmon well with salt and freshly ground black pepper. Spray or brush the bottom of the air fryer basket with vegetable oil and place the salmon fillets inside. Air fry the salmon for 5 minutes. 3. While the salmon is air frying, combine the maple syrup, balsamic vinegar and Dijon mustard in a small saucepan over medium heat and stir to blend well. Let the mixture simmer while the fish is cooking. It should start to thicken slightly, but keep your eye on it so it doesn't burn. 4. Brush the glaze on the salmon fillets and air fry for an additional 5 minutes. The salmon should feel firm to the touch when finished and the glaze should be nicely browned on top. Brush a little more glaze on top before removing and serving with rice and vegetables, or a nice green salad.

Chapter 7

Vegetables and Sides

Chapter 7 Vegetables and Sides

Easy Potato Croquettes

Prep time: 15 minutes | Cook time: 15 minutes | Serves 10

- ◄ ¼ cup nutritional yeast
- ◄ 2 cups boiled potatoes, mashed
- ◄ 1 flax egg
- ◄ 1 tablespoon flour
- ◄ 2 tablespoons chopped
- chives
- ◄ Salt and ground black pepper, to taste
- ◄ 2 tablespoons vegetable oil
- ◄ ¼ cup bread crumbs

1. Preheat the air fryer to 400°F (204°C). 2. In a bowl, combine the nutritional yeast, potatoes, flax egg, flour, and chives. Sprinkle with salt and pepper as desired. 3. In a separate bowl, mix the vegetable oil and bread crumbs to achieve a crumbly consistency. 4. Shape the potato mixture into small balls and dip each one into the bread crumb mixture. 5. Put the croquettes inside the air fryer and air fry for 15 minutes, ensuring the croquettes turn golden brown. 6. Serve immediately.

Shishito Pepper Roast

Prep time: 4 minutes | Cook time: 9 minutes | Serves 4

- ◄ Cooking oil spray (sunflower, safflower, or refined coconut)
- ◄ 1 pound (454 g) shishito, Anaheim, or bell peppers,
- rinsed
- ◄ 1 tablespoon soy sauce
- ◄ 2 teaspoons freshly squeezed lime juice
- ◄ 2 large garlic cloves, pressed

1. Insert the crisper plate into the basket and the basket into the unit. Preheat the unit by selecting AIR ROAST, setting the temperature to 390°F (199°C), and setting the time to 3 minutes. Select START/STOP to begin. 2. Once the unit is preheated, spray the crisper plate and the basket with cooking oil. Place the peppers into the basket and spray them with oil. 3. Select AIR ROAST, set the temperature to 390°F (199°C), and set the time to 9 minutes. Select START/STOP to begin. 4. After 3 minutes, remove the basket and shake the peppers. Spray the peppers with more oil. Reinsert the basket to resume cooking. Repeat this step again after 3 minutes. 5. While the peppers roast, in a medium bowl, whisk the soy sauce, lime juice, and garlic until combined. Set aside. 6. When the cooking is complete, several of the peppers should have lots of nice browned spots on them. If using Anaheim or bell peppers, cut a slit in the side of each pepper and remove the seeds, which can be bitter. 7. Place the roasted peppers in the bowl with the sauce. Toss to coat the peppers evenly and serve.

Sesame Taj Tofu

Prep time: 5 minutes | Cook time: 25 minutes | Serves 4

- ◄ 1 block firm tofu, pressed and cut into 1-inch thick cubes
- ◄ 2 tablespoons soy sauce
- ◄ 2 teaspoons toasted sesame seeds
- ◄ 1 teaspoon rice vinegar
- ◄ 1 tablespoon cornstarch

1. Preheat the air fryer to 400°F (204°C). 2. Add the tofu, soy sauce, sesame seeds, and rice vinegar in a bowl together and mix well to coat the tofu cubes. Then cover the tofu in cornstarch and put it in the air fryer basket. 3. Air fry for 25 minutes, giving the basket a shake at five-minute intervals to ensure the tofu cooks evenly. 4. Serve immediately.

Stuffed Red Peppers with Herbed Ricotta and Tomatoes

Prep time: 10 minutes | Cook time: 20 minutes | Serves 4

- ◄ 2 red bell peppers
- ◄ 1 cup cooked brown rice
- ◄ 2 Roma tomatoes, diced
- ◄ 1 garlic clove, minced
- ◄ ¼ teaspoon salt
- ◄ ¼ teaspoon black pepper
- ◄ 4 ounces (113 g) ricotta
- ◄ 3 tablespoons fresh basil, chopped
- ◄ 3 tablespoons fresh oregano, chopped
- ◄ ¼ cup shredded Parmesan, for topping

1. Preheat the air fryer to 360°F(182°C). 2. Cut the bell peppers in half and remove the seeds and stem. 3. In a medium bowl, combine the brown rice, tomatoes, garlic, salt, and pepper. 4. Distribute the rice filling evenly among the four bell pepper halves. 5. In a small bowl, combine the ricotta, basil, and oregano. Put the herbed cheese over the top of the rice mixture in each bell pepper. 6. Place the bell peppers into the air fryer and roast for 20 minutes. 7. Remove and serve with shredded Parmesan on top.

Crispy Chickpeas

Prep time: 5 minutes | Cook time: 15 minutes | Serves 4

◁ 1 (15 ounces / 425 g) can chickpeas, drained but not rinsed
◁ 2 tablespoons olive oil
◁ 1 teaspoon salt
◁ 2 tablespoons lemon juice

1. Preheat the air fryer to 400ºF (204ºC). 2. Add all the ingredients together in a bowl and mix. Transfer this mixture to the air fryer basket. 3. Air fry for 15 minutes, ensuring the chickpeas become nice and crispy. 4. Serve immediately.

Garlic and Thyme Tomatoes

Prep time: 10 minutes | Cook time: 15 minutes | Serves 2 to 4

◁ 4 Roma tomatoes
◁ 1 tablespoon olive oil
◁ Salt and freshly ground
black pepper, to taste
◁ 1 clove garlic, minced
◁ ½ teaspoon dried thyme

1. Preheat the air fryer to 390ºF (199ºC). 2. Cut the tomatoes in half and scoop out the seeds and any pithy parts with your fingers. Place the tomatoes in a bowl and toss with the olive oil, salt, pepper, garlic and thyme. 3. Transfer the tomatoes to the air fryer, cut side up. Air fry for 15 minutes. The edges should just start to brown. Let the tomatoes cool to an edible temperature for a few minutes and then use in pastas, on top of crostini, or as an accompaniment to any poultry, meat or fish.

Corn and Cilantro Salad

Prep time: 10 minutes | Cook time: 10 minutes | Serves 2

◁ 2 ears of corn, shucked (halved crosswise if too large to fit in your air fryer)
◁ 1 tablespoon unsalted butter, at room temperature
◁ 1 teaspoon chili powder
◁ ¼ teaspoon garlic powder
◁ Kosher salt and freshly ground black pepper, to taste
◁ 1 cup lightly packed fresh cilantro leaves
◁ 1 tablespoon sour cream
◁ 1 tablespoon mayonnaise
◁ 1 teaspoon adobo sauce (from a can of chipotle peppers in adobo sauce)
◁ 2 tablespoons crumbled queso fresco
◁ Lime wedges, for serving

1. Brush the corn all over with the butter, then sprinkle with the chili powder and garlic powder, and season with salt and pepper. Place the corn in the air fryer and air fry at 400ºF (204ºC), turning over halfway through, until the kernels are lightly charred and tender, about 10 minutes. 2. Transfer the ears to a cutting board, let stand 1 minute, then carefully cut the kernels off the cobs and move them to a bowl. Add the cilantro leaves and toss to combine (the cilantro leaves will wilt slightly). 3. In a small bowl, stir together the sour cream, mayonnaise, and adobo sauce. Divide the corn and cilantro among plates and spoon the adobo dressing over the top. Sprinkle with the queso fresco and serve with lime wedges on the side.

Ratatouille

Prep time: 15 minutes | Cook time: 20 minutes | Serves 2 to 3

◁ 2 cups ¾-inch cubed peeled eggplant
◁ 1 small red, yellow, or orange bell pepper, stemmed, seeded, and diced
◁ 1 cup cherry tomatoes
◁ 6 to 8 cloves garlic, peeled
and halved lengthwise
◁ 3 tablespoons olive oil
◁ 1 teaspoon dried oregano
◁ ½ teaspoon dried thyme
◁ 1 teaspoon kosher salt
◁ ½ teaspoon black pepper

1. In a medium bowl, combine the eggplant, bell pepper, tomatoes, garlic, oil, oregano, thyme, salt, and pepper. Toss to combine. 2. Place the vegetables in the air fryer basket. Set the air fryer to 400ºF (204ºC) for 20 minutes, or until the vegetables are crisp-tender.

Asian Tofu Salad

Prep time: 25 minutes | Cook time: 15 minutes | Serves 2

Tofu:
◁ 1 tablespoon soy sauce
◁ 1 tablespoon vegetable oil
◁ 1 teaspoon minced fresh ginger
◁ 1 teaspoon minced garlic
◁ 8 ounces (227 g) extra-firm tofu, drained and cubed

Salad:
◁ ¼ cup rice vinegar
◁ 1 tablespoon sugar
◁ 1 teaspoon salt
◁ 1 teaspoon black pepper
◁ ¼ cup sliced scallions
◁ 1 cup julienned cucumber
◁ 1 cup julienned red onion
◁ 1 cup julienned carrots
◁ 6 butter lettuce leaves

1. For the tofu: In a small bowl, whisk together the soy sauce, vegetable oil, ginger, and garlic. Add the tofu and mix gently. Let stand at room temperature for 10 minutes. 2. Arrange the tofu in a single layer in the air fryer basket. Set the air fryer to 400ºF (204ºC) for 15 minutes, shaking halfway through the cooking time. 3. Meanwhile, for the salad: In a large bowl, whisk together the vinegar, sugar, salt, pepper, and scallions. Add the cucumber, onion, and carrots and toss to combine. Set aside to marinate while the tofu cooks. 4. To serve, arrange three lettuce leaves on each of two plates. Pile the marinated vegetables (and marinade) on the lettuce. Divide the tofu between the plates and serve.

Roasted Radishes with Sea Salt

Prep time: 5 minutes | Cook time: 18 minutes | Serves 4

◄ 1 pound (454 g) radishes, ends trimmed if needed
◄ 2 tablespoons olive oil
◄ ½ teaspoon sea salt

1. Preheat the air fryer to 360°F(182°C). 2. In a large bowl, combine the radishes with olive oil and sea salt. 3. Pour the radishes into the air fryer and roast for 10 minutes. Stir or turn the radishes over and roast for 8 minutes more, then serve.

Crispy Green Beans

Prep time: 5 minutes | Cook time: 8 minutes | Serves 4

◄ 2 teaspoons olive oil
◄ ½ pound (227 g) fresh green beans, ends trimmed
◄ ¼ teaspoon salt
◄ ¼ teaspoon ground black pepper

1. In a large bowl, drizzle olive oil over green beans and sprinkle with salt and pepper. 2. Place green beans into ungreased air fryer basket. Adjust the temperature to 350°F (177°C) and set the timer for 8 minutes, shaking the basket two times during cooking. Green beans will be dark golden and crispy at the edges when done. Serve warm.

Sausage-Stuffed Mushroom Caps

Prep time: 10 minutes | Cook time: 8 minutes | Serves 2

◄ 6 large portobello mushroom caps
◄ ½ pound (227 g) Italian sausage
◄ ¼ cup chopped onion
◄ 2 tablespoons blanched
finely ground almond flour
◄ ¼ cup grated Parmesan cheese
◄ 1 teaspoon minced fresh garlic

1. Use a spoon to hollow out each mushroom cap, reserving scrapings. 2. In a medium skillet over medium heat, brown the sausage about 10 minutes or until fully cooked and no pink remains. Drain and then add reserved mushroom scrapings, onion, almond flour, Parmesan, and garlic. Gently fold ingredients together and continue cooking an additional minute, then remove from heat. 3. Evenly spoon the mixture into mushroom caps and place the caps into a 6-inch round pan. Place pan into the air fryer basket. 4. Adjust the temperature to 375°F (191°C) and set the timer for 8 minutes. 5. When finished cooking, the tops will be browned and bubbling. Serve warm.

Cheesy Loaded Broccoli

Prep time: 10 minutes | Cook time: 10 minutes | Serves 2

◄ 3 cups fresh broccoli florets
◄ 1 tablespoon coconut oil
◄ ¼ teaspoon salt
◄ ½ cup shredded sharp Cheddar cheese
◄ ¼ cup sour cream
◄ 4 slices cooked sugar-free bacon, crumbled
◄ 1 medium scallion, trimmed and sliced on the bias

1. Place broccoli into ungreased air fryer basket, drizzle with coconut oil, and sprinkle with salt. Adjust the temperature to 350°F (177°C) and roast for 8 minutes. Shake basket three times during cooking to avoid burned spots. 2. Sprinkle broccoli with Cheddar and cook for 2 additional minutes. When done, cheese will be melted and broccoli will be tender. 3. Serve warm in a large serving dish, topped with sour cream, crumbled bacon, and scallion slices.

Corn on the Cob

Prep time: 5 minutes | Cook time: 12 to 15 minutes | Serves 4

◄ 2 large ears fresh corn
◄ Olive oil for misting
◄ Salt, to taste (optional)

1. Shuck corn, remove silks, and wash. 2. Cut or break each ear in half crosswise. 3. Spray corn with olive oil. 4. Air fry at 390°F (199°C) for 12 to 15 minutes or until browned as much as you like. 5. Serve plain or with coarsely ground salt.

Lemon-Garlic Mushrooms

Prep time: 10 minutes | Cook time: 10 to 15 minutes | Serves 6

◄ 12 ounces (340 g) sliced mushrooms
◄ 1 tablespoon avocado oil
◄ Sea salt and freshly ground black pepper, to taste
◄ 3 tablespoons unsalted butter
◄ 1 teaspoon minced garlic
◄ 1 teaspoon freshly squeezed lemon juice
◄ ½ teaspoon red pepper flakes
◄ 2 tablespoons chopped fresh parsley

1. Place the mushrooms in a medium bowl and toss with the oil. Season to taste with salt and pepper. 2. Place the mushrooms in a single layer in the air fryer basket. Set your air fryer to 375°F (191°C) and roast for 10 to 15 minutes, until the mushrooms are tender. 3. While the mushrooms cook, melt the butter in a small pot or skillet over medium-low heat. Stir in the garlic and cook for 30 seconds. Remove the pot from the heat and stir in the lemon juice and red pepper flakes. 4. Toss the mushrooms with the lemon-garlic butter and garnish with the parsley before serving.

Roasted Grape Tomatoes and Asparagus

Prep time: 5 minutes | Cook time: 12 minutes | Serves 6

◄ 2 cups grape tomatoes
◄ 1 bunch asparagus, trimmed
◄ 2 tablespoons olive oil
◄ 3 garlic cloves, minced
◄ ½ teaspoon kosher salt

1. Preheat the air fryer to 380ºF(193ºC). 2. In a large bowl, combine all of the ingredients, tossing until the vegetables are well coated with oil. 3. Pour the vegetable mixture into the air fryer basket and spread into a single layer, then roast for 12 minutes.

Fried Zucchini Salad

Prep time: 10 minutes | Cook time: 5 to 7 minutes | Serves 4

◄ 2 medium zucchini, thinly sliced
◄ 5 tablespoons olive oil, divided
◄ ¼ cup chopped fresh parsley
◄ 2 tablespoons chopped fresh
  mint
◄ Zest and juice of ½ lemon
◄ 1 clove garlic, minced
◄ ¼ cup crumbled feta cheese
◄ Freshly ground black pepper, to taste

1. Preheat the air fryer to 400ºF (204ºC). 2. In a large bowl, toss the zucchini slices with 1 tablespoon of the olive oil. 3. Working in batches if necessary, arrange the zucchini slices in an even layer in the air fryer basket. Pausing halfway through the cooking time to shake the basket, air fry for 5 to 7 minutes until soft and lightly browned on each side. 4. Meanwhile, in a small bowl, combine the remaining 4 tablespoons olive oil, parsley, mint, lemon zest, lemon juice, and garlic. 5. Arrange the zucchini on a plate and drizzle with the dressing. Sprinkle the feta and black pepper on top. Serve warm or at room temperature.

Asparagus Fries

Prep time: 15 minutes | Cook time: 5 to 7 minutes per batch | Serves 4

◄ 12 ounces (340 g) fresh asparagus spears with tough ends trimmed off
◄ 2 egg whites
◄ ¼ cup water
◄ ¾ cup panko bread crumbs
◄ ¼ cup grated Parmesan cheese, plus 2 tablespoons
◄ ¼ teaspoon salt
◄ Oil for misting or cooking spray

1. Preheat the air fryer to 390ºF (199ºC). 2. In a shallow dish, beat egg whites and water until slightly foamy. 3. In another shallow dish, combine panko, Parmesan, and salt. 4. Dip asparagus spears in egg, then roll in crumbs. Spray with oil or cooking spray. 5. Place a layer of asparagus in air fryer basket, leaving just a little space in between each spear. Stack another layer on top, crosswise. Air fry at 390ºF (199ºC) for 5 to 7 minutes, until crispy and golden brown. 6. Repeat to cook remaining asparagus.

Broccoli-Cheddar Twice-Baked Potatoes

Prep time: 10 minutes | Cook time: 46 minutes | Serves 4

◄ Oil, for spraying
◄ 2 medium russet potatoes
◄ 1 tablespoon olive oil
◄ ¼ cup broccoli florets
◄ 1 tablespoon sour cream
◄ 1 teaspoon granulated garlic
◄ 1 teaspoon onion powder
◄ ½ cup shredded Cheddar cheese

1. Line the air fryer basket with parchment and spray lightly with oil. 2. Rinse the potatoes and pat dry with paper towels. Rub the outside of the potatoes with the olive oil and place them in the prepared basket. 3. Air fry at 400ºF (204ºC) for 40 minutes, or until easily pierced with a fork. Let cool just enough to handle, then cut the potatoes in half lengthwise. 4. Meanwhile, place the broccoli in a microwave-safe bowl, cover with water, and microwave on high for 5 to 8 minutes. Drain and set aside. 5. Scoop out most of the potato flesh and transfer to a medium bowl. 6. Add the sour cream, garlic, and onion powder and stir until the potatoes are mashed. 7. Spoon the potato mixture back into the hollowed potato skins, mounding it to fit, if necessary. Top with the broccoli and cheese. Return the potatoes to the basket. You may need to work in batches, depending on the size of your air fryer. 8. Air fry at 400ºF (204ºC) for 3 to 6 minutes, or until the cheese has melted. Serve immediately.

Zucchini Fritters

Prep time: 10 minutes | Cook time: 10 minutes | Serves 4

◄ 2 zucchini, grated (about 1 pound / 454 g)
◄ 1 teaspoon salt
◄ ¼ cup almond flour
◄ ¼ cup grated Parmesan cheese
◄ 1 large egg
◄ ¼ teaspoon dried thyme
◄ ¼ teaspoon ground turmeric
◄ ¼ teaspoon freshly ground black pepper
◄ 1 tablespoon olive oil
◄ ½ lemon, sliced into wedges

1. Preheat the air fryer to 400ºF (204ºC). Cut a piece of parchment paper to fit slightly smaller than the bottom of the air fryer. 2. Place the zucchini in a large colander and sprinkle with the salt. Let sit for 5 to 10 minutes. Squeeze as much liquid as you can from the zucchini and place in a large mixing bowl. Add the almond flour, Parmesan, egg, thyme, turmeric, and black pepper. Stir gently until thoroughly combined. 3. Shape the mixture into 8 patties and arrange on the parchment paper. Brush lightly with the olive oil. Pausing halfway through the cooking time to turn the patties, air fry for 10 minutes until golden brown. Serve warm with the lemon wedges.

Tofu Bites

Prep time: 15 minutes | Cook time: 30 minutes | Serves 4

- 1 packaged firm tofu, cubed and pressed to remove excess water
- 1 tablespoon soy sauce
- 1 tablespoon ketchup
- 1 tablespoon maple syrup
- ½ teaspoon vinegar
- 1 teaspoon liquid smoke
- 1 teaspoon hot sauce
- 2 tablespoons sesame seeds
- 1 teaspoon garlic powder
- Salt and ground black pepper, to taste
- Cooking spray

1. Preheat the air fryer to 375ºF (191ºC). 2. Spritz a baking dish with cooking spray. 3. Combine all the ingredients to coat the tofu completely and allow the marinade to absorb for half an hour. 4. Transfer the tofu to the baking dish, then air fry for 15 minutes. Flip the tofu over and air fry for another 15 minutes on the other side. 5. Serve immediately.

Mushrooms with Goat Cheese

Prep time: 10 minutes | Cook time: 10 minutes | Serves 4

- 3 tablespoons vegetable oil
- 1 pound (454 g) mixed mushrooms, trimmed and sliced
- 1 clove garlic, minced
- ¼ teaspoon dried thyme
- ½ teaspoon black pepper
- 4 ounces (113 g) goat cheese, diced
- 2 teaspoons chopped fresh thyme leaves (optional)

1. In a baking pan, combine the oil, mushrooms, garlic, dried thyme, and pepper. Stir in the goat cheese. Place the pan in the air fryer basket. Set the air fryer to 400ºF (204ºC) for 10 minutes, stirring halfway through the cooking time. 2. Sprinkle with fresh thyme, if desired.

Spinach and Cheese Stuffed Tomatoes

Prep time: 20 minutes | Cook time: 15 minutes | Serves 2

- 4 ripe beefsteak tomatoes
- ¾ teaspoon black pepper
- ½ teaspoon kosher salt
- 1 (10-ounce / 283-g) package frozen chopped spinach, thawed and squeezed dry
- 1 (5.2-ounce / 147-g) package garlic-and-herb Boursin cheese
- 3 tablespoons sour cream
- ½ cup finely grated Parmesan cheese

1. Cut the tops off the tomatoes. Using a small spoon, carefully remove and discard the pulp. Season the insides with ½ teaspoon of the black pepper and ¼ teaspoon of the salt. Invert the tomatoes onto paper towels and allow to drain while you make the filling. 2. Meanwhile, in a medium bowl, combine the spinach, Boursin cheese, sour cream, ¼ cup of the Parmesan, and the remaining ¼ teaspoon salt and ¼ teaspoon pepper. Stir until ingredients are well combined. Divide the filling among the tomatoes. Top with the remaining ¼ cup Parmesan. 3. Place the tomatoes in the air fryer basket. Set the air fryer to 350ºF (177ºC) for 15 minutes, or until the filling is hot.

Mashed Sweet Potato Tots

Prep time: 10 minutes | Cook time: 12 to 13 minutes per batch | Makes 18 to 24 tots

- 1 cup cooked mashed sweet potatoes
- 1 egg white, beaten
- ⅛ teaspoon ground cinnamon
- 1 dash nutmeg
- 2 tablespoons chopped
- pecans
- 1½ teaspoons honey
- Salt, to taste
- ½ cup panko bread crumbs
- Oil for misting or cooking spray

1. Preheat the air fryer to 390ºF (199ºC). 2. In a large bowl, mix together the potatoes, egg white, cinnamon, nutmeg, pecans, honey, and salt to taste. 3. Place panko crumbs on a sheet of wax paper. 4. For each tot, use about 2 teaspoons of sweet potato mixture. To shape, drop the measure of potato mixture onto panko crumbs and push crumbs up and around potatoes to coat edges. Then turn tot over to coat other side with crumbs. 5. Mist tots with oil or cooking spray and place in air fryer basket in single layer. 6. Air fry at 390ºF (199ºC) for 12 to 13 minutes, until browned and crispy. 7. Repeat steps 5 and 6 to cook remaining tots.

Cheesy Cauliflower Tots

Prep time: 15 minutes | Cook time: 12 minutes | Makes 16 tots

- 1 large head cauliflower
- 1 cup shredded Mozzarella cheese
- ½ cup grated Parmesan cheese
- 1 large egg
- ¼ teaspoon garlic powder
- ¼ teaspoon dried parsley
- ⅛ teaspoon onion powder

1. On the stovetop, fill a large pot with 2 cups water and place a steamer in the pan. Bring water to a boil. Cut the cauliflower into florets and place on steamer basket. Cover pot with lid. 2. Allow cauliflower to steam 7 minutes until fork tender. Remove from steamer basket and place into cheesecloth or clean kitchen towel and let cool. Squeeze over sink to remove as much excess moisture as possible. The mixture will be too soft to form into tots if not all the moisture is removed. Mash with a fork to a smooth consistency. 3. Put the cauliflower into a large mixing bowl and add Mozzarella, Parmesan, egg, garlic powder, parsley, and onion powder. Stir until fully combined. The mixture should be wet but easy to mold. 4. Take 2 tablespoons of the mixture and roll into tot shape. Repeat with remaining mixture. Place into the air fryer basket. 5. Adjust the temperature to 320ºF (160ºC) and set the timer for 12 minutes. 6. Turn tots halfway through the cooking time. Cauliflower tots should be golden when fully cooked. Serve warm.

Indian Eggplant Bharta

Prep time: 15 minutes | Cook time: 20 minutes | Serves 4

- 1 medium eggplant
- 2 tablespoons vegetable oil
- ½ cup finely minced onion
- ½ cup finely chopped fresh tomato
- 2 tablespoons fresh lemon
- juice
- 2 tablespoons chopped fresh cilantro
- ½ teaspoon kosher salt
- ⅛ teaspoon cayenne pepper

1. Rub the eggplant all over with the vegetable oil. Place the eggplant in the air fryer basket. Set the air fryer to 400ºF (204ºC) for 20 minutes, or until the eggplant skin is blistered and charred. 2. Transfer the eggplant to a resealable plastic bag, seal, and set aside for 15 to 20 minutes (the eggplant will finish cooking in the residual heat trapped in the bag). 3. Transfer the eggplant to a large bowl. Peel off and discard the charred skin. Roughly mash the eggplant flesh. Add the onion, tomato, lemon juice, cilantro, salt, and cayenne. Stir to combine.

Cheese-Walnut Stuffed Mushrooms

Prep time: 5 minutes | Cook time: 10 minutes | Serves 4

- 4 large portobello mushrooms
- 1 tablespoon canola oil
- ½ cup shredded Mozzarella cheese
- ⅓ cup minced walnuts
- 2 tablespoons chopped fresh parsley
- Cooking spray

1. Preheat the air fryer to 350ºF (177ºC). Spritz the air fryer basket with cooking spray. 2. On a clean work surface, remove the mushroom stems. Scoop out the gills with a spoon and discard. Coat the mushrooms with canola oil. Top each mushroom evenly with the shredded Mozzarella cheese, followed by the minced walnuts. 3. Arrange the mushrooms in the air fryer and roast for 10 minutes until golden brown. 4. Transfer the mushrooms to a plate and sprinkle the parsley on top for garnish before serving.

Spiced Honey-Walnut Carrots

Prep time: 5 minutes | Cook time: 12 minutes | Serves 6

- 1 pound (454 g) baby carrots
- 2 tablespoons olive oil
- ¼ cup raw honey
- ¼ teaspoon ground
- cinnamon
- ¼ cup black walnuts, chopped

1. Preheat the air fryer to 360ºF(182ºC). 2. In a large bowl, toss the baby carrots with olive oil, honey, and cinnamon until well coated. 3. Pour into the air fryer and roast for 6 minutes. Shake the basket, sprinkle the walnuts on top, and roast for 6 minutes more. 4. Remove the carrots from the air fryer and serve.

Fried Brussels Sprouts

Prep time: 10 minutes | Cook time: 18 minutes | Serves 4

- 1 teaspoon plus 1 tablespoon extra-virgin olive oil, divided
- 2 teaspoons minced garlic
- 2 tablespoons honey
- 1 tablespoon sugar
- 2 tablespoons freshly squeezed lemon juice
- 2 tablespoons rice vinegar
- 2 tablespoons sriracha
- 1 pound (454 g) Brussels sprouts, stems trimmed and any tough leaves removed, rinsed, halved lengthwise, and dried
- ½ teaspoon salt
- Cooking oil spray

1. In a small saucepan over low heat, combine 1 teaspoon of olive oil, the garlic, honey, sugar, lemon juice, vinegar, and sriracha. Cook for 2 to 3 minutes, or until slightly thickened. Remove the pan from the heat, cover, and set aside. 2. Place the Brussels sprouts in a resealable bag or small bowl. Add the remaining olive oil and the salt, and toss to coat. 3. Insert the crisper plate into the basket and the basket into the unit. Preheat the unit by selecting AIR FRY, setting the temperature to 390ºF (199ºC), and setting the time to 3 minutes. Select START/STOP to begin. 4. Once the unit is preheated, spray the crisper plate with cooking oil. Add the Brussels sprouts to the basket. 5. Select AIR FRY, set the temperature to 390ºF (199ºC), and set the time to 15 minutes. Select START/STOP to begin. 6. After 7 or 8 minutes, remove the basket and shake it to toss the sprouts. Reinsert the basket to resume cooking. 7. When the cooking is complete, the leaves should be crispy and light brown and the sprout centers tender. 8. Place the sprouts in a medium serving bowl and drizzle the sauce over the top. Toss to coat, and serve immediately.

Herbed Shiitake Mushrooms

Prep time: 10 minutes | Cook time: 5 minutes | Serves 4

- 8 ounces (227 g) shiitake mushrooms, stems removed and caps roughly chopped
- 1 tablespoon olive oil
- ½ teaspoon salt
- Freshly ground black pepper, to taste
- 1 teaspoon chopped fresh thyme leaves
- 1 teaspoon chopped fresh oregano
- 1 tablespoon chopped fresh parsley

1. Preheat the air fryer to 400ºF (204ºC). 2. Toss the mushrooms with the olive oil, salt, pepper, thyme and oregano. Air fry for 5 minutes, shaking the basket once or twice during the cooking process. The mushrooms will still be somewhat chewy with a meaty texture. If you'd like them a little more tender, add a couple of minutes to this cooking time. 3. Once cooked, add the parsley to the mushrooms and toss. Season again to taste and serve.

Tamarind Sweet Potatoes

Prep time: 5 minutes | Cook time: 20 to 25 minutes | Serves 4

- 5 garnet sweet potatoes, peeled and diced
- 1½ tablespoons fresh lime juice
- 1 tablespoon butter, melted
- 2 teaspoons tamarind paste
- 1½ teaspoon ground allspice
- ⅓ teaspoon white pepper
- ½ teaspoon turmeric powder
- A few drops liquid stevia

1. Preheat the air fryer to 400ºF (204ºC). 2. In a large mixing bowl, combine all the ingredients and toss until the sweet potatoes are evenly coated. 3. Place the sweet potatoes in the air fryer basket and air fry for 20 t0 25 minutes, or until the potatoes are crispy on the outside and soft on the inside. Shake the basket twice during cooking. 4. Let the potatoes cool for 5 minutes before serving.

Roasted Salsa

Prep time: 15 minutes | Cook time: 30 minutes | Makes 2 cups

- 2 large San Marzano tomatoes, cored and cut into large chunks
- ½ medium white onion, peeled and large-diced
- ½ medium jalapeño, seeded
- and large-diced
- 2 cloves garlic, peeled and diced
- ½ teaspoon salt
- 1 tablespoon coconut oil
- ¼ cup fresh lime juice

1. Place tomatoes, onion, and jalapeño into an ungreased round nonstick baking dish. Add garlic, then sprinkle with salt and drizzle with coconut oil. 2. Place dish into air fryer basket. Adjust the temperature to 300ºF (149ºC) and bake for 30 minutes. Vegetables will be dark brown around the edges and tender when done. 3. Pour mixture into a food processor or blender. Add lime juice. Process on low speed 30 seconds until only a few chunks remain. 4. Transfer salsa to a sealable container and refrigerate at least 1 hour. Serve chilled.

"Faux-Tato" Hash

Prep time: 10 minutes | Cook time: 12 minutes | Serves 4

- 1 pound (454 g) radishes, ends removed, quartered
- ¼ medium yellow onion, peeled and diced
- ½ medium green bell pepper, seeded and chopped
- 2 tablespoons salted butter, melted
- ½ teaspoon garlic powder
- ¼ teaspoon ground black pepper

1. In a large bowl, combine radishes, onion, and bell pepper. Toss with butter. 2. Sprinkle garlic powder and black pepper over mixture in bowl, then spoon into ungreased air fryer basket. 3. Adjust the temperature to 320ºF (160ºC) and air fry for 12 minutes. Shake basket halfway through cooking. Radishes will be tender when done. Serve warm.

Asian-Inspired Roasted Broccoli

Prep time: 10 minutes | Cook time: 15 minutes | Serves 4

Broccoli:
- Oil, for spraying
- 1 pound (454 g) broccoli florets

Sauce:
- 2 tablespoons soy sauce
- 2 teaspoons honey

- 2 teaspoons peanut oil
- 1 tablespoon minced garlic
- ½ teaspoon salt

- 2 teaspoons Sriracha
- 1 teaspoon rice vinegar

Make the Broccoli 1. Line the air fryer basket with parchment and spray lightly with oil. 2. In a large bowl, toss together the broccoli, peanut oil, garlic, and salt until evenly coated. 3. Spread out the broccoli in an even layer in the prepared basket. 4. Air fry at 400ºF (204ºC) for 15 minutes, stirring halfway through. Make the Sauce 5. Meanwhile, in a small microwave-safe bowl, combine the soy sauce, honey, Sriracha, and rice vinegar and microwave on high for about 15 seconds. Stir to combine. 6. Transfer the broccoli to a serving bowl and add the sauce. Gently toss until evenly coated and serve immediately.

Easy Greek Briami (Ratatouille)

Prep time: 15 minutes | Cook time: 40 minutes | Serves 6

- 2 russet potatoes, cubed
- ½ cup Roma tomatoes, cubed
- 1 eggplant, cubed
- 1 zucchini, cubed
- 1 red onion, chopped
- 1 red bell pepper, chopped
- 2 garlic cloves, minced
- 1 teaspoon dried mint
- 1 teaspoon dried parsley
- 1 teaspoon dried oregano
- ½ teaspoon salt
- ½ teaspoon black pepper
- ¼ teaspoon red pepper flakes
- ⅓ cup olive oil
- 1 (8-ounce / 227-g) can tomato paste
- ¼ cup vegetable broth
- ¼ cup water

1. Preheat the air fryer to 320°F(160°C). 2. In a large bowl, combine the potatoes, tomatoes, eggplant, zucchini, onion, bell pepper, garlic, mint, parsley, oregano, salt, black pepper, and red pepper flakes. 3. In a small bowl, mix together the olive oil, tomato paste, broth, and water. 4. Pour the oil-and-tomato-paste mixture over the vegetables and toss until everything is coated. 5. Pour the coated vegetables into the air fryer basket in an even layer and roast for 20 minutes. After 20 minutes, stir well and spread out again. Roast for an additional 10 minutes, then repeat the process and cook for another 10 minutes.

Chili Fingerling Potatoes

Prep time: 10 minutes | Cook time: 16 minutes | Serves 4

- ◀ 1 pound (454 g) fingerling potatoes, rinsed and cut into wedges
- ◀ 1 teaspoon olive oil
- ◀ 1 teaspoon salt
- ◀ 1 teaspoon black pepper
- ◀ 1 teaspoon cayenne pepper
- ◀ 1 teaspoon nutritional yeast
- ◀ ½ teaspoon garlic powder

1. Preheat the air fryer to 400°F (204°C). 2. Coat the potatoes with the rest of the ingredients. 3. Transfer to the air fryer basket and air fry for 16 minutes, shaking the basket at the halfway point. 4. Serve immediately.

Bacon-Wrapped Asparagus

Prep time: 10 minutes | Cook time: 10 minutes | Serves 4

- ◀ 8 slices reduced-sodium bacon, cut in half
- ◀ 16 thick (about 1 pound /
- 454 g) asparagus spears, trimmed of woody ends

1. Preheat the air fryer to 350°F (177°C). 2. Wrap a half piece of bacon around the center of each stalk of asparagus. 3. Working in batches, if necessary, arrange seam-side down in a single layer in the air fryer basket. Air fry for 10 minutes until the bacon is crisp and the stalks are tender.

Tingly Chili-Roasted Broccoli

Prep time: 5 minutes | Cook time: 10 minutes | Serves 2

- ◀ 12 ounces (340 g) broccoli florets
- ◀ 2 tablespoons Asian hot chili oil
- ◀ 1 teaspoon ground Sichuan peppercorns (or black pepper)
- ◀ 2 garlic cloves, finely chopped
- ◀ 1 (2-inch) piece fresh ginger, peeled and finely chopped
- ◀ Kosher salt and freshly ground black pepper, to taste

1. In a bowl, toss together the broccoli, chili oil, Sichuan peppercorns, garlic, ginger, and salt and black pepper to taste. 2. Transfer to the air fryer and roast at 375°F (191°C), shaking the basket halfway through, until lightly charred and tender, about 10 minutes. Remove from the air fryer and serve warm.

Caramelized Eggplant with Harissa Yogurt

Prep time: 10 minutes | Cook time: 15 minutes | Serves 2

- ◀ 1 medium eggplant (about ¾ pound / 340 g), cut crosswise into ½-inch-thick slices and quartered
- ◀ 2 tablespoons vegetable oil
- ◀ Kosher salt and freshly ground black pepper, to
- taste
- ◀ ½ cup plain yogurt (not Greek)
- ◀ 2 tablespoons harissa paste
- ◀ 1 garlic clove, grated
- ◀ 2 teaspoons honey

1. In a bowl, toss together the eggplant and oil, season with salt and pepper, and toss to coat evenly. Transfer to the air fryer and air fry at 400°F (204°C), shaking the basket every 5 minutes, until the eggplant is caramelized and tender, about 15 minutes. 2. Meanwhile, in a small bowl, whisk together the yogurt, harissa, and garlic, then spread onto a serving plate. 3. Pile the warm eggplant over the yogurt and drizzle with the honey just before serving.

Roasted Potatoes and Asparagus

Prep time: 5 minutes | Cook time: 23 minutes | Serves 4

- ◀ 4 medium potatoes
- ◀ 1 bunch asparagus
- ◀ ⅓ cup cottage cheese
- ◀ ⅓ cup low-fat crème fraiche
- ◀ 1 tablespoon wholegrain mustard
- ◀ Salt and pepper, to taste
- ◀ Cooking spray

1. Preheat the air fryer to 390°F (199°C). Spritz the air fryer basket with cooking spray. 2. Place the potatoes in the basket. Air fry the potatoes for 20 minutes. 3. Boil the asparagus in salted water for 3 minutes. 4. Remove the potatoes and mash them with rest of ingredients. Sprinkle with salt and pepper. 5. Serve immediately.

Chapter 8

Vegetarian Mains

Chapter 8 Vegetarian Mains

Crustless Spinach Cheese Pie

Prep time: 10 minutes | Cook time: 20 minutes | Serves 4

◀ 6 large eggs
◀ ¼ cup heavy whipping cream
◀ 1 cup frozen chopped

spinach, drained
◀ 1 cup shredded sharp Cheddar cheese
◀ ¼ cup diced yellow onion

1. In a medium bowl, whisk eggs and add cream. Add remaining ingredients to bowl. 2. Pour into a round baking dish. Place into the air fryer basket. 3. Adjust the temperature to 320ºF (160ºC) and bake for 20 minutes. 4. Eggs will be firm and slightly browned when cooked. Serve immediately.

Garlic White Zucchini Rolls

Prep time: 20 minutes | Cook time: 20 minutes | Serves 4

◀ 2 medium zucchini
◀ 2 tablespoons unsalted butter
◀ ¼ white onion, peeled and diced
◀ ½ teaspoon finely minced roasted garlic
◀ ¼ cup heavy cream
◀ 2 tablespoons vegetable broth
◀ ⅛ teaspoon xanthan gum

◀ ½ cup full-fat ricotta cheese
◀ ¼ teaspoon salt
◀ ½ teaspoon garlic powder
◀ ¼ teaspoon dried oregano
◀ 2 cups spinach, chopped
◀ ½ cup sliced baby portobello mushrooms
◀ ¾ cup shredded Mozzarella cheese, divided

1. Using a mandoline or sharp knife, slice zucchini into long strips lengthwise. Place strips between paper towels to absorb moisture. Set aside. 2. In a medium saucepan over medium heat, melt butter. Add onion and sauté until fragrant. Add garlic and sauté 30 seconds. 3. Pour in heavy cream, broth, and xanthan gum. Turn off heat and whisk mixture until it begins to thicken, about 3 minutes. 4. In a medium bowl, add ricotta, salt, garlic powder, and oregano and mix well. Fold in spinach, mushrooms, and ½ cup Mozzarella. 5. Pour half of the sauce into a round baking pan. To assemble the rolls, place two strips of zucchini on a work surface. Spoon 2 tablespoons of ricotta mixture onto the slices and roll up. Place seam side down on top of sauce. Repeat with remaining ingredients. 6. Pour remaining sauce over the rolls and sprinkle with remaining Mozzarella. Cover with foil and place into the air fryer basket. 7.

Adjust the temperature to 350ºF (177ºC) and bake for 20 minutes. 8. In the last 5 minutes, remove the foil to brown the cheese. Serve immediately.

Broccoli Crust Pizza

Prep time: 15 minutes | Cook time: 12 minutes | Serves 4

◀ 3 cups riced broccoli, steamed and drained well
◀ 1 large egg
◀ ½ cup grated vegetarian Parmesan cheese

◀ 3 tablespoons low-carb Alfredo sauce
◀ ½ cup shredded Mozzarella cheese

1. In a large bowl, mix broccoli, egg, and Parmesan. 2. Cut a piece of parchment to fit your air fryer basket. Press out the pizza mixture to fit on the parchment, working in two batches if necessary. Place into the air fryer basket. 3. Adjust the temperature to 370ºF (188ºC) and air fry for 5 minutes. 4. The crust should be firm enough to flip. If not, add 2 additional minutes. Flip crust. 5. Top with Alfredo sauce and Mozzarella. Return to the air fryer basket and cook an additional 7 minutes or until cheese is golden and bubbling. Serve warm.

Mediterranean Pan Pizza

Prep time: 5 minutes | Cook time: 8 minutes | Serves 2

◀ 1 cup shredded Mozzarella cheese
◀ ¼ medium red bell pepper, seeded and chopped
◀ ½ cup chopped fresh spinach

leaves
◀ 2 tablespoons chopped black olives
◀ 2 tablespoons crumbled feta cheese

1. Sprinkle Mozzarella into an ungreased round nonstick baking dish in an even layer. Add remaining ingredients on top. 2. Place dish into air fryer basket. Adjust the temperature to 350ºF (177ºC) and bake for 8 minutes, checking halfway through to avoid burning. Top of pizza will be golden brown and the cheese melted when done. 3. Remove dish from fryer and let cool 5 minutes before slicing and serving.

Crispy Cabbage Steaks

Prep time: 5 minutes | Cook time: 10 minutes | Serves 4

◄ 1 small head green cabbage, cored and cut into ½-inch-thick slices
◄ ¼ teaspoon salt
◄ ¼ teaspoon ground black pepper

◄ 2 tablespoons olive oil
◄ 1 clove garlic, peeled and finely minced
◄ ½ teaspoon dried thyme
◄ ½ teaspoon dried parsley

1. Sprinkle each side of cabbage with salt and pepper, then place into ungreased air fryer basket, working in batches if needed. 2. Drizzle each side of cabbage with olive oil, then sprinkle with remaining ingredients on both sides. Adjust the temperature to 350ºF (177ºC) and air fry for 10 minutes, turning "steaks" halfway through cooking. 3.Cabbage will be browned at the edges and tender when done. Serve warm.

Roasted Spaghetti Squash

Prep time: 10 minutes | Cook time: 45 minutes | Serves 6

◄ 1 (4 pounds / 1.8 kg) spaghetti squash, halved and seeded
◄ 2 tablespoons coconut oil

◄ 4 tablespoons salted butter, melted
◄ 1 teaspoon garlic powder
◄ 2 teaspoons dried parsley

1. Brush shell of spaghetti squash with coconut oil. Brush inside with butter. Sprinkle inside with garlic powder and parsley. 2. Place squash skin side down into ungreased air fryer basket, working in batches if needed. Adjust the temperature to 350ºF (177ºC) and set the timer for 30 minutes. When the timer beeps, flip squash and cook an additional 15 minutes until fork-tender. 3. Use a fork to remove spaghetti strands from shell and serve warm.

Stuffed Portobellos

Prep time: 10 minutes | Cook time: 8 minutes | Serves 4

◄ 3 ounces (85 g) cream cheese, softened
◄ ½ medium zucchini, trimmed and chopped
◄ ¼ cup seeded and chopped red bell pepper
◄ 1½ cups chopped fresh

spinach leaves
◄ 4 large portobello mushrooms, stems removed
◄ 2 tablespoons coconut oil, melted
◄ ½ teaspoon salt

1. In a medium bowl, mix cream cheese, zucchini, pepper, and spinach. 2. Drizzle mushrooms with coconut oil and sprinkle with salt. Scoop ¼ zucchini mixture into each mushroom. 3. Place

mushrooms into ungreased air fryer basket. Adjust the temperature to 400ºF (204ºC) and air fry for 8 minutes. Portobellos will be tender and tops will be browned when done. Serve warm.

Rosemary Beets with Balsamic Glaze

Prep time: 5 minutes | Cook time: 10 minutes | Serves 2

Beet:
◄ 2 beets, cubed
◄ 2 tablespoons olive oil
◄ 2 springs rosemary, chopped
Balsamic Glaze:
◄ ⅓ cup balsamic vinegar

◄ Salt and black pepper, to taste

◄ 1 tablespoon honey

1. Preheat the air fryer to 400ºF (204ºC). 2. Combine the beets, olive oil, rosemary, salt, and pepper in a mixing bowl and toss until the beets are completely coated. 3. Place the beets in the air fryer basket and air fry for 10 minutes until the beets are crisp and browned at the edges. Shake the basket halfway through the cooking time. 4. Meanwhile, make the balsamic glaze: Place the balsamic vinegar and honey in a small saucepan and bring to a boil over medium heat. When the sauce starts to boil, reduce the heat to medium-low heat and simmer until the liquid is reduced by half. 5. When ready, remove the beets from the basket to a platter. Pour the balsamic glaze over the top and serve immediately.

Cayenne Tahini Kale

Prep time: 5 minutes | Cook time: 15 minutes | Serves 2 to 4

Dressing:
◄ ¼ cup tahini
◄ ¼ cup fresh lemon juice
◄ 2 tablespoons olive oil
Kale:
◄ 4 cups packed torn kale leaves (stems and ribs removed and leaves torn into palm-size pieces)

◄ 1 teaspoon sesame seeds
◄ ½ teaspoon garlic powder
◄ ¼ teaspoon cayenne pepper

◄ Kosher salt and freshly ground black pepper, to taste

1. Preheat the air fryer to 350ºF (177ºC). 2. Make the dressing: Whisk together the tahini, lemon juice, olive oil, sesame seeds, garlic powder, and cayenne pepper in a large bowl until well mixed. 3. Add the kale and massage the dressing thoroughly all over the leaves. Sprinkle the salt and pepper to season. 4. Place the kale in the air fryer basket in a single layer and air fry for about 15 minutes, or until the leaves are slightly wilted and crispy. 5. Remove from the basket and serve on a plate.

Cauliflower Steak with Gremolata

Prep time: 15 minutes | Cook time: 25 minutes | Serves 4

- 2 tablespoons olive oil
- 1 tablespoon Italian seasoning
- 1 large head cauliflower, outer leaves removed and
Gremolata:
- 1 bunch Italian parsley (about 1 cup packed)
- 2 cloves garlic
- Zest of 1 small lemon, plus 1

- sliced lengthwise through the core into thick "steaks"
- Salt and freshly ground black pepper, to taste
- ¼ cup Parmesan cheese

- to 2 teaspoons lemon juice
- ½ cup olive oil
- Salt and pepper, to taste

1. Preheat the air fryer to 400°F (204°C). 2. In a small bowl, combine the olive oil and Italian seasoning. Brush both sides of each cauliflower "steak" generously with the oil. Season to taste with salt and black pepper. 3. Working in batches if necessary, arrange the cauliflower in a single layer in the air fryer basket. Pausing halfway through the cooking time to turn the "steaks," air fry for 15 to 20 minutes until the cauliflower is tender and the edges begin to brown. Sprinkle with the Parmesan and air fry for 5 minutes longer. 4. To make the gremolata: In a food processor fitted with a metal blade, combine the parsley, garlic, and lemon zest and juice. With the motor running, add the olive oil in a steady stream until the mixture forms a bright green sauce. Season to taste with salt and black pepper. Serve the cauliflower steaks with the gremolata spooned over the top.

Zucchini-Ricotta Tart

Prep time: 15 minutes | Cook time: 60 minutes | Serves 6

- ½ cup grated Parmesan cheese, divided
- 1½ cups almond flour
- 1 tablespoon coconut flour
- ½ teaspoon garlic powder
- ¾ teaspoon salt, divided
- ¼ cup unsalted butter, melted

- 1 zucchini, thinly sliced (about 2 cups)
- 1 cup ricotta cheese
- 3 eggs
- 2 tablespoons heavy cream
- 2 cloves garlic, minced
- ½ teaspoon dried tarragon

1. Preheat the air fryer to 330°F (166°C). Coat a round pan with olive oil and set aside. 2. In a large bowl, whisk ¼ cup of the Parmesan with the almond flour, coconut flour, garlic powder, and ¼ teaspoon of the salt. Stir in the melted butter until the dough resembles coarse crumbs. Press the dough firmly into the bottom and up the sides of the prepared pan. Air fry for 12 to 15 minutes until the crust begins to brown. Let cool to room temperature. 3. Meanwhile, place the zucchini in a colander and sprinkle with the remaining ½ teaspoon salt. Toss gently to distribute the salt and let sit for 30 minutes. Use paper towels to pat the zucchini dry. 4. In

a large bowl, whisk together the ricotta, eggs, heavy cream, garlic, and tarragon. Gently stir in the zucchini slices. Pour the cheese mixture into the cooled crust and sprinkle with the remaining ¼ cup Parmesan. 5. Increase the air fryer to 350°F (177°C). Place the pan in the air fryer basket and air fry for 45 to 50 minutes, or until set and a tester inserted into the center of the tart comes out clean. Serve warm or at room temperature.

Broccoli with Garlic Sauce

Prep time: 19 minutes | Cook time: 15 minutes | Serves 4

- 2 tablespoons olive oil
- Kosher salt and freshly ground black pepper, to
Dipping Sauce:
- 2 teaspoons dried rosemary, crushed
- 3 garlic cloves, minced
- ⅓ teaspoon dried marjoram,

- taste
- 1 pound (454 g) broccoli florets

- crushed
- ¼ cup sour cream
- ⅓ cup mayonnaise

1. Lightly grease your broccoli with a thin layer of olive oil. Season with salt and ground black pepper. 2. Arrange the seasoned broccoli in the air fryer basket. Bake at 395°F (202°C) for 15 minutes, shaking once or twice. In the meantime, prepare the dipping sauce by mixing all the sauce ingredients. Serve warm broccoli with the dipping sauce and enjoy!

Fried Root Vegetable Medley with Thyme

Prep time: 10 minutes | Cook time: 22 minutes | Serves 4

- 2 carrots, sliced
- 2 potatoes, cut into chunks
- 1 rutabaga, cut into chunks
- 1 turnip, cut into chunks
- 1 beet, cut into chunks
- 8 shallots, halved
- 2 tablespoons olive oil

- Salt and black pepper, to taste
- 2 tablespoons tomato pesto
- 2 tablespoons water
- 2 tablespoons chopped fresh thyme

1. Preheat the air fryer to 400°F (204°C). 2. Toss the carrots, potatoes, rutabaga, turnip, beet, shallots, olive oil, salt, and pepper in a large mixing bowl until the root vegetables are evenly coated. 3. Place the root vegetables in the air fryer basket and air fry for 12 minutes. Shake the basket and air fry for another 10 minutes until they are cooked to your preferred doneness. 4. Meanwhile, in a small bowl, whisk together the tomato pesto and water until smooth. 5. When ready, remove the root vegetables from the basket to a platter. Drizzle with the tomato pesto mixture and sprinkle with the thyme. Serve immediately.

Sweet Pepper Nachos

Prep time: 10 minutes | Cook time: 5 minutes | Serves 2

- 6 mini sweet peppers, seeded and sliced in half
- ¾ cup shredded Colby jack cheese
- ¼ cup sliced pickled
- jalapeños
- ½ medium avocado, peeled, pitted, and diced
- 2 tablespoons sour cream

1. Place peppers into an ungreased round nonstick baking dish. Sprinkle with Colby and top with jalapeños. 2. Place dish into air fryer basket. Adjust the temperature to 350°F (177°C) and bake for 5 minutes. Cheese will be melted and bubbly when done. 3. Remove dish from air fryer and top with avocado. Drizzle with sour cream. Serve warm.

Air Fryer Veggies with Halloumi

Prep time: 5 minutes | Cook time: 14 minutes | Serves 2

- 2 zucchinis, cut into even chunks
- 1 large eggplant, peeled, cut into chunks
- 1 large carrot, cut into chunks
- 6 ounces (170 g) halloumi
- cheese, cubed
- 2 teaspoons olive oil
- Salt and black pepper, to taste
- 1 teaspoon dried mixed herbs

1. Preheat the air fryer to 340°F (171°C). 2. Combine the zucchinis, eggplant, carrot, cheese, olive oil, salt, and pepper in a large bowl and toss to coat well. 3. Spread the mixture evenly in the air fryer basket and air fry for 14 minutes until crispy and golden, shaking the basket once during cooking. Serve topped with mixed herbs.

Whole Roasted Lemon Cauliflower

Prep time: 5 minutes | Cook time: 15 minutes | Serves 4

- 1 medium head cauliflower
- 2 tablespoons salted butter, melted
- 1 medium lemon
- ½ teaspoon garlic powder
- 1 teaspoon dried parsley

1. Remove the leaves from the head of cauliflower and brush it with melted butter. Cut the lemon in half and zest one half onto the cauliflower. Squeeze the juice of the zested lemon half and pour it over the cauliflower. 2. Sprinkle with garlic powder and parsley. Place cauliflower head into the air fryer basket. 3. Adjust the temperature to 350°F (177°C) and air fry for 15 minutes. 4. Check cauliflower every 5 minutes to avoid overcooking. It should be fork tender. 5. To serve, squeeze juice from other lemon half over cauliflower. Serve immediately.

Cheesy Cabbage Wedges

Prep time: 5 minutes | Cook time: 20 minutes | Serves 4

- 4 tablespoons melted butter
- 1 head cabbage, cut into wedges
- 1 cup shredded Parmesan cheese
- Salt and black pepper, to taste
- ½ cup shredded Mozzarella cheese

1. Preheat the air fryer to 380°F (193°C). 2. Brush the melted butter over the cut sides of cabbage wedges and sprinkle both sides with the Parmesan cheese. Season with salt and pepper to taste. 3. Place the cabbage wedges in the air fryer basket and air fry for 20 minutes, flipping the cabbage halfway through, or until the cabbage wedges are lightly browned. 4. Transfer the cabbage wedges to a plate and serve with the Mozzarella cheese sprinkled on top.

Super Veg Rolls

Prep time: 20 minutes | Cook time: 10 minutes | Serves 6

- 2 potatoes, mashed
- ¼ cup peas
- ¼ cup mashed carrots
- 1 small cabbage, sliced
- ¼ cups beans
- 2 tablespoons sweetcorn
- 1 small onion, chopped
- ½ cup bread crumbs
- 1 packet spring roll sheets
- ½ cup cornstarch slurry

1. Preheat the air fryer to 390°F (199°C). 2. Boil all the vegetables in water over a low heat. Rinse and allow to dry. 3. Unroll the spring roll sheets and spoon equal amounts of vegetable onto the center of each one. Fold into spring rolls and coat each one with the slurry and bread crumbs. 4. Air fry the rolls in the preheated air fryer for 10 minutes. 5. Serve warm.

Baked Turnip and Zucchini

Prep time: 5 minutes | Cook time: 15 to 20 minutes | Serves 4

- 3 turnips, sliced
- 1 large zucchini, sliced
- 1 large red onion, cut into rings
- 2 cloves garlic, crushed
- 1 tablespoon olive oil
- Salt and black pepper, to taste

1. Preheat the air fryer to 330ºF (166ºC). 2. Put the turnips, zucchini, red onion, and garlic in a baking pan. Drizzle the olive oil over the top and sprinkle with the salt and pepper. 3. Place the baking pan in the preheated air fryer and bake for 15 to 20 minutes, or until the vegetables are tender. 4. Remove from the basket and serve on a plate.

Baked Zucchini

Prep time: 10 minutes | Cook time: 8 minutes | Serves 4

- 2 tablespoons salted butter
- ¼ cup diced white onion
- ½ teaspoon minced garlic
- ½ cup heavy whipping cream
- 2 ounces (57 g) full-fat cream cheese
- 1 cup shredded sharp Cheddar cheese
- 2 medium zucchini, spiralized

1. In a large saucepan over medium heat, melt butter. Add onion and sauté until it begins to soften, 1 to 3 minutes. Add garlic and sauté for 30 seconds, then pour in cream and add cream cheese. 2. Remove the pan from heat and stir in Cheddar. Add the zucchini and toss in the sauce, then put into a round baking dish. Cover the dish with foil and place into the air fryer basket. 3. Adjust the temperature to 370ºF (188ºC) and set the timer for 8 minutes. 4. After 6 minutes remove the foil and let the top brown for remaining cooking time. Stir and serve.

Chapter 9

Fast and Easy Everyday Favorites

Chapter 9 Fast and Easy Everyday Favorites

Easy Devils on Horseback

Prep time: 5 minutes | Cook time: 7 minutes | Serves 12

◄ 24 petite pitted prunes (4½ ounces / 128 g)
◄ ¼ cup crumbled blue cheese,
  divided
◄ 8 slices center-cut bacon, cut crosswise into thirds

1. Preheat the air fryer to 400ºF (204ºC). 2. Halve the prunes lengthwise, but don't cut them all the way through. Place ½ teaspoon of cheese in the center of each prune. Wrap a piece of bacon around each prune and secure the bacon with a toothpick. 3. Working in batches, arrange a single layer of the prunes in the air fryer basket. Air fry for about 7 minutes, flipping halfway, until the bacon is cooked through and crisp. 4. Let cool slightly and serve warm.

Southwest Corn and Bell Pepper Roast

Prep time: 10 minutes | Cook time: 10 minutes | Serves 4

For the Corn:
◄ 1½ cups thawed frozen corn kernels
◄ 1 cup mixed diced bell peppers
◄ 1 jalapeño, diced
◄ 1 cup diced yellow onion
◄ ½ teaspoon ancho chile
For Serving:
◄ ¼ cup feta cheese
◄ ¼ cup chopped fresh cilantro
  powder
◄ 1 tablespoon fresh lemon juice
◄ 1 teaspoon ground cumin
◄ ½ teaspoon kosher salt
◄ Cooking spray

◄ 1 tablespoon fresh lemon juice

1. Preheat the air fryer to 375ºF (191ºC). Spritz the air fryer with cooking spray. 2. Combine the ingredients for the corn in a large bowl. Stir to mix well. 3. Pout the mixture into the air fryer. Air fry for 10 minutes or until the corn and bell peppers are soft. Shake the basket halfway through the cooking time. 4. Transfer them onto a large plate, then spread with feta cheese and cilantro. Drizzle with lemon juice and serve.

Bacon Pinwheels

Prep time: 10 minutes | Cook time: 10 minutes | Makes 8 pinwheels

◄ 1 sheet puff pastry
◄ 2 tablespoons maple syrup
◄ ¼ cup brown sugar
◄ 8 slices bacon
◄ Ground black pepper, to taste
◄ Cooking spray

1. Preheat the air fryer to 360ºF (182ºC). Spritz the air fryer basket with cooking spray. 2. Roll the puff pastry into a 10-inch square with a rolling pin on a clean work surface, then cut the pastry into 8 strips. 3. Brush the strips with maple syrup and sprinkle with sugar, leaving a 1-inch far end uncovered. 4. Arrange each slice of bacon on each strip, leaving a ⅛-inch length of bacon hang over the end close to you. Sprinkle with black pepper. 5. From the end close to you, roll the strips into pinwheels, then dab the uncovered end with water and seal the rolls. 6. Arrange the pinwheels in the preheated air fryer and spritz with cooking spray. 7. Air fry for 10 minutes or until golden brown. Flip the pinwheels halfway through. 8. Serve immediately.

Traditional Queso Fundido

Prep time: 10 minutes | Cook time: 25 minutes | Serves 4

◄ 4 ounces (113 g) fresh Mexican chorizo, casings removed
◄ 1 medium onion, chopped
◄ 3 cloves garlic, minced
◄ 1 cup chopped tomato
◄ 2 jalapeños, deseeded and
  diced
◄ 2 teaspoons ground cumin
◄ 2 cups shredded Oaxaca or Mozzarella cheese
◄ ½ cup half-and-half
◄ Celery sticks or tortilla chips, for serving

1. Preheat the air fryer to 400ºF (204ºC). 2. In a baking pan, combine the chorizo, onion, garlic, tomato, jalapeños, and cumin. Stir to combine. 3. Place the pan in the air fryer basket. Air fry for 15 minutes, or until the sausage is cooked, stirring halfway through the cooking time to break up the sausage. 4. Add the cheese and half-and-half; stir to combine. Air fry for 10 minutes, or until the cheese has melted. 5. Serve with celery sticks or tortilla chips.

Garlicky Baked Cherry Tomatoes

Prep time: 5 minutes | Cook time: 4 to 6 minutes | Serves 2

- ◀ 2 cups cherry tomatoes
- ◀ 1 clove garlic, thinly sliced
- ◀ 1 teaspoon olive oil
- ◀ ⅛ teaspoon kosher salt
- ◀ 1 tablespoon freshly chopped basil, for topping
- ◀ Cooking spray

1. Preheat the air fryer to 360°F (182°C). Spritz the air fryer baking pan with cooking spray and set aside. 2. In a large bowl, toss together the cherry tomatoes, sliced garlic, olive oil, and kosher salt. Spread the mixture in an even layer in the prepared pan. 3. Bake in the preheated air fryer for 4 to 6 minutes, or until the tomatoes become soft and wilted. 4. Transfer to a bowl and rest for 5 minutes. Top with the chopped basil and serve warm.

Air Fried Broccoli

Prep time: 5 minutes | Cook time: 6 minutes | Serves 1

- ◀ 4 egg yolks
- ◀ ¼ cup butter, melted
- ◀ 2 cups coconut flower
- ◀ Salt and pepper, to taste
- ◀ 2 cups broccoli florets

1. Preheat the air fryer to 400°F (204°C). 2. In a bowl, whisk the egg yolks and melted butter together. Throw in the coconut flour, salt and pepper, then stir again to combine well. 3. Dip each broccoli floret into the mixture and place in the air fryer basket. Air fry for 6 minutes in batches if necessary. Take care when removing them from the air fryer and serve immediately.

Scalloped Veggie Mix

Prep time: 10 minutes | Cook time: 15 minutes | Serves 4

- ◀ 1 Yukon Gold potato, thinly sliced
- ◀ 1 small sweet potato, peeled and thinly sliced
- ◀ 1 medium carrot, thinly sliced
- ◀ ¼ cup minced onion
- ◀ 3 garlic cloves, minced
- ◀ ¾ cup 2 percent milk
- ◀ 2 tablespoons cornstarch
- ◀ ½ teaspoon dried thyme

1. Preheat the air fryer to 380°F (193°C). 2. In a baking pan, layer the potato, sweet potato, carrot, onion, and garlic. 3. In a small bowl, whisk the milk, cornstarch, and thyme until blended. Pour the milk mixture evenly over the vegetables in the pan. 4. Bake for 15 minutes. Check the casserole—it should be golden brown on top, and the vegetables should be tender. 5. Serve immediately.

Cheesy Baked Grits

Prep time: 10 minutes | Cook time: 12 minutes | Serves 6

- ◀ ¾ cup hot water
- ◀ 2 (1-ounce / 28-g) packages instant grits
- ◀ 1 large egg, beaten
- ◀ 1 tablespoon butter, melted
- ◀ 2 cloves garlic, minced
- ◀ ½ to 1 teaspoon red pepper flakes
- ◀ 1 cup shredded Cheddar cheese or jalapeño Jack cheese

1. Preheat the air fryer to 400°F (204°C). 2. In a baking pan, combine the water, grits, egg, butter, garlic, and red pepper flakes. Stir until well combined. Stir in the shredded cheese. 3. Place the pan in the air fryer basket and air fry for 12 minutes, or until the grits have cooked through and a knife inserted near the center comes out clean. 4. Let stand for 5 minutes before serving.

Easy Air Fried Edamame

Prep time: 5 minutes | Cook time: 7 minutes | Serves 6

- ◀ 1½ pounds (680 g) unshelled edamame
- ◀ 2 tablespoons olive oil
- ◀ 1 teaspoon sea salt

1. Preheat the air fryer to 400°F (204°C). 2. Place the edamame in a large bowl, then drizzle with olive oil. Toss to coat well. 3. Transfer the edamame to the preheated air fryer. Cook for 7 minutes or until tender and warmed through. Shake the basket at least three times during the cooking. 4. Transfer the cooked edamame onto a plate and sprinkle with salt. Toss to combine well and set aside for 3 minutes to infuse before serving.

Easy Cinnamon Toast

Prep time: 5 minutes | Cook time: 20 minutes | Serves 6

- ◀ 1½ teaspoons cinnamon
- ◀ 1½ teaspoons vanilla extract
- ◀ ½ cup sugar
- ◀ 2 teaspoons ground black
- pepper
- ◀ 2 tablespoons melted coconut oil
- ◀ 12 slices whole wheat bread

1. Preheat the air fryer to 400°F (204°C). 2. Combine all the ingredients, except for the bread, in a large bowl. Stir to mix well. 3. Dunk the bread in the bowl of mixture gently to coat and infuse well. Shake the excess off. 4. Arrange the bread slices in the preheated air fryer. Air fry for 5 minutes or until golden brown. Flip the bread halfway through. You may need to cook in batches to avoid overcrowding. 5. Remove the bread slices from the air fryer and slice to serve.

Crispy Green Tomatoes Slices

Prep time: 10 minutes | Cook time: 8 minutes | Makes 12 slices

- ½ cup all-purpose flour
- 1 egg
- ½ cup buttermilk
- 1 cup cornmeal
- 1 cup panko
- 2 green tomatoes, cut into
- ¼-inch-thick slices, patted dry
- ½ teaspoon salt
- ½ teaspoon ground black pepper
- Cooking spray

1. Preheat the air fryer to 400ºF (204ºC). Line the air fryer basket with parchment paper. 2. Pour the flour in a bowl. Whisk the egg and buttermilk in a second bowl. Combine the cornmeal and panko in a third bowl. 3. Dredge the tomato slices in the bowl of flour first, then into the egg mixture, and then dunk the slices into the cornmeal mixture. Shake the excess off. 4. Transfer the well-coated tomato slices in the preheated air fryer and sprinkle with salt and ground black pepper. 5. Spritz the tomato slices with cooking spray. Air fry for 8 minutes or until crispy and lightly browned. Flip the slices halfway through the cooking time. 6. Serve immediately.

Easy Roasted Asparagus

Prep time: 5 minutes | Cook time: 6 minutes | Serves 4

- 1 pound (454 g) asparagus, trimmed and halved crosswise
- 1 teaspoon extra-virgin olive
- oil
- Salt and pepper, to taste
- Lemon wedges, for serving

1. Preheat the air fryer to 400ºF (204ºC). 2. Toss the asparagus with the oil, ⅛ teaspoon salt, and ⅛ teaspoon pepper in bowl. Transfer to air fryer basket. 3. Place the basket in air fryer and roast for 6 to 8 minutes, or until tender and bright green, tossing halfway through cooking. 4. Season with salt and pepper and serve with lemon wedges.

Spicy Air Fried Old Bay Shrimp

Prep time: 7 minutes | Cook time: 10 minutes | Makes 2 cups

- ½ teaspoon Old Bay Seasoning
- 1 teaspoon ground cayenne pepper
- ½ teaspoon paprika
- 1 tablespoon olive oil
- ⅛ teaspoon salt
- ½ pound (227 g) shrimps, peeled and deveined
- Juice of half a lemon

1. Preheat the air fryer to 390ºF (199ºC). 2. Combine the Old Bay Seasoning, cayenne pepper, paprika, olive oil, and salt in a large bowl, then add the shrimps and toss to coat well. 3. Put the shrimps in the preheated air fryer. Air fry for 10 minutes or until opaque. Flip the shrimps halfway through. 4. Serve the shrimps with lemon juice on top.

Classic Poutine

Prep time: 15 minutes | Cook time: 25 minutes | Serves 2

- 2 russet potatoes, scrubbed and cut into ½-inch sticks
- 2 teaspoons vegetable oil
- 2 tablespoons butter
- ¼ onion, minced
- ¼ teaspoon dried thyme
- 1 clove garlic, smashed
- 3 tablespoons all-purpose
- flour
- 1 teaspoon tomato paste
- 1½ cups beef stock
- 2 teaspoons Worcestershire sauce
- Salt and freshly ground black pepper, to taste
- ⅔ cup chopped string cheese

1. Bring a pot of water to a boil, then put in the potato sticks and blanch for 4 minutes. 2. Preheat the air fryer to 400ºF (204ºC). 3. Drain the potato sticks and rinse under running cold water, then pat dry with paper towels. 4. Transfer the sticks in a large bowl and drizzle with vegetable oil. Toss to coat well. 5. Place the potato sticks in the preheated air fryer. Air fry for 25 minutes or until the sticks are golden brown. Shake the basket at least three times during the frying. 6. Meanwhile, make the gravy: Heat the butter in a saucepan over medium heat until melted. 7. Add the onion, thyme, and garlic and sauté for 5 minutes or until the onion is translucent. 8. Add the flour and sauté for an additional 2 minutes. Pour in the tomato paste and beef stock and cook for 1 more minute or until lightly thickened. 9. Drizzle the gravy with Worcestershire sauce and sprinkle with salt and ground black pepper. Reduce the heat to low to keep the gravy warm until ready to serve. 10. Transfer the fried potato sticks onto a plate, then sprinkle with salt and ground black pepper. Scatter with string cheese and pour the gravy over. Serve warm.

Air Fried Tortilla Chips

Prep time: 5 minutes | Cook time: 10 minutes | Serves 4

- 4 six-inch corn tortillas, cut in half and slice into thirds
- 1 tablespoon canola oil
- ¼ teaspoon kosher salt
- Cooking spray

1. Preheat the air fryer to 360ºF (182ºC). Spritz the air fryer basket with cooking spray. 2. On a clean work surface, brush the tortilla chips with canola oil, then transfer the chips in the preheated air fryer. 3. Air fry for 10 minutes or until crunchy and lightly browned. Shake the basket and sprinkle with salt halfway through the cooking time. 4. Transfer the chips onto a plate lined with paper towels. Serve immediately.

Simple and Easy Croutons

Prep time: 5 minutes | Cook time: 8 minutes | Serves 4

- 2 slices friendly bread
- 1 tablespoon olive oil
- Hot soup, for serving

1. Preheat the air fryer to 390ºF (199ºC). 2. Cut the slices of bread into medium-size chunks. 3. Brush the air fryer basket with the oil. 4. Place the chunks inside and air fry for at least 8 minutes. 5. Serve with hot soup.

Beef Bratwursts

Prep time: 5 minutes | Cook time: 15 minutes | Serves 4

- 4 (3-ounce / 85-g) beef bratwursts

1. Preheat the air fryer to 375ºF (191ºC). 2. Place the beef bratwursts in the air fryer basket and air fry for 15 minutes, turning once halfway through. 3. Serve hot.

Honey Bartlett Pears with Lemony Ricotta

Prep time: 10 minutes | Cook time: 8 minutes | Serves 4

- 2 large Bartlett pears, peeled, cut in half, cored
- 3 tablespoons melted butter
- ½ teaspoon ground ginger
- ¼ teaspoon ground cardamom
- 3 tablespoons brown sugar
- ½ cup whole-milk ricotta
- cheese
- 1 teaspoon pure lemon extract
- 1 teaspoon pure almond extract
- 1 tablespoon honey, plus additional for drizzling

1. Preheat the air fryer to 375ºF (191ºC). 2. Toss the pears with butter, ginger, cardamom, and sugar in a large bowl. Toss to coat well. 3. Arrange the pears in the preheated air fryer, cut side down. Air fry for 5 minutes, then flip the pears and air fry for 3 more minutes or until the pears are soft and browned. 4. In the meantime, combine the remaining ingredients in a separate bowl. Whip for 1 minute with a hand mixer until the mixture is puffed. 5. Divide the mixture into four bowls, then put the pears over the mixture and drizzle with more honey to serve.

Crispy Potato Chips with Lemony Cream Dip

Prep time: 20 minutes | Cook time: 15 minutes | Serves 2 to 4

- 2 large russet potatoes, sliced into ⅛-inch slices, rinsed

Lemony Cream Dip:
- ½ cup sour cream
- ¼ teaspoon lemon juice
- 2 scallions, white part only, minced
- Sea salt and freshly ground black pepper, to taste
- Cooking spray
- 1 tablespoon olive oil
- ¼ teaspoon salt
- Freshly ground black pepper, to taste

1. Soak the potato slices in water for 10 minutes, then pat dry with paper towels. 2. Preheat the air fryer to 300ºF (149ºC). 3. Transfer the potato slices in the preheated air fryer. Spritz the slices with cooking spray. You may need to work in batches to avoid overcrowding. 4. Air fry for 15 minutes or until crispy and golden brown. Shake the basket periodically. Sprinkle with salt and ground black pepper in the last minute. 5. Meanwhile, combine the ingredients for the dip in a small bowl. Stir to mix well. 6. Serve the potato chips immediately with the dip.

Parsnip Fries with Garlic-Yogurt Dip

Prep time: 10 minutes | Cook time: 10 minutes | Serves 4

- 3 medium parsnips, peeled, cut into sticks
- ¼ teaspoon kosher salt

Dip:
- ¼ cup plain Greek yogurt
- ⅛ teaspoon garlic powder
- 1 tablespoon sour cream
- 1 teaspoon olive oil
- 1 garlic clove, unpeeled
- Cooking spray
- ¼ teaspoon kosher salt
- Freshly ground black pepper, to taste

1. Preheat the air fryer to 360ºF (182ºC). Spritz the air fryer basket with cooking spray. 2. Put the parsnip sticks in a large bowl, then sprinkle with salt and drizzle with olive oil. 3. Transfer the parsnip into the preheated air fryer and add the garlic. 4. Air fry for 5 minutes, then remove the garlic from the air fryer and shake the basket. Air fry for 5 more minutes or until the parsnip sticks are crisp. 5. Meanwhile, peel the garlic and crush it. Combine the crushed garlic with the ingredients for the dip. Stir to mix well. 6. When the frying is complete, remove the parsnip fries from the air fryer and serve with the dipping sauce.

Chapter *10*

Family Favorites

Chapter 10 Family Favorites

Coconut Chicken Tenders

Prep time: 10 minutes | Cook time: 12 minutes | Serves 4

- Oil, for spraying
- 2 large eggs
- ¼ cup milk
- 1 tablespoon hot sauce
- 1½ cups sweetened flaked coconut
- ¾ cup panko bread crumbs
- 1 teaspoon salt
- ½ teaspoon freshly ground black pepper
- 1 pound (454 g) chicken tenders

1. Line the air fryer basket with parchment and spray lightly with oil. 2. In a small bowl, whisk together the eggs, milk, and hot sauce. 3. In a shallow dish, mix together the coconut, bread crumbs, salt, and black pepper. 4. Coat the chicken in the egg mix, then dredge in the coconut mixture until evenly coated. 5. Place the chicken in the prepared basket and spray liberally with oil. 6. Air fry at 400ºF (204ºC) for 6 minutes, flip, spray with more oil, and cook for another 6 minutes, or until the internal temperature reaches 165ºF (74ºC).

Steak Tips and Potatoes

Prep time: 10 minutes | Cook time: 20 minutes | Serves 4

- Oil, for spraying
- 8 ounces (227 g) baby gold potatoes, cut in half
- ½ teaspoon salt
- 1 pound (454 g) steak, cut into ½-inch pieces
- 1 teaspoon Worcestershire sauce
- 1 teaspoon granulated garlic
- ½ teaspoon salt
- ½ teaspoon freshly ground black pepper

1. Line the air fryer basket with parchment and spray lightly with oil. 2. In a microwave-safe bowl, combine the potatoes and salt, then pour in about ½ inch of water. Microwave for 7 minutes, or until the potatoes are nearly tender. Drain. 3. In a large bowl, gently mix together the steak, potatoes, Worcestershire sauce, garlic, salt, and black pepper. Spread the mixture in an even layer in the prepared basket. 4. Air fry at 400ºF (204ºC) for 12 to 17 minutes, stirring after 5 to 6 minutes. The cooking time will depend on the thickness of the meat and preferred doneness.

Pork Stuffing Meatballs

Prep time: 10 minutes | Cook time: 12 minutes | Makes 35 meatballs

- Oil, for spraying
- 1½ pounds (680 g) ground pork
- 1 cup bread crumbs
- ½ cup milk
- ¼ cup minced onion
- 1 large egg
- 1 tablespoon dried rosemary
- 1 tablespoon dried thyme
- 1 teaspoon salt
- 1 teaspoon freshly ground black pepper
- 1 teaspoon finely chopped fresh parsley

1. Line the air fryer basket with parchment and spray lightly with oil. 2. In a large bowl, mix together the ground pork, bread crumbs, milk, onion, egg, rosemary, thyme, salt, black pepper, and parsley. 3. Roll about 2 tablespoons of the mixture into a ball. Repeat with the rest of the mixture. You should have 30 to 35 meatballs. 4. Place the meatballs in the prepared basket in a single layer, leaving space between each one. You may need to work in batches, depending on the size of your air fryer. 5. Air fry at 390ºF (199ºC) for 10 to 12 minutes, flipping after 5 minutes, or until golden brown and the internal temperature reaches 160ºF (71ºC).

Buffalo Cauliflower

Prep time: 15 minutes | Cook time: 5 minutes | Serves 6

- 1 large head cauliflower, separated into small florets
- 1 tablespoon olive oil
- ½ teaspoon garlic powder
- ⅓ cup low-sodium hot wing sauce
- ⅔ cup nonfat Greek yogurt
- ½ teaspoons Tabasco sauce
- 1 celery stalk, chopped
- 1 tablespoon crumbled blue cheese

1. In a large bowl, toss the cauliflower florets with the olive oil. Sprinkle with the garlic powder and toss again to coat. Put half of the cauliflower in the air fryer basket. Air fry at 380ºF (193ºC) for 5 to 7 minutes, until the cauliflower is browned, shaking the basket once during cooking. 2. Transfer to a serving bowl and toss with half of the wing sauce. Repeat with the remaining cauliflower and wing sauce. 3. In a small bowl, stir together the yogurt, Tabasco sauce, celery, and blue cheese. Serve with the cauliflower for dipping.

Beef Jerky

Prep time: 30 minutes | Cook time: 2 hours | Serves 8

◀ Oil, for spraying
◀ 1 pound (454 g) round steak, cut into thin, short slices
◀ ¼ cup soy sauce
◀ 3 tablespoons packed light

brown sugar
◀ 1 tablespoon minced garlic
◀ 1 teaspoon ground ginger
◀ 1 tablespoon water

1. Line the air fryer basket with parchment and spray lightly with oil. 2. Place the steak, soy sauce, brown sugar, garlic, ginger, and water in a zip-top plastic bag, seal, and shake well until evenly coated. Refrigerate for 30 minutes. 3. Place the steak in the prepared basket in a single layer. You may need to work in batches, depending on the size of your air fryer. 4. Air fry at 180ºF (82ºC) for at least 2 hours. Add more time if you like your jerky a bit tougher.

Bacon-Wrapped Hot Dogs

Prep time: 5 minutes | Cook time: 10 minutes | Serves 4

◀ Oil, for spraying
◀ 4 bacon slices
◀ 4 all-beef hot dogs

◀ 4 hot dog buns
◀ Toppings of choice

1. Line the air fryer basket with parchment and spray lightly with oil. 2. Wrap a strip of bacon tightly around each hot dog, taking care to cover the tips so they don't get too crispy. Secure with a toothpick at each end to keep the bacon from shrinking. 3. Place the hot dogs in the prepared basket. 4. Air fry at 380ºF (193ºC) for 8 to 9 minutes, depending on how crispy you like the bacon. For extra-crispy, cook the hot dogs at 400ºF (204ºC) for 6 to 8 minutes. 5. Place the hot dogs in the buns, return them to the air fryer, and cook for another 1 to 2 minutes, or until the buns are warm. Add your desired toppings and serve.

Fried Green Tomatoes

Prep time: 15 minutes | Cook time: 6 to 8 minutes | Serves 4

◀ 4 medium green tomatoes
◀ ⅓ cup all-purpose flour
◀ 2 egg whites
◀ ¼ cup almond milk
◀ 1 cup ground almonds

◀ ½ cup panko bread crumbs
◀ 2 teaspoons olive oil
◀ 1 teaspoon paprika
◀ 1 clove garlic, minced

1. Rinse the tomatoes and pat dry. Cut the tomatoes into ½-inch slices, discarding the thinner ends. 2. Put the flour on a plate. In a shallow bowl, beat the egg whites with the almond milk until frothy. And on another plate, combine the almonds, bread crumbs, olive oil, paprika, and garlic and mix well. 3. Dip the tomato slices into the flour, then into the egg white mixture, then into the almond mixture to coat. 4. Place four of the coated tomato slices in the air fryer basket. Air fry at 400ºF (204ºC) for 6 to 8 minutes or until the tomato coating is crisp and golden brown. Repeat with remaining tomato slices and serve immediately.

Puffed Egg Tarts

Prep time: 10 minutes | Cook time: 42 minutes | Makes 4 tarts

◀ Oil, for spraying
◀ All-purpose flour, for dusting
◀ 1 (12 ounces / 340 g) sheet frozen puff pastry, thawed
◀ ¾ cup shredded Cheddar

cheese, divided
◀ 4 large eggs
◀ 2 teaspoons chopped fresh parsley
◀ Salt and freshly ground black pepper, to taste

1. Preheat the air fryer to 390ºF (199ºC). Line the air fryer basket with parchment and spray lightly with oil. 2. Lightly dust your work surface with flour. Unfold the puff pastry and cut it into 4 equal squares. Place 2 squares in the prepared basket. 3. Cook for 10 minutes. 4. Remove the basket. Press the center of each tart shell with a spoon to make an indentation. 5. Sprinkle 3 tablespoons of cheese into each indentation and crack 1 egg into the center of each tart shell. 6. Cook for another 7 to 11 minutes, or until the eggs are cooked to your desired doneness. 7. Repeat with the remaining puff pastry squares, cheese, and eggs. 8. Sprinkle evenly with the parsley, and season with salt and black pepper. Serve immediately.

Avocado and Egg Burrito

Prep time: 10 minutes | Cook time: 3 to 5 minutes | Serves 4

◀ 2 hard-boiled egg whites, chopped
◀ 1 hard-boiled egg, chopped
◀ 1 avocado, peeled, pitted, and chopped
◀ 1 red bell pepper, chopped
◀ 3 tablespoons low-sodium salsa, plus additional for

serving (optional)
◀ 1 (1.2 ounces / 34 g) slice low-sodium, low-fat American cheese, torn into pieces
◀ 4 low-sodium whole-wheat flour tortillas

1. In a medium bowl, thoroughly mix the egg whites, egg, avocado, red bell pepper, salsa, and cheese. 2. Place the tortillas on a work surface and evenly divide the filling among them. Fold in the edges and roll up. Secure the burritos with toothpicks if necessary. 3. Put the burritos in the air fryer basket. Air fry at 390ºF (199ºC) for 3 to 5 minutes, or until the burritos are light golden brown and crisp. Serve with more salsa (if using).

Meringue Cookies

Prep time: 15 minutes | Cook time: 1 hour 30 minutes | Makes 20 cookies

- Oil, for spraying
- 4 large egg whites
- 1 cup sugar
- Pinch cream of tartar

1. Preheat the air fryer to 140ºF (60ºC). Line the air fryer basket with parchment and spray lightly with oil. 2. In a small heatproof bowl, whisk together the egg whites and sugar. Fill a small saucepan halfway with water, place it over medium heat, and bring to a light simmer. Place the bowl with the egg whites on the saucepan, making sure the bottom of the bowl does not touch the water. Whisk the mixture until the sugar is dissolved. 3. Transfer the mixture to a large bowl and add the cream of tartar. Using an electric mixer, beat the mixture on high until it is glossy and stiff peaks form. Transfer the mixture to a piping bag or a zip-top plastic bag with a corner cut off. 4. Pipe rounds into the prepared basket. You may need to work in batches, depending on the size of your air fryer. 5. Cook for 1 hour 30 minutes. 6. Turn off the air fryer and let the meringues cool completely inside. The residual heat will continue to dry them out.

Phyllo Vegetable Triangles

Prep time: 15 minutes | Cook time: 6 to 11 minutes | Serves 6

- 3 tablespoons minced onion
- 2 garlic cloves, minced
- 2 tablespoons grated carrot
- 1 teaspoon olive oil
- 3 tablespoons frozen baby peas, thawed
- 2 tablespoons nonfat cream cheese, at room temperature
- 6 sheets frozen phyllo dough, thawed
- Olive oil spray, for coating the dough

1. In a baking pan, combine the onion, garlic, carrot, and olive oil. Air fry at 390ºF (199ºC) for 2 to 4 minutes, or until the vegetables are crisp-tender. Transfer to a bowl. 2. Stir in the peas and cream cheese to the vegetable mixture. Let cool while you prepare the dough. 3. Lay one sheet of phyllo on a work surface and lightly spray with olive oil spray. Top with another sheet of phyllo. Repeat with the remaining 4 phyllo sheets; you'll have 3 stacks with 2 layers each. Cut each stack lengthwise into 4 strips (12 strips total). 4. Place a scant 2 teaspoons of the filling near the bottom of each strip. Bring one corner up over the filling to make a triangle; continue folding the triangles over, as you would fold a flag. Seal the edge with a bit of water. Repeat with the remaining strips and filling. 5. Air fry the triangles, in 2 batches, for 4 to 7 minutes, or until golden brown. Serve.

Berry Cheesecake

Prep time: 5 minutes | Cook time: 10 minutes | Serves 4

- Oil, for spraying
- 8 ounces (227 g) cream cheese
- 6 tablespoons sugar
- 1 tablespoon sour cream
- 1 large egg
- ½ teaspoon vanilla extract
- ¼ teaspoon lemon juice
- ½ cup fresh mixed berries

1. Preheat the air fryer to 350ºF (177ºC). Line the air fryer basket with parchment and spray lightly with oil. 2. In a blender, combine the cream cheese, sugar, sour cream, egg, vanilla, and lemon juice and blend until smooth. Pour the mixture into a 4-inch springform pan. 3. Place the pan in the prepared basket. 4. Cook for 8 to 10 minutes, or until only the very center jiggles slightly when the pan is moved. 5. Refrigerate the cheesecake in the pan for at least 2 hours. 6. Release the sides from the springform pan, top the cheesecake with the mixed berries, and serve.

Pecan Rolls

Prep time: 20 minutes | Cook time: 20 to 24 minutes | Makes 12 rolls

- 2 cups all-purpose flour, plus more for dusting
- 2 tablespoons granulated sugar, plus ¼ cup, divided
- 1 teaspoon salt
- 3 tablespoons butter, at room temperature
- ¾ cup milk, whole or 2%
- ¼ cup packed light brown sugar
- ½ cup chopped pecans, toasted
- 1 to 2 tablespoons oil
- ¼ cup confectioners' sugar (optional)

1. In a large bowl, whisk the flour, 2 tablespoons granulated sugar, and salt until blended. Stir in the butter and milk briefly until a sticky dough forms. 2. In a small bowl, stir together the brown sugar and remaining ¼ cup of granulated sugar. 3. Place a piece of parchment paper on a work surface and dust it with flour. Roll the dough on the prepared surface to ¼ inch thickness. 4. Spread the sugar mixture over the dough. Sprinkle the pecans on top. Roll up the dough jelly roll-style, pinching the ends to seal. Cut the dough into 12 rolls. 5. Preheat the air fryer to 320ºF (160ºC). 6. Line the air fryer basket with parchment paper and spritz the parchment with oil. Place 6 rolls on the prepared parchment. 7. Bake for 5 minutes. Flip the rolls and bake for 5 to 7 minutes more until lightly browned. Repeat with the remaining rolls. 8. Sprinkle with confectioners' sugar (if using).

Elephant Ears

Prep time: 5 minutes | Cook time: 5 minutes | Serves 8

◄ Oil, for spraying
◄ 1 (8 ounces / 227 g) can buttermilk biscuits
◄ 3 tablespoons sugar
◄ 1 tablespoon ground

◄ cinnamon
◄ 3 tablespoons unsalted butter, melted
◄ 8 scoops vanilla ice cream (optional)

1. Line the air fryer basket with parchment and spray lightly with oil. 2. Separate the dough. Using a rolling pin, roll out the biscuits into 6- to 8-inch circles. 3. Place the dough circles in the prepared basket and spray liberally with oil. You may need to work in batches, depending on the size of your air fryer. 4. Air fry at 350°F (177°C) for 5 minutes, or until lightly browned. 5. In a small bowl, mix together the sugar and cinnamon. 6. Brush the elephant ears with the melted butter and sprinkle with the cinnamon-sugar mixture. 7. Top each serving with a scoop of ice cream (if using).

Scallops with Green Vegetables

Prep time: 15 minutes | Cook time: 8 to 11 minutes | Serves 4

◄ 1 cup green beans
◄ 1 cup frozen peas
◄ 1 cup frozen chopped broccoli
◄ 2 teaspoons olive oil

◄ ½ teaspoon dried basil
◄ ½ teaspoon dried oregano
◄ 12 ounces (340 g) sea scallops

1. In a large bowl, toss the green beans, peas, and broccoli with the olive oil. Place in the air fryer basket. Air fry at 400°F (204°C) for 4 to 6 minutes, or until the vegetables are crisp-tender. 2. Remove the vegetables from the air fryer basket and sprinkle with the herbs. Set aside. 3. In the air fryer basket, put the scallops and air fry for 4 to 5 minutes, or until the scallops are firm and reach an internal temperature of just 145°F (63°C) on a meat thermometer. 4. Toss scallops with the vegetables and serve immediately.

Churro Bites

Prep time: 5 minutes | Cook time: 6 minutes | Makes 36 bites

◄ Oil, for spraying
◄ 1 (17¼ ounces / 489 g) package frozen puffed pastry, thawed
◄ 1 cup granulated sugar

◄ 1 tablespoon ground cinnamon
◄ ½ cup confectioners' sugar
◄ 1 tablespoon milk

1. Preheat the air fryer to 400°F (204°C). Line the air fryer basket with parchment and spray lightly with oil. 2. Unfold the puff pastry onto a clean work surface. Using a sharp knife, cut the dough into 36 bite-size pieces. 3. Place the dough pieces in one layer in the prepared basket, taking care not to let the pieces touch or overlap. 4. Cook for 3 minutes, flip, and cook for another 3 minutes, or until puffed and golden. 5. In a small bowl, mix together the granulated sugar and cinnamon. 6. In another small bowl, whisk together the confectioners' sugar and milk. 7. Dredge the bites in the cinnamon-sugar mixture until evenly coated. 8. Serve with the icing on the side for dipping.

Veggie Tuna Melts

Prep time: 15 minutes | Cook time: 7 to 11 minutes | Serves 4

◄ 2 low-sodium whole-wheat English muffins, split
◄ 1 (6 ounces / 170 g) can chunk light low-sodium tuna, drained
◄ 1 cup shredded carrot
◄ ⅓ cup chopped mushrooms

◄ 2 scallions, white and green parts, sliced
◄ ⅓ cup nonfat Greek yogurt
◄ 2 tablespoons low-sodium stone ground mustard
◄ 2 slices low-sodium low-fat Swiss cheese, halved

1. Place the English muffin halves in the air fryer basket. Air fry at 340°F (171°C) for 3 to 4 minutes, or until crisp. Remove from the basket and set aside. 2. In a medium bowl, thoroughly mix the tuna, carrot, mushrooms, scallions, yogurt, and mustard. Top each half of the muffins with one-fourth of the tuna mixture and a half slice of Swiss cheese. 3. Air fry for 4 to 7 minutes, or until the tuna mixture is hot and the cheese melts and starts to brown. Serve immediately.

Fish and Vegetable Tacos

Prep time: 15 minutes | Cook time: 9 to 12 minutes | Serves 4

◄ 1 pound (454 g) white fish fillets, such as sole or cod
◄ 2 teaspoons olive oil
◄ 3 tablespoons freshly squeezed lemon juice, divided
◄ 1½ cups chopped red

◄ cabbage
◄ 1 large carrot, grated
◄ ½ cup low-sodium salsa
◄ ⅓ cup low-fat Greek yogurt
◄ 4 soft low-sodium whole-wheat tortillas

1. Brush the fish with the olive oil and sprinkle with 1 tablespoon of lemon juice. Air fry in the air fryer basket at 390°F (199°C) for 9 to 12 minutes, or until the fish just flakes when tested with a fork. 2. Meanwhile, in a medium bowl, stir together the remaining 2 tablespoons of lemon juice, the red cabbage, carrot, salsa, and yogurt. 3. When the fish is cooked, remove it from the air fryer basket and break it up into large pieces. 4. Offer the fish, tortillas, and the cabbage mixture, and let each person assemble a taco.

Cajun Shrimp

Prep time: 15 minutes | Cook time: 9 minutes | Serves 4

- Oil, for spraying
- 1 pound (454 g) jumbo raw shrimp, peeled and deveined
- 1 tablespoon Cajun seasoning
- 6 ounces (170 g) cooked kielbasa, cut into thick slices
- ½ medium zucchini, cut into ¼-inch-thick slices
- ½ medium yellow squash, cut into ¼-inch-thick slices
- 1 green bell pepper, seeded and cut into 1-inch pieces
- 2 tablespoons olive oil
- ½ teaspoon salt

1. Preheat the air fryer to 400ºF (204ºC). Line the air fryer basket with parchment and spray lightly with oil. 2. In a large bowl, toss together the shrimp and Cajun seasoning. Add the kielbasa, zucchini, squash, bell pepper, olive oil, and salt and mix well. 3. Transfer the mixture to the prepared basket, taking care not to overcrowd. You may need to work in batches, depending on the size of your air fryer. 4. Cook for 9 minutes, shaking and stirring every 3 minutes. Serve immediately.

Meatball Subs

Prep time: 15 minutes | Cook time: 19 minutes | Serves 6

- Oil, for spraying
- 1 pound (454 g) 85% lean ground beef
- ½ cup Italian bread crumbs
- 1 tablespoon dried minced onion
- 1 tablespoon minced garlic
- 1 large egg
- 1 teaspoon salt
- 1 teaspoon freshly ground black pepper
- 6 hoagie rolls
- 1 (18 ounces / 510 g) jar marinara sauce
- 1½ cups shredded Mozzarella cheese

1. Line the air fryer basket with parchment and spray lightly with oil. 2. In a large bowl, mix together the ground beef, bread crumbs, onion, garlic, egg, salt, and black pepper. Roll the mixture into 18 meatballs. 3. Place the meatballs in the prepared basket. 4. Air fry at 390ºF (199ºC) for 15 minutes. 5. Place 3 meatballs in each hoagie roll. Top with marinara and Mozzarella cheese. 6. Place the loaded rolls in the air fryer and cook for 3 to 4 minutes, or until the cheese is melted. You may need to work in batches, depending on the size of your air fryer. Serve immediately.

Appendix 1:

Air Fryer Cooking Chart

Beef					
Item	Temp (°F)	Time (mins)	Item	Temp (°F)	Time (mins)
Beef Eye Round Roast (4 lbs.)	400 °F	45 to 55	Meatballs (1-inch)	370 °F	7
Burger Patty (4 oz.)	370 °F	16 to 20	Meatballs (3-inch)	380 °F	10
Filet Mignon (8 oz.)	400 °F	18	Ribeye, bone-in (1-inch, 8 oz)	400 °F	10 to 15
Flank Steak (1.5 lbs.)	400 °F	12	Sirloin steaks (1-inch, 12 oz)	400 °F	9 to 14
Flank Steak (2 lbs.)	400 °F	20 to 28			

Chicken					
Item	Temp (°F)	Time (mins)	Item	Temp (°F)	Time (mins)
Breasts, bone in (1 ¼ lb.)	370 °F	25	Legs, bone-in (1 ¾ lb.)	380 °F	30
Breasts, boneless (4 oz)	380 °F	12	Thighs, boneless (1 ½ lb.)	380 °F	18 to 20
Drumsticks (2 ½ lb.)	370 °F	20	Wings (2 lb.)	400 °F	12
Game Hen (halved 2 lb.)	390 °F	20	Whole Chicken	360 °F	75
Thighs, bone-in (2 lb.)	380 °F	22	Tenders	360 °F	8 to 10

Pork & Lamb					
Item	Temp (°F)	Time (mins)	Item	Temp (°F)	Time (mins)
Bacon (regular)	400 °F	5 to 7	Pork Tenderloin	370 °F	15
Bacon (thick cut)	400 °F	6 to 10	Sausages	380 °F	15
Pork Loin (2 lb.)	360 °F	55	Lamb Loin Chops (1-inch thick)	400 °F	8 to 12
Pork Chops, bone in (1-inch, 6.5 oz)	400 °F	12	Rack of Lamb (1.5 – 2 lb.)	380 °F	22

Fish & Seafood					
Item	Temp (°F)	Time (mins)	Item	Temp (°F)	Time (mins)
Calamari (8 oz)	400 °F	4	Tuna Steak	400 °F	7 to 10
Fish Fillet (1-inch, 8 oz)	400 °F	10	Scallops	400 °F	5 to 7
Salmon, fillet (6 oz)	380 °F	12	Shrimp	400 °F	5
Swordfish steak	400 °F	10			

Air Fryer Cooking Chart

Vegetables					
INGREDIENT	AMOUNT	PREPARATION	OIL	TEMP	COOK TIME
Asparagus	2 bunches	Cut in half, trim stems	2 Tbsp	420°F	12-15 mins
Beets	1½ lbs	Peel, cut in ½-inch cubes	1Tbsp	390°F	28-30 mins
Bell peppers (for roasting)	4 peppers	Cut in quarters, remove seeds	1Tbsp	400°F	15-20 mins
Broccoli	1 large head	Cut in 1-2-inch florets	1Tbsp	400°F	15-20 mins
Brussels sprouts	1lb	Cut in half, remove stems	1Tbsp	425°F	15-20 mins
Carrots	1lb	Peel, cut in ¼-inch rounds	1 Tbsp	425°F	10-15 mins
Cauliflower	1 head	Cut in 1-2-inch florets	2 Tbsp	400°F	20-22 mins
Corn on the cob	7 ears	Whole ears, remove husks	1 Tbps	400°F	14-17 mins
Green beans	1 bag (12 oz)	Trim	1 Tbps	420°F	18-20 mins
Kale (for chips)	4 oz	Tear into pieces, remove stems	None	325°F	5-8 mins
Mushrooms	16 oz	Rinse, slice thinly	1 Tbps	390°F	25-30 mins
Potatoes, russet	1½ lbs	Cut in 1-inch wedges	1 Tbps	390°F	25-30 mins
Potatoes, russet	1lb	Hand-cut fries, soak 30 mins in cold water, then pat dry	½ -3 Tbps	400°F	25-28 mins
Potatoes, sweet	1lb	Hand-cut fries, soak 30 mins in cold water, then pat dry	1 Tbps	400°F	25-28 mins
Zucchini	1lb	Cut in eighths lengthwise, then cut in half	1 Tbps	400°F	15-20 mins

Appendix 2: Recipes Index

Made in United States
Orlando, FL
06 May 2024

46556274R00057